Assessing Young Children in Inclusive Settings

Assessing Young Children in Inclusive Settings

The Blended Practices Approach

by

Jennifer Grisham-Brown, Ed.D.
University of Kentucky
Lexington, Kentucky

and

Kristie Pretti-Frontczak, Ph.D.
Kent State University
Kent, Ohio

with invited contributors

Baltimore • London • Sydney

Paul H. Brookes Publishing Co.
Post Office Box 10624
Baltimore, Maryland 21285-0624
USA

www.brookespublishing.com

Typeset by Aptara, Inc., Falls Church, Virginia.
Manufactured in the United States of America by
Sheridan Books, Inc., Chelsea, Michigan.

Photographs on pages 1, 37, 61, 91, 149, and 231 courtesy of Jennifer Grisham-Brown. Photograph on page 15 courtesy of Whitney A. Stevenson. Photographs on page 61 and the front cover courtesy of Kenneth Sese. Photograph on pages 121 and 193 courtesy of Carrie Pfeifer-Fiala.

The individuals described in this book are composites or real people who situations are masked and are based on the authors' experiences. In most instances, names and identifying details have been changed to protect confidentiality. Real names and identifying details used with permission.

Library of Congress Cataloging-in-Publication Data

Assessing young children in inclusive settings: the blended practices approach/by Jennifer
  Grisham-Brown and Kristie L. Pretti-Frontczak.
     p.   cm.
  Includes index.
  ISBN-13: 978-1-59857-057-1
  ISBN-10: 1-59857-057-9
  1. Educational tests and measurements.   2. Early childhood education.   3. Inclusive education.
  I. Grisham-Brown, Jennifer.   II. Pretti-Frontczak, Kristie.   III. Title.
  LB3051.A76646 2010
  372.126—dc22
                                                                            2010035947

British Library Cataloguing in Publication data are available from the British Library.

2019 2018

10   9   8   7   6   5

Contents

About the Authors

Jennifer Grisham-Brown Ed.D., Professor, College of Education, Department of Special Education and Rehabilitation Counseling, University of Kentucky, 229 Taylor Education Building, Lexington, Kentucky 40506

Dr. Grisham-Brown is Professor in the Department of Special Education and Rehabilitation Counseling at University of Kentucky, Lexington. She received her doctorate in education from the University of Kentucky. She is Director of the Early Childhood Laboratory at the University of Kentucky, an inclusive early childhood program for children from birth to 5 years of age. Her research interests include authentic assessment, tiered instruction, and inclusion of children with significant disabilities. Dr. Grisham-Brown provides training and technical assistance throughout the United States on these topics. Dr. Grisham-Brown is Cofounder of a children's home and preschool program in Guatemala City called Hope for Tomorrow.

Kristie Pretti-Frontczak, Ph.D., Professor, College of Education, Health, and Human Services, School of Lifespan Development and Educational Sciences, Kent State University, Kent, Ohio 44242

Dr. Pretti-Frontczak is Professor in the School of Lifespan Development and Educational Sciences at Kent State University (KSU), Ohio. She received her doctorate in early intervention from the University of Oregon and has extensive experience in preparing preservice and in-service personnel in recommended practices for working with young children and their families. She directs the Early Childhood Intervention Specialist Program at KSU, where she is responsible for preparing preservice teachers to work with children with disabilities from birth to age 8. Her lines of research center on using authentic assessment practices for accountability and programming, specifically on the utility of the *Assessment, Evaluation, and Programming System for Infants and Children, 2nd Edition* (AEPS®), effective approaches to working with young children in inclusive settings (specifically regarding the efficacy of an activity-based approach and the application of universal design for learning principles), and the link between assessment, individualized goals, and quality curriculum.

Contributors

Teresa L. Brown, M.Ed.
Doctoral Student
Center for Excellence in Early
  Childhood Research and
  Training
Kent State University
150 Terrace Drive
Kent, Ohio 44242

Anna H. Hall, M.Ed.
Doctoral Student
Department of Special Education
  and Rehabilitation Counseling
University of Kentucky
237 C. Taylor Education Building
Lexington, Kentucky 40506

Sarah R. Hawkins, Ed.D
Assistant Professor
Department of Early Childhood,
  Elementary, and Special
  Education
Morehead State University
401 F Ginger Hall
Morehead, Kentucky 40351

Sophia Hubbell, M.A.T.
Doctoral Student
Center for Excellence in Early
  Childhood Research and
  Training
Kent State University
150 Terrace Drive
Kent, Ohio 44242

Ashley N. Lyons. M.Ed
Intervention Specialist
Kent State University
220 White Hall
Post Office Box 5190
Kent, Ohio 44242

Lydia Moore, M.Ed.
Doctoral Student
Center for Excellence in Early
  Childhood Research and Training
Kent State University
150 Terrace Drive
Kent, Ohio 44242

Carrie Pfeiffer-Fiala, M.Ed.
Doctoral Student
Kent State University
4662 Alliance Road
Ravenna, Ohio 44266

Sandra Hess Robbins, M.Ed.
Doctoral Candidate
Center for Excellence in Early
  Childhood Research and Training
Kent State University
150 Terrace Drive
Kent, Ohio 44242

Julie Harp Rutland, M.S.
Special Education
University of Kentucky
103 Adams Lane
Lexington, Kentucky 40511

Nicole R. Shannon, M.Ed.
Doctoral Candidate
School Psychology
Kent State University
150 Terrace Drive
Kent, Ohio 44242

Whitney A. Stevenson, M.S.
Doctoral Student
Fayette County Public Schools
  Early Childhood Department
University of Kentucky
701 East Main Street
Lexington, Kentucky 40502

Foreword

Authenticity—Common Core to
Blend Assessment and Teaching for
Inclusive Education of Young Children

Modern early childhood programs in the United States are beginning to exemplify an integrated system of high-quality care and instruction to gradually replace the "unsystem" for all infants, toddlers, and preschoolers. Over the past 15 years, inclusion of young children with developmental differences and challenging behaviors has become more the rule than the exception.

In increasing numbers of states, "systems of care" encompass many different types of program settings: public and private center-based and home-based child care, Early Head Start and Head Start, and prekindergarten programs. Young children with special needs are being educated with their friends in their local communities. State early learning standards and curriculum frameworks are becoming linked; integrated professional practice standards (e.g., National Association for the Education of Young Children [NAEYC], Division for Early Childhood [DEC], and Head Start) encourage teachers and providers to use both developmentally appropriate and evidence-based approaches with children and families. Finally, we are aligning our actions with our professional philosophies and laws in order to become more ethical and humane.

Blended Practices for Teaching Young Children in Inclusive Settings (Grisham-Brown, Hemmeter, & Pretti-Frontczak, 2005) has proven to be a stellar and indispensable guide for professionals who strive to meet the new trends and mandates to effectively teach and care for all children in everyday settings and routines. *Blended Practices for Teaching Young Children in Inclusive Settings* has become the roadmap for inclusion in the early childhood intervention field.

Despite these positive trends to promote inclusion and system linkages, not all professional practices have changed at the same pace. Perhaps most notable among these "delayed" changes in practice is early childhood measurement. Measurement in early childhood is still dominated by conventional tests and testing practices to the detriment of young children, particularly for determining their eligibility to be included in high-quality programs. However, over the past 10 years, professional beliefs and practices have changed due to the publication and promotion of professional standards—and spurred on by the failure of conventional tests and testing to be helpful in accurately planning and evaluating the outcomes of individual plans for children with developmental differences.

Authentic assessment methods and processes are beginning to be dominant in all types of early childhood intervention programs—and with all children—because they exemplify "best practices" (Bagnato, 2007). Authentic assessment aligns best with the trends to include and educate all children in natural settings. Authentic assessment links with authentic instruction and ensures "blended practices" in everyday environments (Bagnato, Neisworth, & Pretti-Frontczak, 2010).

Thus, the time is ripe in 2010 for the publication of *Assessing Young Children in Inclusive Settings*. Grisham and colleagues have once again produced a superb text and companion volume to their *Blended Practices* volume. It is notable that the concepts of *curriculum* and *curriculum framework* take center stage in a discussion of assessment for early childhood intervention. This text articulates the recent joint early childhood inclusion statement of NAEYC and DEC (2009), which emphasizes access, participation, and supports for all children and encourages blended professional practices about curriculum, standards, instruction, and assessment. *Assessing Young Children* is comprehensive in its coverage and well-illustrated with child vignettes and practical details on ensuring that assessment links to intervention and outcomes. The text fronts the collaboration among families and professionals. Assessment to accomplish the specific purposes and objectives of inclusive early childhood education is one of the primary themes of this text. Chapters 7 and 8 are exemplary in their portrayal of the steps to use "data-based decision-making" to plan individual programs for children and to monitor performance. Chapter 9 demystifies assessment for program accountability.

Over the past decade, the United States has witnessed the implementation of state-funded early care and education programs for all children and the applied program evaluation research which has accompanied them. The outcomes of these modern programs demonstrate clearly that prevention works; inclusion works; and developmentally appropriate practice works—for all children. Authentic assessment methods linked to curriculum standards have been the foundation for most of these successful programs (Bagnato, Salaway, & Suen, 2009).

I have had the professional and personal privilege to conduct national and international professional development workshops for interdisciplinary professionals with both Drs. Grisham-Brown and Pretti-Frontczak on our mutual interests in authentic curriculum-based assessment. These competent and engaging professionals are the new wave of leaders in the early childhood intervention field, and their assessment-linked curriculum framework perspective enabled our workshop participants to readily learn and apply appropriate assessment in their daily work. *Assessing Young Children* has the same engaging material as our workshops.

Readers will find that Grisham-Brown and colleagues have met clearly their stated objective "to guide early childhood intervention teachers in implementing high-quality assessment with children with and without disabilities." Moreover, this text is not just for teachers, but all interdisciplinary professionals who must adhere to the unique philosophy and practices for effective early childhood intervention. *Assessing Young Children* will be welcomed eagerly by all interdisciplinary professionals who seek to use "best practices" for all of our young children, but particularly our most vulnerable.

Stephen J. Bagnato
Professor of Pediatrics & Psychology
Director, Early Childhood Partnerships
University of Pittsburgh/Children's Hospital of Pittsburgh

REFERENCES

Bagnato, S.J. (2007). *Authentic assessment for early childhood intervention: Best practices.* New York: Guilford Press, Inc.

Bagnato, S.J., Neisworth, J.T., & Pretti-Frontczak, K. (2010). *LINKing authentic assessment and early childhood intervention: Best measures for best practices* (2nd ed.). Baltimore: Paul H. Brookes Publishing Co.

Bagnato, S.J., Salaway, J., & Suen, H.K. (2009). *Pre-K Counts in Pennsylvania for Youngster's Early School Success: Authentic Outcomes of Innovative Prevention and Promotion Initiative (2005–2009).* Pittsburgh, PA: Early Childhood Partnerships, University of Pittsburgh/Children's Hospital.

DEC/NAEYC. (2009). *Early childhood inclusion: A joint position statement of the Division for Early Childhod (DEC) and the National Association for the Education of Young Children (NAEYC).* Chapel Hill, NC: The University of North Carolina, FPG Child Development Institute.

Preface

If you ask a group of early childhood interventionists about their greatest challenge teaching in blended classrooms, common responses would include "the paperwork," "data collection," or "getting the (*name of test*) finished on all of the children." Each of these challenges, in some way, is likely associated with assessment. In *Assessing Young Children in Inclusive Settings: The Blended Practices Approach* we define assessment as a process of gathering information about young children for the purpose of making decisions. The intent of using a broad definition is twofold. First, the apparent simplicity of the definition is meant to demystify a set of practices that have challenged all teachers for years. Teachers "gather" all types of information about young children and similarly make many "decisions" on their behalf. Therefore, our hope is that the definition will invoke ideas of practices in which teachers are presently engaged. Second, the aim of using a generic definition is to eliminate the idea that assessment and testing are one in the same. For many, the word *testing*, and therefore in some cases *assessment*, conjures images of young children being forced to follow strict directions to complete uninteresting tasks with adults whom they do not know. Although the *assessment* definition used in *Assessing Young Children in Inclusive Settings* is intended to set the tone for the book, we acknowledge that teachers face real challenges associated with conducting assessment activities with young children in blended classrooms.

It is our perception that the very notion of collecting information about young children is a struggle for some early childhood interventionists. In a field that values positive adult–child interactions, the idea of gathering information about children may seem contradictory to the role as teacher of young children. Frequently, we have heard teachers complain that they "wish they could get the assessment finished so that they can actually teach." This statement is reflective of the fact that some teachers view the two practices separately and incompatible with one another. Our hope is that *Assessing Young Children in Inclusive Settings* clarifies the close relationship between assessment and instruction and highlights practices that are not contrary to their understanding of high-quality interactions with young children.

Additional challenges we address in *Assessing Young Children in Inclusive Settings* are those associated with gathering required *and* needed assessment information within the realities of today's classrooms settings. Teachers feel very real pressure to complete necessary assessment activities associated with eligibility and accountability mandates, sometimes to the detriment of focusing on gathering assessment information for directing and guiding instruction. Layered on these multiple purposes is the stress of collecting required and needed assessment information within the context of early childhood intervention today. Many teachers work in classrooms that meet from 2–5 half days a week, frequently with double sessions on each of those days. Within those classrooms, teachers serve children who have varying abilities, who speak different languages, and who represent various ethnic and cultural backgrounds. In many of these highly diverse classrooms, teachers must address the assessment mandates for different early childhood programs (e.g., public preschool, Head Start, child care). Although the length of the program may be shorter, the group of children more diverse, and the assessment requirements enormous, early childhood teachers share similar, if not greater, assessment responsibilities than their school-age teacher counterparts. In writing *Assessing Young Children in Inclusive Settings*, it was our desire to provide teachers with a realistic set of assessment practices that can be implemented in today's early childhood classrooms.

As with *Blended Practices for Teaching Young Children in Inclusive Settings* (Grisham-Brown, Hemmeter, & Pretti-Frontczak, 2005), our hope is that this companion book will support teachers of young children in facing challenges associated with assessment. More specifically, we hope that our readers find solutions to their daily struggles associated with assessing young children in blended settings in *Assessing Young Children in Inclusive Settings*.

Acknowledgments

We started discussions around writing the companion to *Blended Practices for Teaching Young Children in Inclusive Settings* almost as soon as work on the first text was completed. Our intent to write a companion text stemmed partially out of frustration in finding an assessment text that provided what we perceived to be the necessary information early childhood teachers need to know about conducting assessment with young children, particularly in blended classrooms. Although we knew what the "perfect" assessment text should contain, finding the *time* to write proved a challenge. In order to obtain our goal, we decided to invite our "best and brightest" past and current doctoral students to co-author chapters with us. In theory, this seemed like a win-win situation. In other words, we would get the perfect assessment text written, and our students would have the opportunity to co-author a book chapter. In reality, the challenges and benefits of coordinating such a project was something much more complex. We were challenged by bringing together different writing styles and ideals into a cohesive body of work. There is no doubt that our students were frequently frustrated by our multiple changes to outlines, extensive edits, and ridiculous timelines. Despite these challenges, we believe that those who read *Assessing Young Children in Inclusive Settings* will benefit from the incredible contributions of these fine young professionals. Their insights were refreshing and brought to the book the perspectives of practitioners who are only recently out of the classroom and the voice of parents of young children, some who have disabilities. What resulted from our collective efforts, is a *much* better text, because of the contributions of Teresa Brown, Anna Hall, Sarah Hawkins, Sophia Hubbell, Ashley Lyons, Lydia Moore, Carrie Pfeiffer-Fiala, Sandra Robbins, Julie Rutland, Nicole Shannon, and Whitney Stevenson. Edward Zigler, Yale Scholar and considered by some to be the "Grandfather of Head Start," once said that our responsibility as academicians is to worry less about advancing our own careers and more about mentoring the future generation of researchers in child development. We feel confident that the future of early childhood intervention will be in good hands if the contributors of our book, and others like them, continue to provide leadership in our field.

Jennifer also wishes to thank a number of groups and people who supported her in the development of the book. A person cannot write about how to work with young children if she never spends time with children, families, and early childhood teachers. I am grateful for the children, families, and professionals who continue to teach me about best practices for working with young children and inspire me to continue writing about what I have learned. Diane Haynes and the families and children of the Kentucky Deaf-Blind Project have long provided me with insight into how to approach practices for young children with the most severe disabilities. I am grateful to Charlotte Manno and the staff, families, and children of the University of Kentucky Early Childhood Laboratory, who teach me about the challenges and benefits of implementing high-quality blended early childhood practices in the real world. Finally, to cover photographer Kenneth Sese, Diana Sese, Brenda Riddle, and the staff and children of Hope for Tomorrow Children's Home in Guatemala City, I extend my love and gratitude for teaching me that children everywhere deserve high-quality educational services and that these services are possible anywhere if enough people are willing to make them available. I want to also acknowledge my personal supports that tolerate my long absences and inattentiveness during writing projects. Even 50-year-old women need girlfriends, and I have the best. Thanks to Christy, Rita, Amy, Carolyn, Cathy, Debbie, Donna, Gay, Kathy, Kellye, Lanell, Mary Louise, Melisa, and Sharon for making sure I still have a good time occasionally. To my work colleagues, Katherine, Kim, and Lee Ann, thank you for challenging my thinking about services for young children and for your personal and professional support through the years. I want to acknowledge and thank my co-author, colleague, *and* friend, Kristie. You keep me inspired and excited about our work and manage to make some of what we do fun! My family suffered greatly, with the loss of my father during the writing of this book. At the completion of another big project, I miss his understated praise but am so grateful to the family I do have for their love and support. Thanks to Mom, Milly, Tom, Thomas, Kehla, and Mattie for always reminding me what is most important and to Paul and Kendall for being what is most important. I love you all.

Kristie wishes to thank her longtime friend and mentor, Diane Bricker, who instilled the values of authentic, family-guided assessment practices before it was vogue to engage in such practices. I am also thankful for the 100s of 1,000s of Early Childhood Intervention (ECI) providers who welcome me into their classrooms, their programs, and their lives and share with me invaluable lessons that humble me daily. In particular I would like to thank another longtime friend, Lynn Sullivan, who stretches the boundaries of quality professional development and practice every day and continues to teach me lessons about what will lead to improved practices in the real world. I am also thankful for my international friends and colleagues, particularly those in Singapore, Australia, and New Zealand. They remind me that children are children and we must be diligent in our efforts to remember that all of our practices should have their happiness and well-being as our ultimate goal. As Jennifer mentions, we cannot have success without the professional and personal support around us on a day-to-day basis. I am thankful to my husband for the countless hours he has spent taking care of all the things I have neglected, the hours he has listened to me process what should be contained in a particular chapter, and his seemingly endless patience with hearing stories from the field. I am also thankful for my colleagues at Kent State University (KSU), particularly Melody Tankersley and Sanna Harjusola-Webb, who understand me and support me when I am lacking in patience or time. I also thank the rest of the KSU ECI doctoral cohort. Each of them helped in finding resources for the book, formatted tables and figures, fielded questions about relevance, and did what they could to support our efforts in writing the "perfect" assessment text.

To my Father, Roy Lee Grisham,
whose opinion mattered more than that of anyone to me,
and whose life I try hardest to imitate.
—*JGB*

To families and providers who care each day for young children,
you have the most necessary and challenging roles in their lives,
and as such should be honored.
—*KPF*

CHAPTER 1

Introduction

Jennifer Grisham-Brown and
Kristie Pretti-Frontczak

The trends that guided the development of *Blended Practices for Teaching Young Children in Inclusive Settings* (Grisham-Brown, Hemmeter, & Pretti-Frontczak, 2005), the companion to the present book, were in their infancy in the early 2000s. Those operating early childhood intervention programs were beginning to design plans for supporting children with and without disabilities in the same setting. Early childhood professionals were searching for instructional models to differentiate instruction for children with varying needs in inclusive programs. Administrators and teachers of programs serving young children were beginning to hear about early learning standards and their implication for program development and evaluation. State and program administrators were learning about collecting, reporting, and using accountability data. The implications of having an early childhood accountability system were unknown.

When Grisham-Brown et al. (2005) was written, many topics associated with early childhood assessment were not sufficiently addressed. Our intent has always been to develop a companion book focused solely on assessment (to help address associated material). Since the previous book was published, the basic themes in early childhood have remained essentially the same. However, new legislation has led to changes in how these issues are addressed. Inclusive programming, standards-based education, and accountability remain key themes for early childhood professionals and are more recently affecting assessment practices. The placement of young children in special education classes has been altered by newly defined Child Find regulations that require programs to implement interventions prior to evaluation and determine children's progress toward applied interventions. Increased statewide prekindergarten programs have resulted in a need for comprehensive assessment systems that are tied to early learning standards and link to K–12 assessment systems. The onset of full-fledged accountability assessment in programs serving young children who are at risk for or have disabilities has influenced all components of the assessment process, including diagnosis, program planning, progress monitoring, and program evaluation.

While an overview of assessment was described in Grisham-Brown et al. (2005), the book emphasized designing and delivering high-quality instruction for young children by using a curriculum framework as the overarching guide or model. The specific purpose of *Assessing Young Children in Inclusive Settings: The Blended Practices Approach* is to provide detailed information on the reasons for, and structures associated with, performing high-quality assessment for young children and their families.

In Grisham-Brown et al. (2005), a curriculum framework was described for planning and implementing evidenced-based practices for young children. The curriculum framework consists of four elements: 1) assessment, 2) scope and sequence, 3) activities and instruction, and 4) progress monitoring. In Grisham-Brown et al., emphasis was placed on Elements 2 and 3. *Assessing Young Children in Inclusive Settings: The Blended*

Practices Approach, by contrast, focuses on Elements 1 and 4, with an expanded conceptualization of the term *assessment*. (See Definitions of Key Terms later in this chapter.) Together, the two books provide teachers in blended classrooms with information on how to plan, implement, and evaluate instruction for young children with and without disabilities.

INTENDED AUDIENCE AND USE

Similar to Grisham-Brown et al. (2005), the intended audience for *Assessing Young Children in Inclusive Settings: The Blended Practices Approach* is individuals seeking initial certification in early childhood education (ECE), primarily in blended certification programs. Students in blended certification programs take coursework in typical child development and early childhood special education (ECSE). Their degree allows them to work with children with and without disabilities. Although many states now have some form of blended certification program, some do not. While blended certification may not exist in all states, all states have early childhood programs that serve children with and without disabilities in the same setting. Therefore, both *Assessing Young Children in Inclusive Settings: The Blended Practices Approach* and Grisham-Brown et al. (2005) remain appropriate for programs that offer only ECE or ECSE certifications, and the information in *Assessing Young Children in Inclusive Settings: The Blended Practices Approach* will remain pertinent to future teachers in either certification program.

A secondary audience, teachers currently working in the field of early childhood education, would also benefit from using this book. The information is helpful to early childhood professionals who are striving to move toward more inclusive programming for children. Consultants, principals, and technical assistance providers who work with teachers in inclusive programs will find the information contained in the book useful for providing technical assistance on topics such as conducting authentic assessment, designing data collection systems, and implementing program evaluation. After Grisham-Brown et al. (2005) was published, teachers, consultants, and administrators indicated that they used the book for group studies in their school districts and agencies. For example, teachers read one or two chapters each month and met to discuss the implications in their program, or teachers read chapters and discussed implications for practice in threaded discussions and blogs.

While the main focus of the book is children who participate in center-based early childhood programs and who are between the ages of 3 and 5 years, the basic tenets of the book are appropriate for the broader range of young children. Programs serving children from birth to age 3 and ages 5–8 will find that the principles advocated in *Assessing Young Children in Inclusive Settings: The Blended Practices Approach* are relevant for younger and older groups of children as well. Therefore, universities and programs that emphasize teaching children from birth to age 5 or birth to age 8 will find the book worthwhile.

DEFINITIONS OF KEY TERMS

In an effort to ensure consistency across chapters and between this book and Grisham-Brown et al. (2005), common terms are defined in the sections that follow. In some cases, an explanation is provided for why one term is used instead of another. In defining key terms, an attempt is made to ensure that early childhood professionals from traditionally ECE or ECSE backgrounds will be comfortable with the terms used.

Assessment

Assessment is defined as a process of gathering information for the purposes of making decisions. Often educators talk about "giving tests," "administering assessments," or "using an assessment tool or measure." Each statement relates to the broader activity or process of gathering information about children (e.g., through direct testing, observations, interviews). As well, educators may say, "We're collecting portfolio entries," "We're trying to see if ____ can get special education services," or "We've got to test all of the children because Head Start requires it three times a year." These statements relate to the reasons or purposes assessments are conducted (e.g., to monitor progress, determine eligibility, evaluate a program). Recognizing that assessment is a process that happens for various reasons is essential to understanding the tenets of the book. Assessment, defined broadly, is a process of getting to know a child or a group of children for a variety of purposes. This book discusses the major purposes for conducting assessments and associated recommended practices. Within the curriculum framework, however, the term *assessment* is used as described in Chapter 7 with regard to program planning.

Data-Driven Decision Making

As noted under the definition of *assessment,* teachers engage in assessment processes to make a wide variety of decisions. A related term, particularly with regard to assessment for planning and monitoring purposes, is *data-driven decision making* (DDDM). As Marsh, Pane, and Hamilton stated, DDDM is a model whereby "teachers, principals, and administrators systematically collect and analyze various types of data, including input, process, outcome and satisfaction data, to guide a range of decisions to help improve the success of students and schools" (2006, p. 1). At the heart of making data-driven decisions is the ability to gather and use information for individuals and groups of young children. A five-step process is suggested to guide teachers in making such decisions. The first step is observation, and the second step is documentation, both of which are described at length in Chapter 2. The third, fourth, and fifth steps—summarizing (i.e., numerically, narratively, and visually), analyzing, and interpreting, respectively—are described in Chapter 7.

Early Childhood Intervention

As noted throughout the book, theories, practices, recommendations, research, and so forth, from the fields of ECE and ECSE are blending. Thus, we use a more blended term to refer to the larger context in which teachers work and are trained and in which programs are situated. *Early childhood intervention* refers to a wide range of services provided for children from birth through age 8.

Teacher

While the strategies presented here are designed for use by all early childhood professionals, there is generally one professional who has primary responsibility for children's education. That person may be referred to as the provider, educator, or interventionist. In this book, that professional is referred to as the *teacher,* a term that was selected over other commonly used terms in early childhood education for two reasons. First, *teacher* implies a level of professionalism that other terms do not. Given the importance of children's early years, it is imperative that staff who work with young children have the same educational credentials as staff who educate older learners. Using *teacher,* it is hoped, makes a statement about that importance. Second, *teacher* is used because the focus of the book is on how to assess young children in educational settings. The term *teacher* is most closely associated with those settings.

Blended Practices

In Grisham-Brown et al. (2005), *blended practices* are described as "the integration of practices that can be used to address the needs of all children in inclusive settings" (p. 3). Blended practices imply the merging of theories and philosophies from ECE and ECSE to support young children from diverse backgrounds with varying abilities. The current book emphasizes strategies for gathering information about young children that 1) combine recommendations from professional organizations that represent ECE and ECSE, 2) consider the importance of gathering information on all children regardless of ability, and 3) take into account the need for common assessment practices versus multiple assessment practices when serving children in inclusive programs.

Collaborative Partnerships

While the teacher is recognized as the professional instructional leader in early childhood settings, it is essential for all who work with young children to participate in the assessment process. *Collaborative partnerships,* consisting of professionals, paraprofessionals, and nonprofessionals, should gather assessment information and make decisions about the children with whom they work. These teams may include a teacher, an assistant, an administrator, and volunteers who support the entire class. For individual children, team members may include medical personnel (e.g., neurologist, nurse), therapists (e.g., physical, occupational, speech), and itinerant teachers (e.g., vision, hearing). Regardless of the team's composition, each member should be involved in the assessment process and the child's family and other familiar caregivers should guide each team. Throughout the book, team roles and models of assessing children are discussed. Central to each discussion is the notion that team members need to cooperate (i.e., create collaborative partnerships) with each other by sharing information, being willing to step outside of their traditional roles, and making meaningful contributions to the decision-making process.

HISTORICAL TRENDS

Two trends have affected early childhood intervention assessment since the mid-1980's. Historically, traditional ECE and ECSE approaches to conducting assessment with young children have shaped assessment practices for children with and without disabilities. More recently, the accountability of government-funded early childhood programs has affected how, when, and where young children are assessed.

Approaches to Assessment

Practices for assessing young children were generated from two historical perspectives in ECE and ECSE. Early childhood education, following a constructivist theory of development, emphasizes naturalistic assessment practices. Most assessments described in ECE literature occur in group settings using informal assessment strategies (e.g., observation) (Schultz, Kagan, & Shore, 2009). In this type of assessment, teachers follow children's leads and gather information as the children engage in classroom activities and routines. The primary purpose for conducting assessments from an ECE perspective is to plan instruction for a group of young children.

The ECSE field has emphasized assessment of individual children across traditional developmental domains (McLean, Wolery, & Bailey, 2004). Informal assessment practices are more recently recommended by ECSE professionals. However, historically, conventional assessment approaches have been implemented with young children who have disabilities. Conventional assessment practices (see Chapter 2) rely more on the use of tests to make decisions about young children. The primary purposes of conducting assessment with young children with disabilities have been to determine the children's eligibility for special education services and to design individualized family service plans and individualized education programs.

In short, professionals from the ECE field have used *informal* assessment approaches to focus on *groups* of children, while professionals from the ECSE field have used *formal* assessment approaches to focus on *individual* children. The purpose of this book is to merge practices from both fields to design an assessment framework that 1) recognizes the need for multiple assessment methods (i.e., formal and informal assessment), 2) provides information about the individual needs of children as well as the needs of groups of children, and 3) answers multiple questions about young children (e.g., eligibility for services, program planning, progress monitoring).

Emphasis on Accountability

Assessment in blended early childhood intervention programs has been affected by the recent emphasis on accountability. The primary programs that provide services to young children have different requirements for program accountability, complicating early childhood professionals' jobs because of variation in 1) the types of assessment tools used (i.e., authentic versus conventional), 2) the frequency of data collection (e.g., Head Start requires data collection three times a year, whereas the Office of Special Education Programs requires data collection at program entrance and exit), and 3) the ways data are used (e.g., local versus federal decision making). Schultz et al. (2009) compared mandates related to early childhood standards and associated assessment activities for child care, Head Start, state-funded prekindergarten, and special education. (See Table 1.1 for an overview of program differences.)

Schultz et al. (2009) identified the challenges to states, programs, teachers, and families when trying to address multiple mandates. States have difficulty managing multiple data systems and reporting and interpreting data from multiple sources. Blended programs face challenges in adequately training teachers to administer multiple measures and to meet separate sets of mandates. Teachers are challenged to conduct various types of assessment activities, depending on how children's programs are funded. Families may be confused by the abundance of requests from multiple sources for information about their children.

Multiple mandate challenges are relevant to any discussion about assessment. States, programs, teachers, and families are dealing with the realities of a complicated accountability system that heavily affects their assessment practices. *Assessing Young Children in Inclusive Settings: The Blended Practices Approach* should influence any future guidance about assessment provided.

OVERVIEW OF MAJOR BOOK SECTIONS

The overarching definition of *assessment* used throughout the book is that "assessment is a process of gathering information for purposes of making decisions" (Early Childhood Research Institute on Measuring Growth and Development, 1998, p. 2). This definition provides the foundation for the organization of the book. Because the first part of the definition refers to a *process* and the second part to a *purpose,* the book is divided into

Table 1.1. Early childhood standards for various early childhood programs and associated accountability mandates

Program standards	Child care	Head Start	State-funded pre-K	Special education
Program quality standards	State licensing standards (49 states) State Quality Rating & Improvement Systems (QRIS) (14 states + 29 pilots)	Federal program performance standards	State program standards (39 states)	Federal Individuals with Disabilities Education Act (IDEA) regulations State program standards
Assessing local program quality	State licensing visits	Federal Program Review Instrument for Systems Monitoring (PRISM)	State program monitoring (30 states)	State program reviews
Standards for children's learning	State early learning guidelines (49 states)	Federal child outcomes framework	State early learning guidelines (49 states)	Three functional goals (federal)
Child assessments	No current requirements	Progress toward Head Start outcomes reported three times per year	State pre-K assessments (13 states)	States report % of children in five categories

From Schwtz, T., Kagan, S.L., & Shore, R. (2009). *Taking stock: Assessing and improving early childhood learning and program quality* (p. 18). Washington, DC: National Early Childhood Accountability Task Force; adapted by permission.

Key: IDEA, Individuals with Disabilities Education Act of 1990 (PL 101-476).

two corresponding major sections: Section I—Recommended Practices (process) and Section II—Reasons for Conducting Assessment (purpose). An overview of Section I and Section II follows.

Process: Section I, Recommended Practices

Section I describes the process for conducting assessment of young children in blended classrooms. The process is guided by recommended practices described by professional organizations that represent young children, expert committees that direct policy related to early childhood issues, and/or legislation enacted to oversee programs for young children. A review of recommendations by these entities resulted in six common assessment themes. Recommendations include the use of assessment practices that are 1) authentic, 2) ongoing, 3) developmentally appropriate, 4) individualized, 5) natural, and 6) multifactored (Pretti-Frontczak, Bagnato, & Macy, in press). Table 1.2 illustrates how professional organizations, expert committees, and/or legislation promote each of the recommendations.

Recommended practices are highlighted in Chapters 2 through 5. Chapter 2 provides a discussion of how to conduct and document *authentic* assessment. The chapter differentiates authentic and conventional assessment and describes the ways in which authentic assessment can be collected through observation and interview. The chapter concludes with strategies for documenting information collected through authentic assessment. Chapter 3 focuses on the importance of family involvement in the assessment process. The chapter outlines various roles families might assume during the assessment process, as well as existing tools for gathering information from families about issues related to promoting their child's development. Chapter 4 discusses assessing diverse learners, with a focus on children from culturally and linguistically different backgrounds and children with severe and multiple disabilities. Considerations for assessing diverse groups of children are described, along with recommended practices for ensuring that accurate assessment information is collected. Finally, Chapter 5 highlights the importance of determing the technical adequacy of assessment instruments. The chapter defines terminology associated with technical adequacy, describes differences between various types of early childhood assessments, and explains strategies for interpreting conventional assessment instruments.

Purpose: Section II, Reasons for Conducting Assessment

Section II focuses on the reasons for conducting assessments with young children. Chapter 6 is concerned with the identification of young children who have special needs, emphasizing the processes of Child Find, screening, and diagnostic assessment. Recommended practices for conducting screening and diagnostic assessment are highlighted, and examples of instruments that can be used are provided. Chapter 7 includes information

Table 1.2. Policy recommendations for early childhood assessment practices

Assessment recommendations	DEC	NAEYC	NECATF	NRC	IDEA	NCLB	Other
Authentic	X			X			
Ongoing	X	X	X	X	X	X	Head Start Bureau, NASP
Developmentally appropriate	X	X	X	X			Head Start Bureau, NASDSE, NASP
Individualized	X	X	X	X	X	X	Head Start Bureau, NASP
Natural	X	X	X	X	X		Head Start Bureau
Multifactored	X	X	X	X	X	X	Head Start Bureau, NASDSE, NASP

Key: DEC, Division for Early Childhood; IDEA, Individuals with Disabilities Education Act; NAEYC, National Association for the Education of Young Children; NASDSE, National Association of State Directors of Special Education; NASP, National Association of School Psychologists; NCLB, No Child Left Behind; NECATF, National Early Childhood Accountability Task Force; NRC, National Research Council.

on how to plan programs for young children served in blended classrooms. Information on how to gather assessment information to plan for groups of children, as well as individual children, is provided, and commonly used assessment tools for program planning assessment purposes are described. In Chapter 8, issues about how to gather information for the purpose of monitoring children's progress are emphasized. The chapter describes how teachers collect, interpret, and make instructional decisions based on the ongoing data they collect on children in their classrooms. Finally, Chapter 9 discusses issues with assessment for the purpose of evaluating early childhood intervention programs. The chapter describes reasons for conducting program evaluations as well as the strategies for doing so. Issues associated with accountability assessments also are discussed.

SUMMARY

This book is intended to guide early childhood intervention teachers in implementing high-quality assessment for children with and without disabilities. A thorough understanding and implementation of the practices discussed in the book should result in improved services for young children and their families.

REFERENCES

Early Childhood Research Institute on Measuring Growth and Development. (1998). *Theoretical foundations of the Early Childhood Research Institute on Measuring Growth and Development: An early problem-solving model* (Vol. 6). Minneapolis: University of Minnesota.

Grisham-Brown, J.L., Hemmeter, M.L., & Pretti-Frontczak, K. (2005). *Blended practices for teaching young children in inclusive settings.* Baltimore: Paul H. Brookes Publishing Co.

Marsh, J.A., Pane, J.F., & Hamilton, L.S. (2006). *Making sense of data-driven decision making in education.* Retrieved January 24, 2010, from http://www.rand.org/pubs/occasional_papers/2006/RAND_OP170.pdf

McLean, M., Wolery, M., & Bailey, D.B., Jr. (2004). *Assessing infants and preschoolers with special needs* (3rd ed.). Upper Saddle River, NJ: Pearson.

Pretti-Frontczak, K., Bagnato, S., Macy, M., & Sexton, D. (in press). Data driven decision-making to plan programs and promote performance in early childhood intervention: Applying best professional practice standards. In *Early childhood intervention: Programs and policies for special needs children,* (Vols. 1–3). New York: Praeger.

Schultz, T., Kagan, S.L., & Shore, R. (2009). *Taking stock: Assessing and improving early childhood learning and program quality.* Washington, DC: National Early Childhood Accountability Task Force.

SECTION I

Recommended Practices

CHAPTER 2

Authentic Assessment

Whitney A. Stevenson,
Jennifer Grisham-Brown, and
Kristie Pretti-Frontczak

Ms. Charlotte is a first-year teacher for the Fort Lauderdale Public School System. She teaches in a preschool program that serves 3- and 4-year-old children who are at risk due to economic factors and children who have been diagnosed with disabilities. Ms. Charlotte's degree is in preschool special education. She took a class in college on the assessment of young children with special needs. In that class, she was taught to administer several tools commonly used to screen and diagnose children's disabilities, such as the Battelle (Newborg, 2005), the Developmental Indicators for the Assessment of Learning (DIAL-3; Mardell-Czudnowski & Goldenberg, 1998), and the Peabody Picture Vocabulary Test (PPVT; Dunn & Dunn, 1981). When she started teaching, she felt prepared to conduct assessments of young children. Once she was in the classroom, however, her supervisor began asking for data on children's performance on individual goals, as well as the expected curricular outcomes of the class of children she was teaching. Ms. Charlotte soon realized that she could not repeatedly re-administer a test like the Battelle as a way of obtaining the type of data expected by her administrator. Also, she began to understand that the information she obtained from these tests did not necessarily yield information that was useful in selecting her teaching goals. In other words, the tests she was using were not aligned with the curriculum. Ms. Charlotte needed a new strategy for gathering information about the children in her class.

The dilemma described in the preceding vignette is common for teachers working in blended early childhood settings after being trained in traditional early childhood education (ECE) and early childhood special education (ECSE) programs. As mentioned in Chapter 1, traditional ECSE programs tend to focus on the use of conventional assessment practices. As described in the vignette, the assessment instruments Ms. Charlotte learned to administer in her teacher training program serve a purpose in early childhood intervention (see Chapter 6 for details) but not her supervisor's purpose. Ms. Charlotte's supervisor wants data showing progress of both individual children and the group as a whole. She recognizes the mismatch between what she knows and what she needs to do. Rather, a sound understanding of authentic assessment practices, as they apply to planning instruction, would be beneficial to Ms. Charlotte as she addresses her administrator's request.

Authentic assessment is the primary method for collecting information on young children. As the field of early childhood continues to move toward authentic assessment practices, early childhood intervention teachers must understand how to document observations and interactions with young children, as well as appreciating the importance of the information (data) they are gathering. Authentic assessment provides teachers the opportunity to assess a child's skills and behaviors during everyday routine events and activities.

In this book, *assessment* is broadly defined as gathering information for purposes of making decisions. While the decisions and reasons for conducting assessment were described in Chapter 1, Chapter 2 focuses on the process of collecting information about young children using authentic assessment practices. In the first section, authentic assessment is described, differences between authentic and conventional assessment are discussed, and advantages of authentic assessment are overviewed. The second section focuses on how teachers can engage in authentic assessment practices by observing children in their natural environments and conducting interviews with family members. In the third, and final, section of Chapter 2, strategies for documenting authentic assessment practices are highlighted including written narratives, permanent records, and counts and tallies.

AUTHENTIC ASSESSMENT

Most early childhood intervention teachers are familiar with the term *authentic assessment*. However, their perceptions of what it means to implement authentic assessment in the classroom may vary. In this section, authentic assessment is defined, how it differs from conventional assessment is discussed, and its advantages are illustrated.

Definition

"Authentic performance assessments are methods of documenting children's skills, knowledge, and behaviors using actual classroom-based experiences, activities, and products" (Meisels, Liaw, Dorfman, & Nelson, 1995, p. 279). Authentic assessment is the practice of assessing children in their natural environment (e.g., home, school, child care center) on functional skills that are needed in that environment, with materials that are part of that environment, by people with whom the children are familiar. Authentic assessment is known as play-based, naturalistic, and performance-based assessment (Grisham-Brown, Hallam, & Pretti-Frontczak, 2008). According to Bagnato and Yeh-Ho, authentic assessment refers "to the systematic recording of developmental observations over time about the naturally occurring behaviors and functional competencies of young children in daily routines by familiar and knowledgeable caregivers in the child's life" (2006, p. 29).

The shift from conventional assessment to authentic assessment has had an impact on the field of early childhood intervention. Notable early childhood organizations, the National Association for the Education of Young Children (NAEYC) and the Division of Early Childhood (DEC) have published recommended practices defining what authentic assessment in early childhood intervention should encompass. NAEYC states that authentic assessment methods should be ongoing; inclusive of multiple methods; developmentally appropriate; culturally and linguistically responsive; authentic; useful; inclusive of families; and connected to specific, beneficial purposes (Bredecamp & Copple, 2009). DEC guiding principles conclude that "assessment methods and materials must accommodate children's developmental disability-specific characteristics" (Neisworth & Bagnato, 2004, p. 46).

Difference Between Authentic
Assessment and Conventional Assessment

One way to better understand authentic assessment is to contrast it with conventional assessment. While authentic assessment "elicits demonstrations of knowledge and skills in ways that resemble 'real life' tasks"

(Southeastern Regional Vision for Education, 1995, p. 5), conventional assessment is "the administration of a highly structured array of testing tasks by an examiner in a contrived situation through the use of scripted examiner behaviors and scripted child behaviors in order to determine a normative score for purposes of diagnosis" (Bagnato, Neisworth, & Pretti-Frontczak, in press). Although conventional assessments "require the same procedures be used for all who are being assessed" (McLean, Wolery, & Bailey, 2004. p. 23), authentic assessment can be used on children with and without disabilities; individual needs are taken into account. Table 2.1 illustrates the major differences between authentic assessment and conventional assessment practices.

Because scores from conventional assessment are used to "sort" children, no exceptions or adaptations are made for any children, including those with disabilities. Another disadvantage of conventional assessment is that no consideration is given as to whether a child is familiar with the testing environment and/or the person administering the assessment. Synder, Wixson, Talapatra, and Roach state that "traditional norm-referenced cognitive and developmental assessments are generally administered using

Table 2.1.   Overview of authentic assessment and conventional assessment practices

	Authentic assessment	Conventional assessment
Who administers?	Individuals who are familiar with the child (e.g., teacher, caregiver, therapist, family member)	Individuals unfamiliar with the child (e.g., physician, school psychologist or diagnostician, psychiatrist, therapist, teacher whom child/family does not know)
Where administered?	Places where child spends time and is familiar to the child (i.e., natural environments such as home, school, child care)	Places unfamiliar to child; may include outpatient clinics, therapy offices, doctor offices, classrooms child has not visited or attended
How administered?	Strategies that are nondisruptive to child's daily routines; child does not know that he or she is being assessed (e.g., observation, family interview)	Strategies that disrupt the child's daily routines and remove him or her from the natural environment; child is asked to perform behaviors "upon command"
What is to be assessed?	Functional behaviors in which the child needs to participate, such as daily routines and activities (e.g., physically manipulate objects to participate in snack)	Tasks that represent skills across developmental domains (e.g., making a block pyramid is a common task in the cognitive area)
What materials are used during administration?	Materials that are part of the routine in which the child is being observed	Materials from a test kit
How are families involved?	Family serves numerous roles in the assessment process (See Chapter 3.)	Family is generally involved only by receiving information about the results of the assessment

> **BOX 2.1**
>
> ## Summary of common concerns with conventional assessment
>
> - Assessment does not meet recommended practice standards.
> - There is no evidence base for use in early childhood intervention.
> - Items and procedures are not matched to the objectives of the program and are often insensitive to gains made by children.
> - Assessment may lead to biased, unfair, and inaccurate conclusions regarding a child's capabilities given the requirement to follow standardized procedures (i.e., a child's ability or inability is confused with their ability or inability to perform).
> - Test items are not functional, do not directly link to instructional efforts, and may narrow curricular efforts.
>
> (Bagnato et al., in press; Macy, Bagnato, Lehman, and Salaway, 2007; Neisworth and Bagnato, 2004)

unfamiliar materials outside of children's natural (family and school) contexts" (2008, p. 26), which can affect a child's assessment score. Box 2.1 summarizes these concerns with conventional assessment.

Advantages of Authentic Assessment

One of the major advantages of authentic assessment is that the information gathered on young children provides a true measure of what the child can do in an environment where he or she feels comfortable and secure. Unlike conventional assessment, authentic assessment does not rely on whether a child correctly responds to questions or activities, but rather provides documentation of numerous components of a child's learning. Thus, authentic assessment documents "the progress children make, their strengths, and the ways they learn and solve problems" (Grubb & Courtney, 1996, p. 5), whereas conventional assessment tests a one-time snapshot of skill mastery. Authentic assessment allows teachers and other professionals to gather needed information about a child through observations, portfolios, interviews, and curriculum-based assessments (Diffily & Fleege 1993; Grisham-Brown, Hemmeter, & Pretti-Frontczak, 2005; McNair, Thomson, & Williams, 1998). In this way, authentic assessment allows the teacher to understand each child's developmental level and plan a learning environment to meet the needs of every child, regardless of ethnicity, disability, or language. Conventional assessments, on the other hand, only gather information on whether a child can or cannot demonstrate a skill, making planning and individualizing instruction within a group difficult.

As previously discussed, the first major advantage of using authentic assessment is that the assessment occurs where a child commonly spends time, often referred to as the natural environment. The natural environment provides assessors with the opportunity to observe without putting the stresses of unfamiliar adults, places, materials, and activities on children. When children feel comfortable and relaxed, in a familiar setting, accurate documentation of their skills will be obtained. "Teaching, learning, and assessment are intricately woven together in the classrooms where children grow and learn" (Solley, 2007, p. 35).

The second advantage of authentic assessment is the clear link between information gathered about children and what is taught. A teacher who knows what skills children need to work on can prepare the environment so the children have planned opportunities to practice those skills. During the planned opportunities, the teacher observes children as they engage in activities and documents the children's skills using written descriptions or counts and tallies. Teachers can also use the information gathered from "unplanned" moments that occur during the day as documentation of a child's skill level or behavior. For example, a child who is working on verbal communication with peers may spontaneously walk up and greet a peer who has come to school. Although the interaction was not planned, it still provides an opportunity for observing and documenting verbal interactions.

Unlike conventional assessment, authentic assessment also provides a third advantage by promoting collaboration. In authentic assessment, teachers, families, and other personnel are encouraged to work together to gather information about the child. Collaboration during assessment allows relationships to be built between early childhood professionals and families (Keilty, LaRocco, & Casell, 2009). Positive, trusting relationships among everyone working with the child foster the opportunity for better understanding of all aspects of the child's life. Once established, these relationships afford the possibility for ongoing, open communication. "Assessment should be a continuing process of parent–professional dialogue because these partners in children's education need to maintain contact, share concerns, report progress and problems, monitor and review events, and jointly celebrate success" (Wolfendale, 1998, p. 357). The various inputs from families and professionals help to ensure that the goals and objectives written for a child, whether the child is typical or has a special need, are accurate and on target.

ENGAGING IN AUTHENTIC ASSESSMENT PRACTICES

Implementing authentic assessment requires that teachers learn an important set of skills and procedures. These procedures include observing children in their natural environment and interviewing families and others who know the children well. This section discusses how to collect information on young children using observation and interview, as well as advantages and disadvantages of the two techniques.

Gathering Information

Observing young children is a major component of authentic assessment practices. Observation, however, is more than writing down a specific event or activity in which a child is engaged. Observation is also more than a random recording of a child's skills or behavior. Rather, observation involves watching an interaction, activity, or event in which a child is engaged to gain information about the child. Professionals (i.e., teachers, therapists, and interventionists) must consider the *who, what,* and *how* of observation (Grisham-Brown et al., 2005). For instance, when a team consisting of teacher, teacher assistant, and therapists are working in a classroom, decisions need to be made about each person's role in observation. Ideally, all members of the educational team will share observation responsibilities. It may be necessary, however, to develop a schedule or assign particular team members either to areas of the classroom and/or to particular children. All too often teachers may assume others are watching and reflecting on children's play and actions, when without direction, such observations are not occurring.

In addition to determining who will observe, it is important for teachers to consider *what* to observe. Children's growth, development, and dispositions are on display 24/7. In other words, they are constantly showing us what they know, what they like, and what they struggle with. The number of "things" that could be observed is endless and can lead to watching without purpose or forced observations to see whether a child can demonstrate a preset number of arbitrary skills. To avoid these pitfalls, teachers need to clearly define what they are watching for. For example, is the teacher observing how a child interacts with other children, how he or she uses objects and toys, or how long he or she can remain with a group? If a child is playing at the water table and splashing, pouring, sharing, and so forth, which behavior should be observed, noted, and considered important? In other words, what should the teacher pay attention to?

Finally, teachers need to consider *how* they will conduct an observation. Observations can occur spontaneously or be planned (Dodge, Colker, & Heroman, 2002). Teachers may observe children individually, in small groups, or in large groups. Teachers can observe by watching, by engaging in parallel play, or even by giving the child simple directives and asking questions. Regardless of the degree of spontaneity or planning, the size of the group, or the teachers' roles, teachers should remember to observe children over time, people, materials, and settings. (Children act differently under different circumstances.) Further, when conducting observations, teachers must be discreet so that they can gain an objective picture of the child's development. When a teacher provides too much encouragement, support, or directions, a child's functional and spontaneous actions remain unknown. Also, knowing a child has mastered a skill but does not demonstrate it is just as informative as knowing the child can perform the skill.

Finally, while observation is considered an authentic assessment strategy, observations can be conducted in an *in*authentic manner. Sometimes referred to as analogue observations (Knoff, 1992), *in*authentic observations are contrived. Analogue observations occur when the teacher sets up mock situations in an attempt to elicit and observe the demonstration of a specific behavior. *Authentic* observations occur during children's natural play activities. Teachers watch children and observe any behaviors that occur during the activities.

While the advantages of observations include getting specific examples of children's developmental skills, providing an understanding of how children function in a group setting, and showing progress toward individual goals and objectives, there are disadvantages. Direct observation can be very time consuming. Writing anecdotal notes, recording running records, and completing checklists take time for classroom personnel, especially for a classroom of 20 children, both with and without disabilities, and only two teachers. In such cases, writing an anecdotal note for each child, documenting each encounter between two children, and completing checklists for 20 children can be daunting and time-consuming tasks. Another disadvantage of direct observation is that a professional performing an observation may lack experience and, therefore, not understand the importance of leaving out biases, making nonobjective comments, and making sure what is documented is meaningful.

Conducting Interviews

Interviewing is a second authentic assessment strategy. Interviewing has been described as "family information gathering" (Banks, Santos, & Roff, 2003) and is a method of collecting important pieces of information about young children from those who know the children best and are considered a child's first teacher (DiNatale, 2002). It is crucial to interview families regarding their perceptions of, as well as pertinent background information that might affect, the child's development. Through the interviews, families can provide information regarding how a child functions in settings other than school or child care, and teachers can gain meaningful information from families about children's preferences. Regardless of whether the child has a disability, family interviews play a critical role in how the teacher develops and writes individualized goals for the child. Through the interviews, teachers can gain insight into the family's priorities and concerns for the child, which can help with goal writing.

Banks et al. (2003) indicated that the family's cultural and/or linguistic background and the relationship between the family and teacher influenced the quality of information gathered during family interviews. Therefore, teachers need to be aware of their own cultural competence as they interact with families. Any cultural or linguistic biases a teacher has regarding a family need to be acknowledged before the teacher can expect to have effective interaction with the family. As well, teachers need to recognize the impact that 1) a family's cultural background may have on the amount and type of information that the family is willing to share and 2) a family's linguistic background may have on how well the family understands and answers the questions posed during the interview.

The relationship between the family and teacher also affects the quality of the interview. Family–teacher relationships are enhanced when teachers are sensitive to the needs of the family. One way to foster a solid relationship is to schedule a family interview at the convenience of the family, thus, making family participation more likely. Another way is to talk with and listen to families while documenting their comments and concerns thereby confirming the family's important role in the process of providing the best education for the child.

When interviewing and talking with families, it is important that teachers know that information can be gathered through structured questions and unstructured statements. An example of a structured question is "What type of activities does your child enjoy at home?" while an example of an unstructured (more open-ended) statement is "Tell me about your child." Hanson and Lynch (1989) suggest that teachers use more open-ended questions when they initially meet families, as open-ended questions make families more comfortable. Later, as the relationship between a family and teacher grows, the family will be more willing to answer more structured questions. Box 2.2 summarizes guidelines and suggestions for family interviewing.

As mentioned, the advantages of family interviewing include learning about the child in his or her home environment and hearing what skills the family views as priorities. Families may become empowered with regard to their child's education when the family's priorities are discussed in relation to the child's needs (Dichtelmiller & Ensler, 2004). Teachers should arrange to meet families at times and locations that are convenient for them, thereby increasing the likelihood of attendance. Also, when scheduling a time for the interview, teachers should remember that families may have limited availability and that even a short interview can result in useful information. By preparing for the interview process and taking families'

BOX 2.2

Guidelines and suggestions for family interviewing

1. Consider adopting a conversational approach when interviewing families (Summers et al., 1990).
2. Make the purpose of the interview clear to families prior to conducting the interview (Winton & Bailey, 1988).
3. Establish rapport with families prior to gathering information (Dunst & Deal, 1992).
4. Utilize open-ended and closed-ended questions.
5. Remember that family information gathering is voluntary and be sensitive in asking for details.
6. Talk to as many family members as possible.
7. "Funnel" the information by starting with broad concerns and then getting more specific. Summarize what families say to ensure that you are accurately interpreting what they say.

From Banks, R.A., Santos, R.M., & Roff, V. *Young Exceptional Children* (6, 11) pp. 11–19. Copyright ©2003 by SAGE Publications. Adapted by permission of SAGE Publications.

schedules into consideration, an early childhood intervention teacher makes the interview a positive experience in which valuable information is gathered.

A disadvantage of interviewing families has to do with scheduling and attendance. For various reasons, such as unemployment, lack of transportation, and work schedules, finding a time to interview a family face-to-face can prove difficult. Although a face-to-face meeting is often the best way to communicate with families, other modes of communication can work. For example, phone conferences can provide crucial information (Hearron & Hildenbrand, 2005), and e-mail and texting have become options for brief exchanges of information.

Although scheduling and attendance may pose a problem for family interviews, the teacher must remain understanding of the situation. If family members have had a negative experience in school or they are worried about leaving work to attend a meeting, a flexible teacher can be the start of a new, positive school experience. However, if there are families that miss appointments and do not return phone calls for unknown reasons, it is critical that the teacher continue to keep communication open. Understanding that "at times the teacher initiates the communication, but at other times the parent initiates the contact" (Worham, 2008, p. 270) also is important when meaningfully involving families in the assessment process.

DOCUMENTING AUTHENTIC ASSESSMENT PRACTICES

It is important that teachers learn strategies for effectively documenting observations and interviews. Information gathered from observing young children and interviewing their caregivers can be documented through *written descriptions*, *permanent records*, and *counts or tallies*. Each strategy for documenting is described in the following section.

Written Descriptions

Written descriptions are a variety of strategies used by teachers to document children's observed behavior. Types of written descriptions include anecdotal notes, running records, and ABC analysis. Nevertheless, it is important that teachers remember that what is being documented must be measurable and observable. Also, it is essential that teams identify natural opportunities during the day to gather information. For instance, because snack time is a time of conversation and interaction between children, observing and documenting a child's social initiations could naturally occur during that routine. The teacher might sit at the targeted child's table and record any behaviors that would show progress toward the goal. After a verbal exchange between the targeted child (say, Reba) and a peer (Taylor), the teacher might write: *During snack time, Reba asked Taylor to give her a napkin. After Taylor handed her the napkin, Reba said "thank you."* Reba's statements demonstrate evidence of her ability to initiate social interactions with her peers. Finally, it is important for classroom teachers and therapists to decide how often data will be collected. In Chapter 8, detailed information about how often performance monitoring data should be collected is provided. In general, while data on individual goals need to be collected on a daily basis, gathering information on all general outcomes for all children might occur on a tri-annual basis.

Anecdotal notes are brief, written accounts of behaviors, events, or activities that record a child's skill level and are written after the behavior or event takes place (Ratcliff, 2001). The notes should be detailed, precise, and nonsubjective, omitting observer thoughts and feelings (McNair et al., 1998). Figure 2.1 provides an example of an anecdotal note taken from a preschool classroom, which lists the child's name, date, and observer, along with statements about the child's day. While writing anecdotal notes

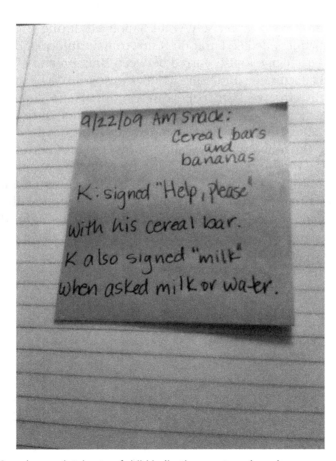

Figure 2.1. Sample anecdotal note of child indicating wants and needs.

is a quick form of documentation, it is important that educational team members develop strategies that indicate what information they want to document and how they want to do so. Do classroom teachers carry self-adhesive notes in their pockets, or is there designated paper available around the room for documentation? Do teachers have notebooks labeled "anecdotal notes" that all educational team members use? By answering these types of questions and deciding on other documentation procedures ahead of time, recording a spontaneous, meaningful event in the classroom should be easier for the teacher.

An example of when to use an anecdotal note could be when a teacher has a child who is working on answering "wh" questions and the opportunity for the child to demonstrate these skills spontaneously arises during small-group time. The teacher creates an anecdotal note, on a self-adhesive note, based on observing the child answering "wh" questions while interacting with another adult. She then posts the sticky note in a notebook, along with others written notes throughout the week in her classroom.

Table 2.2 provides a sample of an anecdotal note written about answering "wh" questions. In Example 1, the teacher, Mr. Bryce, details the verbal exchange between the child, Braxton, and the teacher, Ms. Lynn. Mr. Bryce's written account describes precisely what happened during circle time. Example 2 is much less detailed and does not contain information about the specific verbal exchange that occurred between Braxton and Ms. Lynn. Example 1 clearly documents Braxton's abilities to answer "wh" questions.

At the end of the week, teachers can tear out all anecdotal notes written and place them in each child's folder or portfolio. During the child's conference, the teacher may share a copy of the anecdotal notes with the child's family. Documented observations now serve as both family communication and performance monitoring. By collecting meaningful anecdotal notes over days, weeks, and months, the educational team soon has a variety of written accounts of a child's developmental skills (Diffily & Fleege, 1993) and should be able to make valid decisions about that child's development (McNair et al., 1998). Figure 2.2 provides two examples of anecdotal notes in a child's portfolio.

Table 2.2. Sample anecdotal notes documenting a child answering "wh" questions

Example 1: An objective, specific account of Braxton answering "wh" questions	Example 2: A subjective, nonspecific account of Braxton answering "wh" questions
10-22-2009 During group circle time, Braxton correctly answered the question "What animal is this?" by saying "bird." He also answered the question "Where is the cow?" correctly by responding "behind the barn." Ms. Lynn asked him the questions. —Mr. Bryce	10-22-2009 It was surprising that Braxton could answer any questions at circle time due to his behavior. He kept jumping in Ms. Lynn's lap. He did finally answer two "wh" questions about the book. —Mr. Bryce

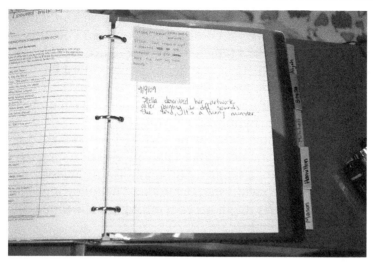

Figure 2.2. Examples of anectdotal notes in child's portfolio.

Running records are another written description strategy teachers may use to gather information. Wortham states a running record "is a more detailed narrative of a child's behavior that includes the sequence of events" (2008, p. 119). For instance, a child has a goal of verbally taking turns with a peer and a teacher notices the child conversing with another child about the plastic flowers in the dramatic play flower shop. The teacher may move to the area and conduct a running record. The teacher's documentation begins with writing down the exact verbal turn taking between the children. After a few minutes, if the children move to another area or if the conversation ends, the observation is complete and the running record documents the child's goal of verbal turn taking with a peer. Figure 2.3 provides an example of the running record that describes this dramatic play flower shop interaction; Robb's verbal turn-taking skills

---

Activity: Flower Shop in Dramatic Play (center-time)

Targeted Child: Robb

Date: 6-03-09

Length of observation: 5 minutes

Robb and Sudanthi were playing in the flower shop in the dramatic play area. As Robb walks around the table to pick up flowers, he looks at Sudanthi and asks, "Do you have a blue flower?" Sudanthi, sitting in a chair, keeps her head down while filling a basket with flowers and says, "Yes, I have one blue flower." Robb stops walking around the table and looks at Sudanthi and says, "I like blue. It's my favorite color." Sudanthi without looking up from her basket responds, "Me, too." Robb walks over and stands next to Sudanthi. Looking in her basket, he says, "Can I have your blue flower?" Sudanthi looks up and says, "No, I want it in my basket. I am getting married to Donovan. You can have a pink one." Robb says, "No," and walks away from the table.

Figure 2.3. Sample running record.

are documented during his conversation and interaction with Sudanthi while discussing flowers. By recording the words and actions, a teacher has a detailed description of a targeted behavior. Once completed, the running record is placed in the child's folder as progress-monitoring data that evidence the child's verbal turn-taking goal.

A final written description strategy of documenting children's behaviors during observations is by conducting an ABC analysis. "ABC" stands for the **a**ntecedent (what happens before the targeted behavior), the targeted **b**ehavior, and the **c**onsequence (what happens after the targeted behavior occurs) (Wortham, 2008). Using an ABC analysis can be helpful in understanding a number of behaviors in a classroom. The following vignette is an example of what a teacher might observe during a circle time activity.

As circle begins, the observer watches Zacharia and notices that Edwin accidentally steps on Zacharia's fingers while standing for the movement activities at circle. (It is noted that Zacharia regularly chooses not to stand up and participate in movement activities.) Once Zacharia's fingers are stepped on, she swings and hits both Edwin and Miguel who are sitting on either side of her. Zacharia is immediately removed from circle and taken to the book area. Once in the book area, the observer notices Zacharia smiling and looking through books. The teacher who takes the child to the book area tells her to look at books quietly and then leaves.

When completing the ABC analysis, the *antecedent* is that Zacharia's fingers get stepped on, the *behavior* is hitting, and the *consequence* is being taken to the book area where she sits alone looking at books. Figure 2.4 provides an example of this ABC analysis for this scenario. By evaluating this situation using an ABC analysis, the teaching staff may begin to understand the child's behavior and reconsider their rules regarding movement activities (e.g., Does every child need to participate?) and their strategies for handling inappropriate behaviors (e.g., Does going to the book area reinforce these behaviors?).

Name: Zacharia Michaels   School: Mid-Town Early Learning Village

Date: 5/13/2010   Observer: Travis Lawson—Teacher

Targeted Behavior: Hitting

Antecedent	Behavior	Consequence
Zacharia's fingers are stepped on during movement activity at circle.	Zacharia hits both children sitting next to her.	Zacharia is moved to the book area by a teacher to look at books by herself.

Figure 2.4. Sample ABC analysis.

While an ABC analysis can provide insight into children's behavior and classroom strategies, a disadvantage of this form of observation is that it can be difficult to always catch the "ABCs" of a situation. If a teacher was targeting a behavior and was concentrating on watching the child, then recording the antecedent, behavior, and consequence would be easy. However, if a teacher is not specifically watching a child, it would be difficult to record the needed information. Thus, it would be more effective to use an ABC analysis during a planned observation.

Permanent Records

A permanent record is used to keep track of a child's data, work samples, and progress over a certain period. One way that a permanent record can be organized is through a portfolio. Portfolios are another authentic documentation method that teachers can use to monitor a child's development. Meadows and Karr-Kidwell state that a portfolio "is a record of a child's progress of learning including how a child thinks, questions, analyzes, and interacts" (2001, p. 44). While there are a number of ways to organize a portfolio, Grubb and Courtney (1996) suggest using developmental domains to organize the many samples collected. The documentation samples can include artwork, anecdotal notes, running records, checklists, and pictures (Diffily & Fleege, 1993).

Remembering that all children in an early childhood classroom should have goals and objectives written, we can see how portfolios can play an important role in organizing and documenting a child's progress over time. For instance, when a child starts preschool the teacher will document how he or she writes his or her name. If the teacher (and family) determines that this is an area of growth for the child, the teacher will keep original or photocopies of samples of the child's name writing, thus documenting the child's progress throughout the year in the portfolio.

In addition, using a portfolio to document progress provides one common place for teachers to store a child's work. As all teachers in the classroom gather information, a portfolio can help keep everything organized. It is also important that teachers decide what documentation to include in the portfolio. By *not* limiting entries to necessary pieces that document a child's progression toward goals and objectives, teachers will soon see their portfolios become overwhelming and lose effectiveness. If this happens, "portfolios may not be representative of what the student knows and can do on a regular basis" (Grubb & Courtney, 1996, p. 8), and the work samples and descriptive information in the portfolio may not represent the child's true abilities (Grubb & Courtney). If, however, teachers plan what, how, and when items will be placed, the portfolio can be effective for documenting children's growth and development. The vignette that follows demonstrates how a teacher can purposefully use a portfolio as an authentic assessment method. Figure 2.5 provides an example of the artwork to be placed in the child's portfolio in regards to the vignette.

Figure 2.5.　Example of a work sample for the portfolio.

Together, two preschool teachers plan the activity My Family Books *to enhance name writing and naming body parts. Currently, three children in the class are working on these objectives. During classroom center time, the teachers provide children with stapled books (made from folded construction paper with the words* My Family Book *written on the front) and markers. The teachers monitor the activity. When the targeted children come to participate (either together or individually), one of the teachers takes the opportunity to sit with the child to gather data. As the children are working on their books, the teacher prompts the child to draw his or her family. If the child completing the activity needs verbal prompts to identify the body parts, the teacher says, "Point to your head." As the child points to the body part, the teacher labels what the child has done. Once the picture is completed, the teacher makes a photocopy (complete with date) and places it in the child's portfolio. In this way, the picture becomes a meaningful piece of the portfolio because it documents the child's progress of naming body parts.*

Counts or Tallies

Counts and tallies are used to track the number of times a behavior occurs. Checklists, event samples, time samples, rating scales, and rubrics all use counts and/or tallies. A checklist, one strategy to gather information, can be a valuable tool for a teacher who is assessing the developmental progress of every child in his or her classroom or of a number of children in the classroom who are working toward the same goal. Using a checklist, "teachers can quickly and easily observe groups of children, and check the

Table 2.3. Sample checklist for Playdough activity

Activity: Playdough Date: 8/12/2010	Number recognition (1–10)	Letter recognition (letters in name only)
Abbi	1–4, 7, 10	A, i
Bryce	✓	B, r, e
Macy	✓	✓
Zeke	1, 2	E

behavior or skill each child is demonstrating at a particular moment" (Ratcliff, 2001, p. 67). One checklist method is to prepare a list of the children and the goal(s) to be monitored and place it near the appropriate activity table or area in the classroom. For example, if several children are being assessed on naming and labeling alphabet letters and numbers, the teacher may prepare a checklist to monitor individual children's skill levels in seeking to reach this goal during small-group activities. As another example, when children are at the table working with playdough, a teacher can take the opportunity to ask the children to label the numbers or letters on the cookie cutters. As the children label the given letters and numbers, the teacher can mark off on the checklist what each child knows regarding alphabet and number recognition. Even if one teacher leaves the table, the checklist can remain readily available at the table for the next teacher, staff person, or therapist to record children's responses. By following this method, over time all targeted children will have the opportunity to engage in the activity, and their alphabet and number knowledge will be documented. Table 2.3 provides an example of a checklist that can be used during a playdough activity.

If a teacher wants to document the frequency of a behavior (how often it occurs), the duration (how long it lasts), the latency (how long it takes for it to begin), and/or the endurance (how many times it is repeated), then event sampling may be the documentation strategy that is chosen (Grisham-Brown et al., 2005). Event sampling can be used to document a variety of behaviors from aggressiveness to "social skills, affective expressions, cognitive attributes, creativity, and enhancement to self" (Mindes, 2007, pp. 83–84). Teachers can determine ahead of time the "events" they want to observe and prepare an observation sheet to record counts or tallies. Asking for assistance is an example of a behavior that could be measured using event sampling. Tally marks can represent each incidence in which a child says "I need help." At the end of a day (or any other designated period), the teachers would have data on the number of times the child actually asked for assistance.

Event sampling can be challenging to use when behaviors occur at a high frequency. For instance, in the preceding example, if a teacher was in the bathroom or changing diapers when the child asked for assistance, the teacher might forget to mark the sheet when entering the classroom. If the child asked for assistance twice on the playground and the teacher did not have the data sheet, the teacher might forget to mark it upon returning to the classroom. These examples illustrate why it is important for teachers to think about how to collect these data ahead of time.

Another count and tally strategy, time sampling, "involves recording the occurrence of a behavior at a given time or time interval" (McLean et al., 2004, p. 558). In time sampling, teachers count or tally how many times a targeted behavior occurs within a given period, providing the frequency of a behavior within that period. For example, if a teacher wanted to monitor how often a child was on task during classroom work time, she may record that child's behavior every 2 minutes during a 15-minute interval. The teacher could use a timer to remind her to look up every 2 minutes to observe whether the child is on task. However, for the meaning of the data to remain clear, it is important that the recorded behavior be clearly defined by the teacher.

Time sampling includes having a set time scheduled to observe a behavior. Therefore, teachers may be more likely to record data if a time is preassigned to a particular teacher. Time sampling also allows planned observation during times and events in which the targeted behavior is most likely to occur. For example, if a child has to be reminded repeatedly at lunch to stay in her seat, teachers may want to conduct a time sampling for that behavior during lunch.

One disadvantage of time sampling is that it requires teachers to have a procedure in place to track the time intervals. In a busy classroom or on the playground, keeping track of when to mark a tally may be forgotten. Therefore, with time sampling, a teacher needs to keep the tally sheet close and be prepared to mark when cued by the timer. If the teacher is unexpectedly called to leave the room during the time interval, he or she needs to ensure that another teacher is aware of the target behavior and can take over the tallying.

Another way for teachers to record a child's behavior is by using rating scales and rubrics, which "allow teachers to record observations, inferences, or judgments quickly based on predetermined definitions of behavior" (Grisham-Brown et al., 2005, p. 133). Teachers have to determine prior to the observation what behavior or skill will be observed and what criteria will be used for "rating" it. Rating the behavior can range from circling a number showing how many times the child performed the targeted behavior to denoting "always, sometimes, never" if the behavior occurred. An example of when to use a rating scale would be in the case of a teacher wanting to monitor the progress of a child's attending skills. In this scenario, the teacher may develop a rating scale of "always, sometimes, never," based on the child's target behavior of staying on task for 10 minutes during three choice-time activities. The teacher may then use the scale to monitor the child over several days. This exercise would give the teacher a better understanding of the child's attending skills—does the child attend "always, sometimes, [or] never." To use the rating method correctly, the teacher must have a clear understanding of what skill or behavior is to be assessed and what rating scale rating will accurately measure it, lest inaccurate and nonmeaningful data be collected.

A rubric, like a rating scale, also provides a quick way for teachers to monitor behaviors. In developing rubrics, teachers "create standards and rules for judging performance" (Mindes, 2007, pp. 150–151). These standards can be based on developmentally appropriate skill levels or state and/or agency requirements. Once teachers decide what behaviors will be assessed, they can circle the criterion that best matches the behavior they observed from the child. For example, if a teacher wants to monitor a child's progress toward the writing standards of the teacher's agency, he or she could develop a rubric for, and define writing at, each level: novice, apprentice, intermediate, proficient, and mastery. A teacher would then read the criteria under each level and circle where the child is developmentally. Figure 2.6 is an example of a writing rubric.

When using rating scales and rubrics, teachers can quickly document more than one child's behavior on a predetermined skill. However, because of the predetermined criteria, a true picture of the behavior may not be provided. Without the richness of observational notes and comments, the most accurate portrayal of what a child can do may be lost. Jablon, Dombro, and Dichtelmiller state that when using a rating scale "you evaluate a complex behavior in a simple way and, therefore, see only one part of a bigger picture" (2007, p. 82). To see the bigger picture, data needs to be gathered through a variety of strategies: checklists, ABC analysis, time sampling, and anecdotal notes.

SUMMARY

Collecting information about young children by means of authentic assessment methods is a recommended practice and has numerous advantages over conventional assessment. While the characteristics of conventional assessments decrease the likelihood that useful, accurate information will be collected, authentic assessment provides early childhood intervention teachers with valuable information about children that affects classroom instruction and activities.

Throughout the chapter, authentic assessment practices have been described and highlighted. It is important to remember that through meaningful observation and family interviews, a variety of useful information can be gathered about a child. However, for observations and interviews to be effective, teachers need to consider a variety of questions: What is the target behavior? What information needs to be gathered? How will the information be documented and filed? Teachers also need to remember that with authentic assessment practices, activities and instruction can be planned ahead of time to prompt a child's skill or behavior. For instance, if fine motor skills need to be assessed, the teacher can plan a small-group activity of string beads that will address the target skill. However, authentic assessment practices can also be used to document the

Novice	Apprentice	Intermediate	Proficient	Mastery
• Simultaneously brings hands to midline • Brings two objects together at or near midline • Grasps hand-size object with either hand using ends of thumb, index, and second fingers • Grasps fat crayon/marker/other tool and scribbles on paper	• Holds object with one hand while the other hand manipulates • Holds crayon, marker, pencil, or other writing implement using the thumb and first two fingers; may move whole arm across writing surface to write or draw • Uses scribble writing or letter-like forms to represent words or ideas; assigns meaning to scribbles • Copies simple written shapes after demonstration (e.g., circle, cross, T); shape should resemble the demonstrated model; any writing implement is acceptable (e.g., chalk, crayon, marker, paintbrush)	• Uses three-finger grasp to hold writing implement (experiments with grasp when using a variety of writing tools) • Produces simple texts using letter-like forms (writing includes lines and circles) • Draws using representational figures (i.e., drawings to represent people, places, events, and objects) recognizable to others or child is able to describe or label features of the drawings • Prints pseudoletters (i.e., produces characters that resemble letters and words, starting at the top of the page and moving downward from left to right on each line. Do not need to be actual letters or words.) • Produces simple texts using scribble writing (e.g., tries to write name at top of paper with lines)	• Adjusts body position when writing • Adjusts paper position when writing • Draws or writes with crayon, marker, pencil, or other writing implement using three-finger grasp—fingers near point of implement, moving the implement primarily with finger movements rather than whole arm movements; child is able to position writing implement with one hand by moving fingers of the writing hand rather than using two hands • Copies complex shapes (e.g., rectangle, square, triangle) from a drawn model (e.g., drawn on cards, paper, sidewalk) • Copies three letters (i.e., upper- or lowercase letter from model; printing errors okay; letters recognizable) • Copies first name (i.e., from model; letters in correct order; printing errors okay; name is recognizable) • Prints three letters (i.e., upper- or lowercase without model; printing errors okay; recognizable) • Copies familiar words (e.g., own name, *mom, dog*)	• Uses two hands to manipulate objects, each hand performing different movements • Writes common words using three-finger grasp (i.e., moving implement with fingers while wrist and forearm remain stable on writing surface) • Consistently shows evidence of directionality (top to bottom, left to right) • Prints first name or familiar words without a model; letters must be in correct order; errors are permissible, but words are recognizable • Uses invented spellings (i.e., uses phonemic-based spelling where letters match how the word sounds vs. conventional spelling rules)

Figure 2.6. Sample of a handwriting rubric from novice to mastery. (From Grisham-Brown, J.L., ridgley, R., Pretti-Frontczak, K., Litt, C., & Nielson, A. [2006]. Promoting positive outcomes for young children in inclusive classrooms: A preliminary study of children's progress toward pre-writing standards. *Journal of Early and Intensive Behavior Intervention,* 3[1], 171–190; reprinted by permission.)

spontaneous, unpredictable interactions and activities that occur through-out the day, prompting a child's targeted skill or behavior.

The chapter provided many examples and strategies for gathering information on children's behavior and skills. By using written descriptions (anecdotal records, running records, ABC analysis), permanent records (portfolios), and counts and tallies (checklists, event and time sampling, rating scales and rubrics), early childhood intervention teachers can be sure they are authentically gathering information, documenting, and assessing the skills and behaviors of the children in their classrooms.

REFERENCES

Bagnato, S.J. (2005). The authentic alternative for assessment in early intervention: An emerging evidence-based practice. *Journal of Early Intervention, 28,* 17–22.

Bagnato, S.J., Neisworth, J.T., & Pretti-Frontczak, K. (2010). *LINKing Authentic Assessment and Early Childhood Intervention: Best Measures for Best Practices* (2nd ed.). Baltimore: Paul H. Brookes Publishing Co.

Bagnato, S.J., & Yeh-Ho, H. (2006). High-stakes testing with preschool children: Violation of professional standards for evidence-based practice in early childhood intervention. *KEDI International Journal of Educational Policy, 3*(1), 23–43.

Banks, R.A., Santos, R.M., & Roff, V. (2003). Discovering family concerns, priorities, and resources: Sensitive family information gathering. *Young Exceptional Children, 6*(11), 11–19.

Bredekamp, S., & Copple, C. (Eds.). (2009). Developmentally appropriate practice in early childhood programs [Rev. ed.]. Washington, DC: National Association for the Education of Young Children.

Dichtelmiller, M.L., & Ensler, L. (2004). Infant/toddler assessment: One program's experience. *Beyond the Journal. Journal of the National Association for the Education of Young Children.* Retrieved from http://www.journal.nayec.org/btj/2004 01/dichtel.asp

Diffily, D., & Fleege, P.O. (1993). *Sociodramatic play: Assessment through portfolio.* Retrieved from http://eric.ed.gov/

DiNatale, L. (2002). Developing high-quality family involvement programs in early childhood settings. *Young Children, 57,* 90–96.

Dodge, D.T., Colker, L.J., & Heroman, C. (2002). *The creative curriculum for preschool* (4th ed.). Washington, DC: Teaching Strategies.

Dunn, L., & Dunn, L. (1981). *Peabody picture vocabulary test-revised (PPVT).* Circle Pines, MN: American Guidance Service.

Dunst, C.J., & Deal, A.G. (1995). Needs-based family-centered intervention practices. In C.J. Dunst, C.M. Trivette, & A.G. Deal (Eds.), *Supporting and strengthening families, Volume I: Methods, strategies and practices.* Cambridge, MA: Brookline.

Grisham-Brown, J., Hallam, R., & Pretti-Frontczak, K. (2008). Preparing Head Start personnel to use a curriculum-based assessment. *Journal of Early Intervention, 30,* 271–281.

Grisham-Brown, J., Hemmeter, M.L., & Pretti-Frontczak, K. (2005). *Blended practices for teaching young children in inclusive settings.* Baltimore: Paul H. Brookes Publishing Co.

Grubb, D., & Courtney, A. (1996). *Developmentally appropriate assessment of young children: The role of portfolio assessments.* Retrieved from http://eric.ed.gov/

Hanson, M.J., & Lynch, E.W. (1989). Assessing child and family needs. In M.J. Hanson & E.W. Lynch (Eds.), *Early intervention: Implementing child and family services for infants and toddlers who are at-risk or disabled* (pp. 130–154). Austin, TX: PRO-ED.

Hearron, P.F., & Hildebrand, V. (2005). *Guiding young children* (7th ed.). Upper Saddle River, NJ: Pearson.

Jablon, J.R., Dombro, A.L., & Dichtelmiller, M.L. (2007). *The power of observation* (2nd ed.). Washington, DC: Teaching Strategies.

Keilty, B., LaRocco, D.J., & Casell, F.B. (2009). Early interventionists' reports on authentic assessment methods through focus group research. *Topics in Early Childhood Special Education, 28,* 244–256.

Knoff, H.M. (1992). Assessment of social-emotional functioning and adaptive behavior. In E.V. Nuttall, I. Romero, & J. Kalesnik *Assessing and screening preschoolers: Psychological and educational dimensions* (pp. 121–144). Needham Heights, MA: Allyn and Bacon.

Macy, M., Bagnato, S. J., Lehman, C., & Salaway, J. (2007). *Research foundations of conventional tests and testing to ensure accurate and representative early intervention eligibility.* Pittsburgh, PA: Early Childhood Partnerships.

Mardell-Czudnowski, C., & Goldenberg, D. (1998). *Developmental indicators for the assessment of learning* (3rd ed.) (DIAL-3). Circle Pines, MN: American Guidance Service.

McLean, M., Wolery, M., & Bailey, D.B., Jr. (2004). *Assessing infants and preschoolers with special needs* (3rd ed.). Upper Saddle River, NJ: Pearson.

McNair, S., Thomson, M., & Williams, R. (1998). *Authentic assessment of young children's developing concepts in mathematics and science.* Retrieved from http://eric.ed.gov/

Meadows, S., & Karr-Kidwell, P.J. (2001). *The role of standardized tests as a means of assessment of young children: A review of related literature and recommendations of alternative assessments for administrators and teachers.* Retrieved from http://eric.ed.gov/

Meisels, S.J., Liaw, F., Dorfman, A., & Nelson, R.F. (1995). The work sampling system: Reliability and validity of a performance assessment for young children. *Early Childhood Research Quarterly, 10,* 277–296.

Mindes, G. (2007). *Assessing young children.* (3rd ed.). Upper Saddle River, NJ: Pearson.

Neisworth, J.T., & Bagnato, S.J. (2004). The mismeasure of young children: An authentic assessment alternative. *Infants and Young Children, 17,* 198–212.

Neisworth, J.T., & Bagnato, S.J. (2005). DEC recommended practices: Assessment. In S. Sandall, M.L. Hemmeter, B.J. Smith, & M.E. McLean (Eds.), *DEC recommended practices: A comprehensive guide for practical application in early intervention/early childhood special education* (pp. 45–70). Missoula, MT: Division of Early Childhood.

Newborg, J. (2005). *Battelle developmental inventory* (2nd ed.). Itasca, IL: Riverside.

Ratcliff, N. J. (2001). Using authentic assessment to document the emerging literacy skills of young children. *Childhood Education, 78,* 66–69.

Solley, B.A. (2007). On standardized testing: An ACEI position paper. *Childhood Education, 84,* 31–37.

Southeastern Regional Vision for Education. (1995, April). *Assessment in early childhood education: Status of the issue* (ED 383452). Retrieved from http://eric.ed.gov/

Summers, J.A., Dell'Oliver, C., Turnbull, A.P., Benson, H.A., Santelli, E., Campbell, M., & Siegel-Causey, E. (1990). Examining the IEFSP process: What are the family and practitioner preferences? *Topics in Early Childhood Special Education, 10,* 78–99.

Synder, P.A., Wixson, C.S., Talapatra, D., & Roach, A.T. (2008). Instruction-focused strategies to support response-to-intervention frameworks. *Assessment for Effective Intervention, 34(1),* 25–34. doi: 10.1177/1534508408314112

Winton, P.J., & Bailey, D.B. (1988). Early intervention training related to family interviewing. *Topics in Early Childhood Special Education, 10,* 50–62.

Wolfendale, S. (1998). Involving parents in child assessments in the United Kingdom. *Childhood Education, 76,* 355–358.

Wortham, S.C. (2008). *Assessment in early childhood education* (5th ed.). Upper Saddle River, NJ: Pearson.

CHAPTER 3

Family Involvement in the Assessment Process

*Anna H. Hall, Julie Harp Rutland,
and Jennifer Grisham-Brown*

Ms. Caroline initially met 4-year-old Eva's parents on a home visit at the beginning of the school year. While on the visit, she learned a little about the types of activities that Eva enjoys, such as playing on the swing set and roughhousing with her daddy. Ms. Caroline also found out that there are some times during the day that are difficult for Eva's family. As a member of a young family, Eva has two other siblings, one who is 2 years old and one who is 2 months old. Eva's mom works part time and her dad full time. On days when mom and dad have to be at work at the same time, they have difficulty getting everyone ready and out the door. Although the oldest of the children, Eva requires a great deal of attention while eating breakfast and has trouble getting dressed. In fact, when her mom or dad asks her to put on her shoes or coat, Eva will not comply with their requests without a great deal of coaxing.

Now in the third week of school, Ms. Caroline has begun to notice that Eva's mom looks stressed and Eva distressed when they regularly arrive at the Rainbow Early Childhood Development Center 10–15 minutes late. On two occasions now, Eva's mom has shared how "difficult" the mornings have been. As Ms. Caroline completes the classroom-based assessment of Eva and prepares for upcoming parent conferences, she reflects on these experiences and considers the importance of this information in working with Eva's family on identifying priority goals.

Like many teachers, Ms. Caroline is beginning to understand how conversations and interactions with families provide valuable information for planning young children's educational programs. When assessing a child, the teacher must consider the context of the relationships in the many environments in which the child lives and interacts (Bronfenbrenner, 1979). More specifically, teachers must remember that a child's overall development is affected by the interaction between the child's immediate family/community environment and the society in which he or she lives. These facts support how crucial it is to include families as active participants in the assessment process.

While programs that serve young children emphasize the importance of family involvement in all aspects of the educational program, in reality families' roles in the assessment process are often very narrow. All too often families are involved in the assessment process by simply answering a few questions about their child's developmental history and/or listening while their child's teacher tells them about how their child performed on an assessment. Limiting families' involvement in the assessment process to these simple roles underestimates the importance of the information they can provide and how involvement can benefit the families.

The purpose of Chapter 3 is to promote family involvement in the assessment process. The chapter is divided into five main sections. First, the theories that support family involvement in the assessment process are discussed, along with how the research has shaped and guided methods for involving families. Second, the legal mandates regarding family involvement are described. Third, the specific roles of the families are listed, and strategies are provided for improving communication with families.

Fourth, various tools designed for gathering assessment information from families are reviewed including structured and unstructured approaches. Fifth, considerations for gathering reliable information from families are provided to help maximize learning outcomes for children.

INVOLVING FAMILIES IN THE ASSESSMENT PROCESS

Better understanding of the importance of family involvement in the assessment process begins with the ideology behind current recommended practices in the early childhood intervention field. Early childhood intervention is grounded by a strong theoretical foundation (Bandura, 1977; Bronfenbrenner, 1979; Gardner, 1997; Knowles, 1984) that focuses on the child not only as the learner, but also as a member of a family and within the systems and factors that affect the family members' lives. The Ecological Systems Theory, the Adult Learning Theory, and family-centered practices will be discussed in this part of the chapter.

Ecological Systems Theory

To understand a child's development, one must consider the different relationships and the many environments that the child experiences as part of his or her everyday life. The Ecological Systems Theory (Bronfenbrenner, 1979) explains the relationships among different social units and the broad impact of these social supports. The theory defines complex "layers" of the environment, each having an effect on a child's development. Bronfenbrenner depicts these layers as concentric, with the child and family in the innermost circle. The child and family unit is nested in a broader circle of informal social units that consist of relatives, friends, neighbors, child care providers, and other close acquaintances. These units are nested in larger social units, which include neighborhoods, churches, social organizations, and child care centers. Still further, the larger social units are embedded in even larger social systems consisting of governments and other decision-making bodies that could potentially affect the child. A fundamental tenet of the Ecological Systems Theory is that there is interaction both within and between levels so that events occurring in one unit will affect what occurs in another unit.

The interaction between factors in the child's immediate family/community environment and the society in which they live influences their development. As changes or conflicts in any one layer affect the other layers, indirect influences bear upon a child's development as much as more direct influences do. For example, in a poor economy, a child's parent may be forced to work two jobs in order to make ends meet, and the child suffers from lack of parent–child interaction due to a wide-ranging societal problem.

The Ecological Systems Theory is important to consider when working with families during the assessment process because the teacher may need to ask specific questions to learn about a child's different influences and experiences. For example, the teacher may need to ask about the family's support system and the ability of the family to consistently carry out intervention plans in the home setting. To conduct an accurate assessment, teachers must consider not only the child in the immediate environment, but also interactions within and between environments. These environments may include the home, school, child care center, and parents' workplaces. Parents as well as caregivers, teachers, and other professional personnel have played typical roles in the assessment process. The importance of multiple influences on the child, however, may also include relatives, friends, neighbors, parents' co-workers, and communities, as well as how interactions among these influences may directly or indirectly affect a child's development.

Adult Learning Theory

Because the focus of early childhood intervention is the broader context of family and not the child, interactions with adults are as important as interactions with children. Designed to better understand the education of adults, Adult Learning Theory (Knowles, 1984) was first introduced by Malcolm Knowles in the 1970s and is based on the following assumptions: Adults are self-directed learners, life experience and knowledge contribute to adult learning, adults learn when they perceive a need to know something, and learning must be relevant. Therefore, the Adult Learning Theory can help teachers understand what may motivate parents and other familiar caregivers to participate in setting individual goals during the assessment process (Marquardt & Waddill, 2004; Mezirow, 1981).

More applicable to early childhood intervention, Knowles suggested that as self-directed learners, adults are resistant to decisions and strategies that are determined without the participation of the adult. In these circumstances, feelings of ill will can result rather than inclusion as part of a team of collaborators. Finally, the Adult Learning Theory assumes learners are motivated by intrinsic factors (Knowles, 1984). They learn what they want to learn based on what is important to them at any particular time in life. In response to Adult Learning Theory, early childhood educators should consider what is important to families and try to meet those needs. When planning assessments, teachers need to consider the type of involvement that families would like to play in the assessment process and the extent to which they would like to be involved. By valuing the information provided by families, assessment can be designed to be functional within the context of their typical daily routines and focus on the family as a whole.

Family-Centered Practices

The field of early childhood intervention has evolved in its view of families, starting with *child-centered practices*, moving to *family-guided practices*, and finally arriving at *family-centered practices*. Family-centered practices involve a set of beliefs, principles, and values for supporting and strengthening the capacity of families to promote and enhance the development of their children (Dunst, 2002). A few of the tenets of family-centered practices include the recognition and respect for 1) the family as the expert on the child, 2) the family as the ultimate decision maker for the child and family, 3) the family as the constant in the child's life with teachers being a temporary relationship, 4) the family's choice in level of participation, 5) the family's priorities and concerns as the propeller for goals and outcomes, and 6) the family's cultural beliefs and values (Baird & Peterson, 1997). Family-centered practices use models that conceptualize and implement learning strategies focusing on the child within everyday settings and social relationships. As children may respond differently in environments and with people with whom they are unfamiliar, it is important to use family-centered practices that will result in more reliable measures.

Research indicates that using family-centered practices during the assessment process yields higher reported satisfaction and family well-being (Dunst, 1985; Dunst, Bruder, Trivette, & Hamby, 2006) and better outcomes for children (Dunst) than the traditional child-centered approach. As the field of early childhood intervention has evolved in its views, so have practices. It is important to implement the tenets of family-centered practices in all aspects of early childhood intervention including the assessment process. Respect must be given to the family as the expert in providing valuable information about their child and to using family priorities and concerns as the foundation for planning.

The common thread in the aforementioned foundational theories and practices of early childhood intervention (Bronfenbrenner, 1979; Dunst, 1985; Knowles, 1984) is the recognition of the family's role as important and relevant. Theories and practices that are grounded in research contribute to assessment processes that are functional and support the family's ability to promote the child's development because they lead to feelings of empowerment, which in turn lead to better outcomes for children (Hoover-Dempsey et al., 2005). Without careful attention to the important influence of the child's family, the success of early intervention is likely compromised (Dunst, 1985).

LEGAL MANDATES

In response to research, and shaped by foundational theories and philosophies, legislative mandates in early childhood intervention that require the involvement of families are now present. These trends include legislation in early childhood special education/early intervention, Head Start and Early Head Start. For example, a key component of the federal special education law, the Education of All Handicapped Children Act (PL 94-142), together with its subsequent amendments, references the need for parent involvement. With each reauthorization, Congress has affirmed the commitment to family involvement leading to what is now known as the Individuals with Disabilities Education Act (IDEA; U.S. Department of

---

BOX 3.1

Examples of the importance of family as stated in IDEA

Sample phrase from PL 94-142—Education of All Handicapped Children Act: "Parents should be provided training through a not-for-profit agency to enable them to participate more effectively with professionals in meeting educational needs of their child."

Sample phrase from PL 99-457—Education of All Handicapped Children Act Amendments of 1986: "To enhance the capacity of families to meet the special needs of their infants and toddlers with handicaps."

Sample phrase from PL 105-17—Individuals with Disabilities Education Act Amendments of 1997: "a family-directed assessment of the resources, priorities, and concerns of the family and the identification of the supports and services necessary to enhance the family's capacity to meet the developmental needs of the infant or toddler. . . ."

Sample phrase from PL 108-446—Individuals with Disabilities Education Improvement Act of 2004: "a written individualized family service plan developed by a multidisciplinary team, including the parents, as required by subsection (e). . . ."

Health and Human Services, 2009). See Box 3.1 for examples of how the importance of families has been stated in PL 94-142 and continuing through each of the amendments.

Early intervention (Part C of IDEA), which serves children birth through 2 years of age, requires that the family is part of the team that develops the individualized family service plan (IFSP). Families are not only expected to be present, but also expected to describe daily routines, their children's likes and dislikes, the typical interactions that take place within the context of relationships, and how these descriptions affect their parenting and support of their child with disabilities. In fact, one element of the IFSP is a statement of the child's current levels of cognitive, physical, communication, social-emotional, and adaptive development, which can be provided only by or through the family.

As children transition from Part C (early intervention) to part B of IDEA, families of children 3–5 years of age often struggle with the change from family-centered services to child-centered education programs where the school assumes the primary educational responsibility. IDEA requires a 6-month transition period from Part C to Part B to assist families with these changes in services. During the transition, meetings are held with families and evaluations of the child are conducted. Extra time is allowed for conversations among parents, teachers, and specialists to ensure a positive transition for the child (Johnson, 2001).

Another example of a mandated program that focuses on the family is the Head Start program, which provides grants to local public and private nonprofit and for-profit agencies to provide comprehensive child-development services to economically disadvantaged children and their families. Head Start promotes school readiness by supporting the social and cognitive development of children through the provision of educational, health, nutritional, social, and other services to enrolled children and families (U.S. Department of Health and Human Services, 2009). The main focus of Head

Start is helping preschoolers develop the early reading and math skills they need to be successful in school. Parents are engaged in their children's learning and help them progress toward their educational, literacy, and employment goals. The Head Start program places a strong emphasis on the involvement of families (U.S. Department of Health and Human Services). Head Start standards state the need for agencies to maintain regular communication with families including periodic meetings to discuss assessment results and student progress. Progress reports must be distributed to families in an understandable, uniform format and, if possible, in a language that parents understand. Head Start also encourages direct participation of parents and community members in its implementation. The goal of parent participation is to allow parents to become full partners in the education of their children (U.S. Department of Health and Human Services).

Furthermore, the Early Head Start program was established to serve children from birth to 3 years of age in recognition of the growing evidence that the earliest years are extremely important to a child's growth and development. Early Head Start promotes healthy prenatal outcomes, enhances infant and toddler development, and empowers the family to function in a healthy manner. One way that Early Head Start promotes family involvement is through home visits. During home visits, Early Head Start workers reinforce the parent's ability to support their child's cognitive, social, emotional, and physical development. Strengths-based parent education is also provided to encourage parents to be their child's first teacher (U.S. Department of Health and Human Services, 2009).

INVOLVING FAMILIES IN THE ASSESSMENT PROCESS

Family involvement in the assessment process is a necessary component of successful early childhood intervention; however, it must be respected as a choice for families. Families may choose to participate in the assessment process at varying levels. One of the tenets of family-centered practices is recognition of and respect for the family as the expert of the child (Baird & Peterson, 1997). In other words, families know their children best; therefore, it is important to welcome their involvement regardless of the level.

There are many ways in which families can be "invited" to participate in the assessment process. Possible roles families can play include 1) creating opportunities for parents to be *consumers* by providing them with important information about their child's development, 2) asking families to share their story or be *informants* through the process, 3) *teaming* with families as they assist with the assessment process, and/or 4) allowing them to be the *advocate* as they describe hopes and dreams for their child. Each of these roles is described in the sections that follow.

Consumer

All families have the right to receive important information about their child's education. Teachers should discuss issues with families that relate to curriculum framework design, implementation, and evaluation, such as the underlying philosophy of their teaching. Families should also receive information that will support their child's development when their child is not in school (Grisham-Brown, Hemmeter, & Pretti-Frontczak, 2005).

Families need information about the school's philosophy of early childhood education in order to understand how children are learning important concepts while engaged in play. Teachers need to share with families how content and individualized goals are being addressed. Oftentimes, there is a disconnect between home and school, and new strategies are needed to bridge the gap. Visual representations of learning opportunities related to targeted behaviors and/or standards can be used to inform parents about their child's school experiences. These visual representations are referred to as embedding schedules (Grisham-Brown et al., 2005; Hemmeter & Grisham-Brown, 1997; Pretti-Frontczak & Bricker, 2004). Embedding schedules include target behaviors that will be addressed for the child, activities that occur throughout the school day, and examples of specific behaviors that the child can demonstrate/practice within a designated activity. By sending embedding schedules home, the teacher is providing another opportunity for the families to be consumers in the assessment process. Table 3.1 is an example of a classroom embedding schedule.

Lesson planning forms are another strategy used by teachers to help families understand how important concepts and standards are being addressed through play. The forms include the daily classroom schedule with accompanying activities that will occur throughout the day, standards or broad outcomes for all children that will be the focus of each activity, and suggestions for how the family can promote the identified outcomes at

Table 3.1. Sandy's target behaviors/embedding schedule

Schedule of activities	Count objects	Practice fine motor skills	Interact appropriately with peers
Greeting circle	Count friends and days on the calendar	Help teacher put CD in the stereo	Greet peers by name
Small group	Count objects to go on art project	Button shirt prior to art project	Ask peers to pass objects using appropriate manners
Snack	Count pieces of cereal or snack of the day	Open milk carton	Share important happenings in her life
Centers/ work time	Count objects around the room such as cars in the block area	Make bead necklace to be used in dramatic play	Invite friends to play in a center
Outdoor play	Count butterflies	Button/snap/zip coat before going out to play	Join friends in a game of tag

Table 3.2. Lesson planning form

Schedule/activities	Learning outcomes	Home activities
Greeting circle • Story: Olivia • Finger play: "This little piggy went to market" • Movement: Parachute	• Enjoys and values reading • Actively participates in conversation • Shows rhythm while moving	• Read stories about animal characters • Do finger plays with family members
Small group • Farm paintings	• Uses tools for writing and drawing • Explores cause and effect	• Go through old magazines and make a farm animal collage

Snack
• Fruit salad
• Milk
	• Identify different colors and shapes
	• Begin to recognize nutritional food choices
		• Prepare applewiches
		  1. Spread peanut butter on two round slices of apple.
		  2. Put cheese slice in the middle and eat like a sandwich.

Centers/work time • Blocks: Farm • Dramatic play: Grocery store • Reading: Animal books	• Take turns with others • Take on pretend roles and situations	• Talk about how food gets to the grocery store from the farm • Build a barn using blocks
Outdoor play • Farm animals in the sandbox	• Make believe with objects	• Go to a local farm to see the animals

home. Table 3.2 provides an example of a lesson planning form that teachers may send home to families on a weekly basis.

Along with sharing targeted behaviors and daily activities, teachers are required to share assessment information with parents in a variety of settings. A child's progress toward individual goals can be shared formally during parent meetings or informally through notes and phone calls. Teachers need to use multiple ways to communicate with families due to the differences in family schedules, preferences, literacy levels, and primary language. School web sites, teacher blogs, e-mail, and texting are all new technologies that can also assist teachers in communicating with families.

If a child has an IFSP or an individualized education program (IEP) in place, meetings are held to share the child's progress with the parents. During these meetings, parents may be informed that their child has reached proficiency for an individualized goal and that it is time to create a new goal. If the child has not yet reached proficiency, plans could also be made to adjust goals or continue work on goals already in place.

Often, parent conferences are held on a regular basis for all children so that the teacher can share assessment results and talk with parents about their child's strengths and weaknesses. At these conferences, for example, teachers may show parents their child's journal illustrating writing growth over time or they may explain the results from a formal curriculum-based assessment (CBA). Parent conferences can also serve as a time for parents to inform teachers about their child. Involving families in such bidirectional sharing of information allows further connections to be made between home and school (Cheatham & Ostrosky, 2009).

Sharing information, whether it is in person, through hand-written notes, or through some form of technology, is critical. Teachers also can share valuable information with families by extending learning opportunities to the home. Families are better equipped to help their child when they are provided with in-home learning activities and with suggestions for ways to promote the child's individualized targeted behaviors within their daily routines. For example, if a child is working on fine motor skills as a targeted behavior, the teacher may suggest that the child be given small foods to pick up during mealtimes, such as dry cereal or raisins, or provide the family with developmentally appropriate art activities that will further develop the child's fine motor skills. Teachers should also be well versed in child development issues, such as toilet training, sleep schedules, and sibling relationships, in order to provide parents with reasonable explanations for the presence of such issues (Grisham-Brown et al., 2005; Katz, 1996).

Although it is vital for families to receive information about school policies, curriculum design, and targeted behaviors, teachers should be careful not to limit families' role in the assessment process to that of the consumer. Both structured and unstructured approaches to assessment often fail to include the family as an active participant. It is important to remember that families are their child's first teacher and that they know their child best. Therefore, families should play an active role in the assessment process, working together with the teacher and specialists to play additional roles such as informant, team member, and/or advocate.

Informant

Families can provide critical information about their child from their very unique perspectives. National Association for the Education of Young Children guidelines recommend that families be involved in early childhood programs as *receivers* and *providers* of information (Bredekamp & Copple, 1997). The DEC recommended practices also emphasize family–professional partnerships (Sandall, Hemmeter, Smith, & McLean, 2005). It is important to use families as informants in the assessment process because they have almost constant contact with their child and interact with the child in many different contexts (Vangalder, 1997). These experiences allow families to provide teachers with various types of information that can aid in the design and implementation of valid assessments.

Families can share information about their child's temperament and physical needs, which may help the teacher understand a child's reaction to different assessment situations. For example, a child who tends to be anxious might perform better on CBAs than on structured assessments. A child who has poor fine motor skills may struggle with pen and paper assessments but perform well with oral questioning.

Families also can share information about their child's daily routine. Teachers need to know about these routines in order to have reasonable, culturally sensitive expectations for the child, especially regarding self-help issues. For example, in some cultures mothers assist their child with using utensils for many years, while in other cultures mothers encourage independent feeding skills at a young age. When discussing routines, it is helpful to talk with families about how they encourage and limit their child at home. Learning about styles of encouragement and limiting can give insight into the child's behavior and reactions in the classroom (McWilliam, Casey, & Sims, 2009). If a child is accustomed to receiving extrinsic rewards for motivation at home, he or she may have a hard time adjusting to intrinsic rewards used in the classroom. The child may be confused about the different types of encouragement used by parents and teacher and may require some explanation. Limits and consequences will most likely vary between home and school as well. While some homes will use physical punishment, schools are required to use more natural consequences, such as removing the child from a troublesome situation.

It is helpful for teachers to learn about the dynamics of a family to better understand the child and his or her behaviors in the classroom. Family relationships and varying types of social-emotional interaction can affect the child's performance on classwork and assessments. Gaining information about the family's history and the child's previous life experiences can help teachers provide more accurate assessment. For example, if the child has recently lost an important family member, he or she may feel reserved and be more reluctant to answer open-ended questions on an assessment. In contrast, the child may perform well on an assessment that encourages drawing freely and expressing feelings without words.

Information about the family's community involvement and cultural background can help build rapport with the family and child and enable the teacher to provide appropriate resources during the assessment process. (See Chapter 4.) Teachers should consider a child's cultural background in economic, social, and occupational terms instead of focusing solely on ethnicity and race (Westphal, 1989), an idea that will be discussed in detail later in the chapter under *Sensitivity towards diversity*.

Understanding each family's priorities and goals for its child, along with the family's strengths, needs, and resources, allows teachers to plan, implement, and evaluate each child as an individual (Vangalder, 1997), ensuring that the assessment process is accurate and valid. For example, a family's priority may be for the child to improve in the area of language development. Understanding this priority would help the teacher when developing the classroom curriculum and individual goals for the child. More importantly, when teachers acknowledge family's priorities and goals for their child, the families are more likely to feel that their needs are validated and, therefore, will carry through any suggestions regarding teaching the priority in other environments.

Families also can share their child's preferences and tell the teacher what "works" with their child in order to help teachers develop assessments and interventions that are tailored to students' individual needs. If a student prefers working in a quiet setting, a teacher may allow the child to move to the hallway to be assessed. Students who have strong interests, such as sports or animals, may perform better on assessments that are developed with their interests in mind. As well, children may have preferences about how adults interact with them, the type of environment in which they work best, and the type of materials that motivate them.

Team Member

Families, as collaborative members during the assessment process, can be instrumental in identifying the best assessment strategies and approaches for their children. Therefore, families must be invited to participate in all aspects of the assessment process (Boone & Crais, 1999), including planning the assessment, participating in interviews, helping gather information and testing the child, and helping to determine whether the information collected is representative of their child's actual abilities.

By participating, gathering information, and rating specific behaviors in their children, parents have increased their awareness of their child's development (Dinnebeil & Rule, 1994) thus enhancing their contributions to the development of intervention plans and decision making (Brinckerhoff & Vincent, 1987). The family, along with the teacher and specialists, can develop a more accurate picture of the child by compiling and interpreting their multiple observations of the child (Vangalder, 1997). For example, when teachers use the Assessment, Evaluation, and Programming System for Infants and Children (AEPS®), Second Edition (Bricker, 2002), as an assessment, families are asked to make observations of their child in the home or in other familiar settings and fill out a family report about their children's level of independence on each developmental skill. Family involvement in AEPS may improve program planning or progress monitoring. Figure 3.1 illustrates a portion of the AEPS Family Report II, where parents marked each skill with an "Y" if they feel that their child performs the skill or action described in the question, an "S" if they feel that their child sometimes performs the skill or action, and an "N" if they feel that their child does not perform the skill or action yet.

Multiple observations, including those from families can also be collected using the Transdisciplinary Play-Based Assessment and Intervention (TPBA/I2; Linder, 2008). The arena approach to assessment includes families as equal team members along with professionals from various disciplines. One purpose of involving families in this assessment is to determine eligibility for special education services.

TPBA/I2 is a flexible, holistic process that meets the needs of the individual child and the family. In the arena model, one team member is authorized to interact with the child using novel and familiar toys in a natural

Cognitive Area

Cognitive skills are those that involve mental processes and reasoning. These skills include problem solving, counting, recalling, imitating categorizing, and pre-reading.

11. Does your child pretend play with other children? (F1) NOTE: Place a "Y," "S," or "N" by items a through c:

   _S_ a. Does your child pretend to be someone else and tell other children who they can pretend to be? For example, your child says, "I'll be the bus driver and you be the kid." (F1.1)

   _S_ b. Does your child act out a pretend story or event? For example, your child says he or she is going fishing and then pretends to catch some fish and cook them. (F1.2)

   _Y_ c. Does your child use pretend objects or motions to play? For example, your child pretends to brush hair without a brush. (F1.3)

12. Does your child play games following rules? (F2) | S |

13. Does your child count at least 20 objects (G1) | N |

Figure 3.1. Completed a portion of the AEPS Family Report II title. (From Bricker, D., Pretti–Frontczak, K., Johnson, J.J., & Strake, E. [2002]. *Assessment, Evaluation, and Programming System for Infants and Children (AEPS), Second Edition: Volume I. AEPS Administration guide.* Baltimore: Paul H. Brookes Publishing Co.; reprinted by permission.)

setting, while the other team members gather information through observation of the child and use developmental guidelines to help interpret the assessment. Using these guidelines and age tables related to each of the developmental domains, the team interprets their cumulative information to determine the ability level of the child. Results from the assessment help develop effective individualized goals. The results also help teachers determine strategies for promoting higher levels of skills or more functional behaviors (Adrienne & McCollum, 1992; Linder, 2008).

Active family involvement does not mean abdicating professionals of their responsibilities. It is still the responsibility of teachers and specialists to help families choose a reasonable course of action for achieving targeted behaviors. All team members should be actively involved in suggesting and providing appropriate options for individualized goals (Berman & Shaw, 1995). Families are the most familiar with their child, but they are not always familiar with appropriate interventions or developmentally appropriate practices. It is the job of the teachers and specialists to share their expertise and to help guide families and facilitate teamwork when working together. Involving families in the TPBA/I2 assessment process as team members leads to a report that seems honest to those families and, ultimately, leads them toward appropriate solutions and resources (Berman & Shaw).

Advocate

Although professionals in the field of early childhood intervention have a great interest in the children they serve and teach, families have the greatest vested interest in their children. They must live with the results and strategies that are developed from the assessment. Therefore, families may confirm or refute assessment information, based on their knowledge and understanding of their child's abilities and characteristics. Their advocacy may be achieved through gathering information and commenting on their child's behaviors and performance during assessment, asking questions about the methods used during the evaluation, and making sure they clearly understand the process (Berman & Shaw, 1995). To provide support, families must be advocates for their children throughout each step of the assessment process, including planning the evaluation, gathering information, and analyzing the results. Family advocacy at times may be as simple as assuring that the time of day and the length of observations are appropriate and in the best interest of the child. Families can provide a fresh perspective on how services should be delivered (Thegan & Weber, 2002) and must be supported in their efforts to develop skills to communicate concerns, goals, placement options, and many other types of key information that is relevant to the assessment process.

Benefits to Families and Children

When families are fully involved in the assessment process, there are improved outcomes for both children and families. The term *outcomes* refers to the end result of services. It is important that outcomes be functional, or meaningful to children and families in their everyday lives and routines across a variety of settings. In addition to the outcomes that are directly related to core content, parent involvement also contributes to better attitudes about school (Epstein, 2000).

Another result of family involvement in the assessment process is increased family satisfaction. Using family-centered practices, such as including families in assessment, leads to feelings of empowerment (Hanft & Pilkington, 2000) and a higher level of parents' well-being (Dunst et al., 2006). In addition, involving families in the assessment process increases the likelihood of learning outcomes that are meaningful to the family, which increases the likelihood of the family addressing targeted skills within typical routines using strategies developed from information gained during the assessment.

APPROACHES FOR GATHERING
ASSESSMENT INFORMATION FROM FAMILIES

Information can be gathered from families with unstructured and structured approaches. Using a combination of these approaches, teachers can gather valuable information about children's strengths and weaknesses as well as monitor their progress toward important learning outcomes. Unstructured approaches involve asking open-ended strategies that allow families the opportunity to provide as little or as much information as they desire. Structured approaches include those which are linked to the use of CBA tools in planning instruction.

Unstructured Approaches

Interviews, informal observations, and open-ended questioning are examples of unstructured approaches to gather information. Formal measurement tools may not provide all of the necessary information to clearly depict the strengths and concerns of each child and family, thereby hindering the development of strategies that are functional (Dunst & McWilliam, 1988). On the other hand, unstructured approaches, such as the Routines-Based Interview (McWilliam et al., 2009) or the Asset-Based Context Matrix (Wilson, Mott, & Batman, 2004), provide a framework for gathering information on the family routines, interests, interactions, and participation in everyday activities. A Routines-Based Interview focuses on discussing the family's daily routines and asking parents to share their satisfaction with each routine. The interview is often conducted using an "open" form that does not specify the routine being discussed and a "structured" form that lists the specific routine and questions to ask the family. While discussing daily routines with parents, the teacher records the family's level of satisfaction with their child's engagement during each of the routines. Routines that may be discussed during a Routines-Based Interview include waking up, diapering/dressing, feeding/meals, getting ready to go/traveling, hanging out/watching TV, bath time, outdoors, and nap/bed time.

Similarly, the Asset-Based Context Matrix focuses on the context of natural environments or routines in which the child interacts and lives. The model focuses on using the child's interests and assets within daily activities to promote new opportunities for growth. Information about the child is gathered through observations, interactions, and conversations with the family. Once the information is gathered, teachers and families enter the information into a matrix that can be easily used to develop goals and interventions. Information obtained through these less formal measures can provide a clearer picture of each unique child and assist in developing strategies that will be functional (Wilson & Mott, 2006).

Different techniques are used by teachers when communicating with families. Some use a conversational approach, while others use direct questioning or forms for interviewing. Research suggests that the conversational approach, which gives parents conversational control, better reflects actual family goals (Cheatham & Ostrosky, 2009) and the use of open-ended questions helps to create mutual trust and free-flowing communication (Reedy & Walls, 1996).

The use of open-ended questions is important when unstructured approaches are employed to gather limitless information from families. Open-ended questions are those that cannot be answered by a simple "Yes" or "No" or one-word answer, but instead invite the family to expand on their answers in order to share more information about their child. Table 3.3 contains examples of closed-ended questions and how they can be converted into open-ended questions.

Table 3.3. Using open-ended questions vs. closed-ended questions

Topic	Closed-ended	Open-ended
Self-help	Does your child bathe him- or herself?	How is your child involved with bath time?
Literacy	Does your child identify letters?	How does your child interact with print?
Numeracy	Does your child know how to count?	How does your child use numbers in his or her daily routines?
Communication	How many words does your child say?	How does your child get his or her wants and needs met?

Structured Approaches

Structured approaches for gathering assessment information from families are associated with CBAs. Curriculum-based assessments are designed to measure specific skills for families and teachers to determine the child's current level of development. Some CBAs have specific forms and/or processes for involving families in their children's assessment. Active family involvement in the assessment process is built into CBAs through the use of reports, interviews, family albums, developmental record books, profiles, narrative family reports, and conferencing. Table 3.4 describes how selected CBAs involve families in the assessment process.

CONSIDERATIONS FOR GATHERING RELIABLE INFORMATION FROM FAMILIES

There are many issues teachers must consider when gathering information from families. How will the information be gathered? How will the teacher get families to be open and forthcoming with information? How is information about the family best used to help the child? Understanding family involvement in the assessment process and how to use effective communication skills can help teachers answer these questions. It is also important that teachers have knowledge of scheduling needs and unique needs of diverse groups in order to collect reliable information. Finally, it is important for teachers to understand how to define family priorities, set individual goals, and plan programs with families in mind.

Understanding Levels of Family Involvement

As previously discussed, one of the tenets of family-centered philosophy is the recognition and respect for the families' choice in how they want to be involved in the assessment process. Assessment practices should encourage and support varying levels of family involvement (i.e., from involving the family as receivers of information to using the family as important informants, team members, and advocates).

Table 3.4.   Description of how select CBAs involve families in the assessment process

CBA	Description
Assessment, Evaluation, and Programming System for Infants and Young Children (AEPS), Second Edition (Bricker, 2002)	The Family Report has two sections: Family Routines and Family Observations. A process for involving families in the development of individualized goals is provided.
BRIGANCE Inventory for Early Development-II (Brigance, 2004)	A developmental record book with a color coding system is used to inform families of their children's progress. The recording system helps families and teachers identify individualized goals.
Carolina Curriculum for Preschoolers with Special Needs (CCPSN), Second Edition (Johnson-Martin, Attermeier, & Hacker, 2004)	Regular conferences are held to maintain family participation. Families are included in discussions about their child's intervention program and planned activities.
Creative Curriculum Developmental Continuum Assessment (Trister-Dodge, Colker, & Heroman, 2002)	Suggestions for gathering information about child and family are provided (e.g., routines, culture). The Child Progress and Summary form is provided to families to demonstrate child's progress
Hawaii Early Learning Profile (HELP) (Furano, O'Reily, Hosaka, Inastuda, & Allman, 2006)	The Help Chart and HELP Family Participation format facilitates parent involvement by giving the family choice of how much they want to be involved in their child's assessment and planning.
The Ounce Scale (Meisels, Marsden, Dombro, Weston, & Jewkes, 2003)	Albums serve to gather information from the family including photographs, drawings, and written information. Developmental Profiles and Standards help teachers work with families during conferences to evaluate children's progress and identify goals.
Transdisciplinary Play-Based Assessment and Intervention (TPBA/I2), 2nd Edition (Linder, 2008)	Information is gathered from families through the Child and Family History Questionnaire and the Family Assessment of Child Functioning Daily Routines Rating form.
Work Sampling System, 4th Edition (WSS) (Meisels, Marsden, Dichtelmiller & Jablon, 2001)	Ongoing assessment is summarized three times per year (fall, winter, spring) for each child. An easy-to-read report is given to families to share the results. An optional narrative family report is provided, but no specific role is assigned to the parent to help gather information to use as part of the process.

Kansas Inservice Training System. (2010). *Curriculum-based assessments for measuring early childhood outcomes*. Parsons, KS: Kansas University Center on Developmental Disabilities. Retrieved from http://www.kskits.org/ta/ECOOutcomes/index.shtml

Effective Communication Strategies

Regardless of whether structured or unstructured assessment approaches are utilized, the assessment information gathered will be most useful if teachers use effective communication strategies. It is important to maintain a very clear and open level of communication with families in order to maximize the amount of information collected. "Communication is noticeably enhanced when the following indicators are observed: (a) warmth, (b) empathy, (c) respect, (d) genuineness, (e) listening, and (f) concrete practicality" (Maring & Magelky, 1990, p. 606). Warmth and empathy may be achieved by signaling openness through body language, such as keeping one's arms uncrossed and sitting close to the family members instead of across from them. It also may increase the family's comfort level if the teacher reflects on what families say and restate their concerns to show understanding. Finally, asking questions that encourage families to speak their minds and share their concerns will help teachers learn valuable information about the child (Topping, & Hoffman, 2002). Trained assessment providers know that by using effective communication strategies, more opportunities to gain new information will be created.

In gathering information, it is important that teachers use a variety of communication methods with families. Teachers can communicate with families informally through phone calls, e-mails, or written notes or more formally through home visits, conferences, or team meetings (Grisham-Brown et al., 2005). Teachers often use anecdotal records to record a child's developmental milestones. For example, if the teacher notices Sandy tying her shoe for the first time independently, she may note her achievement with the date and time so she can share the information with Sandy's family during a conference and record her fine motor skill development.

Formal and informal communications with families are opportunities to demonstrate a belief in the value of a successful partnership between home and school (Studer, 1993). When teachers communicate effectively with families, a level of intimacy and understanding develops that allows teachers to obtain more accurate and useful information during the assessment process (Reedy & Walls, 1996). Mutual give and take in a parent–teacher relationship develops a sharing of trust as well as information (Reedy & Walls).

Considerate Scheduling

In making family involvement in the assessment process a priority, teachers must consider the unique scheduling needs of each family. Many families have work schedules and transportation needs that can cause attending meetings during the school day a hardship. Therefore, teachers should evaluate each family's scheduling needs on an individual basis and consider alternative options for communicating with families who cannot attend meetings during school hours.

The first consideration for involving families should be giving plenty of advance notice and sending reminders to the family, so that they can make arrangements to attend. It may be helpful for some families to hold meetings in the evening or at a time when a baby sitter can be provided at the school. Home visits work well for families with transportation needs, and conference calls can replace face-to-face meetings when not all parties involved can arrange a suitable meeting time.

Sensitivity Toward Diversity

Another tenet of the family-centered approach is respecting differences in beliefs and values (Baird & Peterson, 1997). Families cannot be treated as if they are all the same because they will vary in their ideas about strategies, treatment, causes of illness, independence, discipline, and child rearing. Families also differ in their cultural values and the amount of support that they receive from their relatives and communities. Understanding how a family is organized/structured and defined can help teachers become sensitive to the unique needs of the child during the assessment process. Developing a relationship with families before engaging in formal assessment practices can help teachers plan and carry out a more accurate assessment based on each child's individual goals.

Families of children with multiple, low-incidence, or severe disabilities may require special considerations during the assessment process. These children will most likely have an IFSP or IEP in place to guide the assessment planning, and a team will be assembled to work together to determine the child's developmental goals. Family involvement is mandated during this process, and these families will most likely require frequent updates on their child's progress.

Just as culture can determine the definition of family structure and authority within the family, it also may affect who is included on the intervention team. Families often extend beyond parents and siblings and can include grandparents, aunts, uncles, and many other people who have an important role in the child's life (Berman & Shaw, 1995).

Cultural values and experiences influence children's lives and unique identities and guide behavior, emotions, and thinking (Gollnick & Chinn, 2005). Teachers must understand that cultural awareness reaches beyond racial, ethnic, and linguistic diversity. Teachers must consider the primary language of the family, their reading abilities, and cultural factors (e.g., sharing personal family information may be taboo in some cultures) when selecting strategies for gathering information (Lo, 2008). When families share information with teachers about their culture and traditions, teachers can use the information to enrich their curriculum and make families feel involved. The teacher becomes a colearner with the students as they share about the special parts of their culture. If the teacher is aware of a language barrier, one way he or she can help is to make sure to have an interpreter available for the family and child during the assessment process.

Defining Priorities

Family priorities, or the ways in which families prefer practices in early childhood education, and family concerns, areas that family members identify as problems, are key elements to the development of the goals and curriculum for all children (McGonigel, Woodruff, & Roszmann-Millican, 1994). Furthermore, recommended practice suggests that goals be derived from the priorities and concerns of families (Sandall et al., 2005). Family priorities and concerns that are directly and indirectly related to the child's development should be documented so that the family is viewed as a whole. Then, strategies that occur within the context of everyday routines (classroom activities, family activities, and community) should be developed to reflect these priorities and concerns. A curriculum that is designed in response to the priorities and concerns of families empowers families to enhance the development of their child (Hanft & Pilkington, 2000). Assessment should be based on the family's priorities and concerns and should reflect what the family wants to gain from the assessments.

Setting Individual Goals

Taking into consideration the priorities and concerns of families and their children, it is clear that each child is a unique individual with distinctive needs and interests. Recommended practice suggests that all children need individualized goals and instruction (Grisham-Brown et al., 2005). Strategies must be implemented in developmentally appropriate environments and include activities and experiences that are based on the child's interests.

Program Planning

Assessment should be used to make decisions about program planning. As part of the assessment process, families may share information about their child's hobbies and interests, which may be helpful in determining themes of study in the classroom. Children are much more engaged in the program when it revolves around their areas of interest. For example, if many families share that their children enjoy taking care of their pets at home, inviting a veterinarian to speak to the class may be an exciting opportunity for the children to extend their learning. If other families share their children's interest in cars and trucks, then transportation may be an obvious focus of study.

When teachers consider field-trip opportunities, knowledge about the students' families is important. Families can be wonderful learning resources when teaching students about the communities in which they live. Families also can offer inexpensive learning experiences by inviting children to their farms, offices, or other places of employment. Finally, families can offer helpful information when planning celebrations in the classroom. It is important to be respectful of family traditions and cultural values when planning celebrations, especially those that revolve around traditional holidays. Family traditions within the classroom can help children experience multiculturalism in a unique way.

SUMMARY

Chapter 3 provides suggestions and strategies on how teachers can fully involve families in the assessment process. First, teachers need to understand the theories and philosophies that support family involvement as well as the laws that mandate the inclusion of families in the assessment process. Theories and philosophies discussed in the chapter include the Ecological Systems Theory, the Adult Learning Theory, and family-centered philosophy.

The chapter has also described four different ways that families can be involved in the assessment process. Although the role of parent as consumer is important, the roles of informant, team member, and advocate must also be considered. The benefits families receive from being fully involved in the assessment process include better outcomes for children and families and feelings of empowerment for parents.

A discussion of unstructured and structured approaches for gathering assessment information from families was provided. Unstructured approaches use less formal methods, such as interviews, informal observations, and open-ended questioning, to obtain information. Structured approaches are associated with existing assessment tools and include formal methods for gathering information from families about their children's development and/or otherwise involving families in the assessment process. Considerations for gathering reliable information from families were also discussed. These considerations include understanding levels of family involvement, using effective communication strategies, being considerate of scheduling issues, showing sensitivity toward diversity, defining priorities, setting individual goals, and developing the curriculum.

REFERENCES

Adrienne, F., & McCollum, J. (1992). *Transdisciplinary arena assessment process viewing guide. A resource for teams.* (Report No. EC 302 429). Lightfoot, VA: Child Development Resources. (ERIC Document Reproduction Service No. ED361959).

Baird, S., & Peterson, J. (1997). Seeking a comfortable fit between family-centered philosophy and infant–parent interaction in early intervention: Time for a paradigm shift? *Topics in Early Childhood Special Education, 17*(2), 139–165.

Bandura, A. (1977). *Social learning theory.* Englewood Cliffs, NJ: Prentice-Hall.

Berman, C., & Shaw, E. (1995). *Family directed child evaluation and assessment under IDEA; lessons from families and programs.* (Report No. ES 308 439). Chapel Hill, NC: National Early Childhood Technical Assistance System. (ERIC Document Reproduction Service No. ED451578).

Boone, H., & Crais, E. (1999). Strategies for family-driven assessment and intervention planning. *Young Exceptional Children, 3*(1), 2–12.

Bredekamp, S., & Copple, C. (Eds.). (1997). *Developmentally appropriate practice in early childhood programs* (Rev. ed.). Washington, DC: National Association for the Education of Young Children.

Bricker, D. (2002). *Assessment, evaluation, and programming system for infants and children (AEPS).* Baltimore: Paul H. Brookes Publishing Co.

Brigance, A. (2004). *BRIGANCE Inventory for Early Development-II (IED-II, 0–7 yrs).* North Billerica, MA: Curriculum Associates, Inc.

Brinckerhoff, J., & Vincent, L. (1987). Increasing parental decision-making at the individualized educational program meeting. *Journal of the Division for Early Childhood, 11*(1), 46–58.

Bronfenbrenner, U. (1979). *The ecology of human development,* Cambridge, MA: Harvard University Press.

Cheatham, G.A., & Ostrosky, M.M. (2009). Listening for details of talk: Early childhood parent–teacher conference communication facilitators. *Young Exceptional Children, 13*(1), 36–49.

Dinnebeil, L.A., & Rule, S. (1994). Congruence between parents' and professionals' judgments about the development of young children with disabilities: A review of the literature. *Topics in Early Childhood Special Education, 14*(1), 1–25.

Dunst, C.J. (1985). Rethinking early intervention. *Analysis and Intervention in Developmental Disabilities, 5,* 165–201.

Dunst, C.J. (2002) Family-centered practices: Birth through high school. *Journal of Special Education, 36,* 139–147.

Dunst, C.J., Bruder, M.B., Trivette, C.M., & Hamby, D.W. (2006). Everyday activity settings, natural learning environments, and early intervention practices. *Journal of Policy and Practice in Intellectual Disabilities, 3*(1), 3–10.

Dunst, C.J., & McWilliam, R.A. (1988). Cognitive assessment of multiply handicapped young children. In T. Wachs & R. Sheehan (Eds.), *Assessment of developmentally disabled children* (pp. 213–238). New York: Plenum Press.

Epstein, J. (2000). *School and family partnerships: Preparing educators and improving schools.* Boulder, CO: Westview.

Furano, S., O'Reily, A., Hosaka, C., Inatsuda, T., Allman, T., & Zeesloft, B. (1999). Hawaii Early Learning Profile (HELP) for preschoolers. Palo Alto, CA: VORT Corporation.

Gardner, H. (1977). The first seven...and the eighth. *Educational Leadership, 55,* 12–15.

Gollnick & Chinn, (2005). *Multicultural education in a pluralistic society* (7th ed.). Columbus, Ohio: Upper Saddle River.

Grisham-Brown, J., Hemmeter, M.L., & Pretti-Frontczak, K. (2005). *Blended practices for teaching young children in inclusive settings.* Baltimore: Paul H. Brookes Publishing Co.

Hanft, B.E., & Pilkington, P.E. (2000). Therapy in natural environments: The means or end goal for early intervention? *Infants and Young Children, 12*(4), 1–13.

Hemetter, M.L., & Grisham-Brown, J. (1997). Developing children's language skills in inclusive early childhood classrooms. *Dimensions of Early Childhood, 25*(3), 6–13.

Hoover-Dempsey, K.V., Walker, J.M., Sandler, H.M., Whetsel, D., Green, C.L., Wilkins, A.S., et al. (2005). Why do parents become involved? Research findings and implications. *The Elementary School Journal, 106*(2), 105–130.

Johnson, C.D. (2001). Transition: Making it a process rather than an event. *Educational Audiology Review, 18*(3), 5–11.

Johnson-Martin, N., Attermeier, S., & Hacker, B. (2004). *Carolina curriculum for preschoolers with special needs* (2nd ed.). Baltimore: Paul H. Brookes Publishing Co.

Kansas Inservice Training System. (2007). *Curriculum-based assessments for measuring early childhood outcomes.* Parsons, KS: Kansas University Center on Developmental Disabilities. Available from www.kskits.org

Katz, L.G. (1996). Child development knowledge and teacher preparation: Confronting assumptions. *Early Childhood Research Quarterly, 11*(2), 135–146.

Knowles, M.S. (1984). *Androgogy in action: Applying modern principles of adult learning.* San Francisco: Jossey-Bass Publishers.

Linder, T. (2008). *Transdisciplinary Play-Based Assessment and Intervention (TPBA/I2).* Baltimore: Paul H. Brookes Publishing Co.

Lo, L. (2008). Expectations of Chinese families of children with disabilities towards American schools. *The School Community Journal, 18*(2), 73–90.

Maring, G.H., & Magelky, J. (1990). Effective communication: key to parent/community. *Reading Teacher, 43*(8), 606–607.

Marquardt, M., & Waddill, D. (2004). The power of learning in action learning: A conceptual analysis of how the five schools of adult learning theories are incorporated within the practice of action learning. *Action Learning: Research and Practice, 1*(2), 185–202.

McGonigel, M.J., Woodruff, G., & Roszmann-Millican, M. (1994). The transdisciplinary team: A model for family-centered early intervention. In L.J. Johnson, R.J. Gallagher, M.J. LaMontagne, J.B. Jordan, J.J. Gallagher, P.L. Hutinger, & M.B. Karnes (Eds.), *Meeting early intervention challenges: Issues from birth to three* (2nd ed., pp. 95–131). Baltimore: Paul H. Brookes Publishing Co.

McWilliam, R., Casey, A.M., & Sims, J. (2009). The routines-based interview: A method for gathering information and assessing needs. *Infants & Young Children, 22*(3), 224–233.

Meisels, S.B., Marsden, D.B., Dichtelmiller, M.K., & Jablon, J.R. (2001). *Work sampling system (WSS).* New York: Pearson Assessments.

Meisels, S.B., Marsden, D.B., Dombro, A.L., Weston, D.R., & Jewkes, A.M. (2003). *The ounce scale.* New York: Pearson Early Learning.

Mezirow, J. (1981). A critical theory of adult learning and education. *Adult Education, 32*(1), 3–24.

Pretti-Frontczak, K., & Bricker, D. (2004). *An activity-based approach to early intervention* (3rd ed.). Baltimore: Paul H. Brookes Publishing Co. (ERIC Document Reproduction Service No. ED491762).

Reedy, Y.B., & Walls, R. (1996). *Obtaining information through basic communication.* (Report No. PS 024 884). New Orleans: Head Start Association's 23rd Annual

Training Conference. (ERIC Document Reproduction Service No. ED402104).

Sandall, S., Hemmeter, M.L., Smith, B.J., & McLean, M. (2005). *DEC recommended practices: A comprehensive guide.* Longmont, CO: Sopris West.

Studer, J. (1993). Listen so that parents will speak. *Childhood Education, 70*(2), 74–76.

Thegan, K., & Weber, L. (2002). *Family support: a solid foundation for children (more than a nice thing to do!).* (Report No. PS 030 871). Raleigh, NC: North Carolina Partnership for Children. (ERIC Document Reproduction Service No. ED472026).

Topping, D.J., & Hoffman, S.J. (2002). Helping teachers become teacher researchers. *Journal of Reading Education, 27*(3), 20–29.

Trister-Dodge, D., Colker, L.J., & Heroman, C. (2002). *Creative Curriculum for Preschool* (4th ed.). Mt. Ranier, MD: Gryphon House.

U.S. Department of Health and Human Services. (2009). Administration for children & families. Retrieved August 26, 2009, from http://www.hhs.gov/

Vangalder, C.J. (1997). *CARE: Caregiver assistance, resources and education. A case study of a family-centered assessment and intervention model.* (Report No. EC 305 546). Holland, MI: Holland Public School District. (ERIC Document Reproduction Service No. ED407787).

Westphal, S. (1989, Winter). Notes on the First National ICC Parents' Meeting. *Early Childhood Bulletin,* 3–4.

Wilson, L.L., & Mott, D.W. (2006). Asset-based context matrix: an assessment tool for developing contextually-based child outcomes. *CASEtools, 2*(4), 1–12.

Wilson L.L., Mott, D.W., & Battman, D. (2004). The asset-based context matrix: A tool for assessing children's learning opportunities and participation in natural environments. *Topics in Early Childhood Special Education, 24*(2), 110–120.

CHAPTER 4

Recommended Practices for Assessing Children with Diverse Abilities

Sandra Hess Robbins,
Kristie Pretti-Frontczak, and
Jennifer Grisham-Brown

Miss Jaden is a teacher in an inclusive preschool classroom serving children both with and without disabilities in a culturally and linguistically diverse neighborhood. At the start of the school year, Miss Jaden has 12 children registered to attend her classroom. Five of the children have identified disabilities, including speech delay, autism, cerebral palsy, Down syndrome, and hearing impairment, and two of them are considered to have multiple disabilities. Within the group of 12 children registered to start preschool in Miss Jaden's class, seven different cultural backgrounds are represented, with 4 of the children primarily speaking languages other than English. Miss Jaden understands that it is her responsibility to assess each child in an individually appropriate and nonbiased way; however, Miss Jaden also recognizes the challenge of assessing children who do not understand English, cannot hear instructions when they are given, cannot verbalize a response, and are physically unable to complete the tasks associated with the assessment instruments. Furthermore, Miss Jaden realizes that her resources are limited and that the school district has inadequate funds for additional resources and support. Miss Jaden is very worried about how she is going to design a high-quality learning experience for all of the children when she is unsure of even where to begin facilitating an appropriate, nonbiased assessment process for a group of children with such diverse abilities.

According to the U.S. Department of Education (2006), more than 2 million young children with disabilities are served throughout the United States each year. Recommended practices emphasize that young children with disabilities be included and taught in natural and least restrictive environments (LREs; Etscheidt, 2006; Sandall, Hemmeter, Smith, & McLean, 2005)—in other words, in places where, and activities in which, children without disabilities of the same age and their families would participate (Jackson, Pretti-Frontczak, Harjusola-Webb, Grisham-Brown, & Romani, 2009; Raab & Dunst, 2004). As the number of children with disabilities who are served in community settings has increased, so has the overall diversity of the population of young children being served. In terms of language alone, reports indicate that the number of children who are dual-language learners is rising, as is their proportion to the rest of the population (Ballantyne, Sanderman, & McLaughlin, 2008). For instance, in a single district in Michigan that serves 12,000 students, 85 different languages are spoken. In fact, one early childhood center in the state serves 329 children who speak 35 different languages.

As a result of demographic changes, the push for LRE and inclusion, and the growing need for out-of-the-home care, early childhood programs are increasingly faced with assessing and meeting the needs of children with progressively more diverse abilities (Copple & Bredekamp, 2009; Durand, 2008). Diversity, in its broadest sense, comes in the form of genders, ages, cultures, languages, socioeconomic status, family configurations, religions, geographical locations, preferences, interests, and abilities. All of these aspects of diversity affect the assessment process.

The purpose of this chapter is to promote the recommended assessment practices discussed in Chapter 1 as they apply to children with diverse abilities. The text that follows is divided into four main sections. The first section illustrates the need to work as a member of a transdisciplinary team when assessing young children with diverse abilities. The second section provides an overview of the challenges and general considerations for assessing these children. In the third section, specific recommendations and suggestions are made for the assessment process. Finally, the fourth section concludes the chapter with a discussion of the measures available for assessing young children with diverse abilities. Practices for serving children with severe or multiple disabilities (or both), children with diverse cultural experiences, and children who are dual- or multilanguage learners will be emphasized throughout the chapter.

TRANSDISCIPLINARY TEAMING

In a transdisciplinary approach to professional collaboration, teams (which always include the family) attempt to maximize communication and collaboration by crossing disciplinary boundaries and engaging in a simultaneous assessment process (King et al., 2009; Woodruff & Mcgonigel, 1988). Transdisciplinary teams are more necessary than ever when serving young children who have severe or multiple disabilities, who come from diverse cultural backgrounds, or who are dual- or multilanguage learners. Specifically, when assessing young children with diverse abilities, a transdisciplinary approach allows the team to ensure much needed expertise in collaborative problem solving and joint decision making. For example, when determining how and when to transition a child who is tube fed to oral feeding, no single team member will possess all of the expertise or information necessary to make a decision regarding the initial feeding problem, the nutritional needs of the child, or the readiness of the child and family for the transition.

All of the team members need to understand that they represent or come from different philosophical or training orientations. Team members are likely to represent medical (e.g., neurologists, nurses, audiologists), educational (e.g., early interventionists, interpreters), or therapeutic (e.g., occupational and physical therapists, speech-language pathologists) models. In addition, teams serving young children with diverse abilities are likely to include specialists with expertise in particular disabilities or disorders (e.g., vision, hearing, dual-language acquisition, autism). Therefore, team members must understand that individual training, philosophical beliefs, and past experiences will influence all aspects of working with a young child and their family. For example, some team members may feel that modifications or adaptations to the "testing" procedures are in order because standardized testing presents bias and does not provide an accurate picture of a child's performance. Others may think that standardized testing produces the most objective results—that when accommodations are made, standardization is broken and the norms reported for the test no longer apply. The team is thus put into a situation where some members believe and trust in one set of assessment practices and other team members advocate for another. To work effectively, particularly with regard to assessment, team members need to recognize these differences and use open communication to reach consensus on how best to address various issues.

Effective transdisciplinary teams recognize that the most central participant is the child's family (Bruder & Bologna, 1993). As discussed in Chapter 3, family-centered practice is recommended in early childhood intervention within and across the provision of all services (Sandall et al., 2005). Families should be viewed as experts on their children. Particularly in the case of young children with diverse abilities, parents and other caregivers can provide valuable information about the children's functioning at home and in the community that would be extremely difficult, if not impossible, to gather by other means. Families are the team members who can best describe the children's capabilities, challenges, and developmental history. Given their clear understanding of the child's interests and abilities, families can also help make decisions about which assessments are most appropriate (McLean, Wolery, & Bailey, 2004). Finally, family members can support the administration of assessments because they are best able to interact with the child and to elicit the child's optimal level of functioning (Bagnato & Simeonsson, 2007). During the assessment process, teams must share responsibilities and ensure that families are involved to the extent they desire in all aspects of assessment, including planning the assessment, administration of assessment measures, summarization and interpretation of findings, application of planning intervention, and identification of services. Chapter 6 provides additional information about how transdisciplinary teams participate in play-based assessments as a strategy for making the eligibility process more authentic.

In general, transdisciplinary teams need to understand that development 1) is interrelated (Allen & Marotz, 2010); 2) is heavily influenced by culture (Klingner, Blanchett, & Harry, 2007; Shonkoff & Phillips, 2000); 3) is best understood when the child is viewed as a whole and within the context of his or her family and community (Bronfenbrenner, 1977); and 4) even when atypical, can result in patterns of predictable responses that should be considered when drawing conclusions or making decisions (Ferrell, 1998).

As teams adopt such a framework, they will find that their assessment practices will change in terms of which assessments are used, who administers the assessment, how assessment information is summarized, and how assessment information is used to make decisions. For example, a number of specialists, experts, caregivers, educators, and therapists may be involved in assessing children with diverse abilities. As a family moves through the assessment process, each "assessor" may ask similar questions regarding the child's developmental history, family concerns, and past treatments. It is unnecessary for a family to answer these common questions multiple times. Further, each assessor may generate their own report and set of recommendations. When team members write individual reports, they are unaware of whether their recommendations are in conflict or support the suggestions of others, often times leaving families on his or her

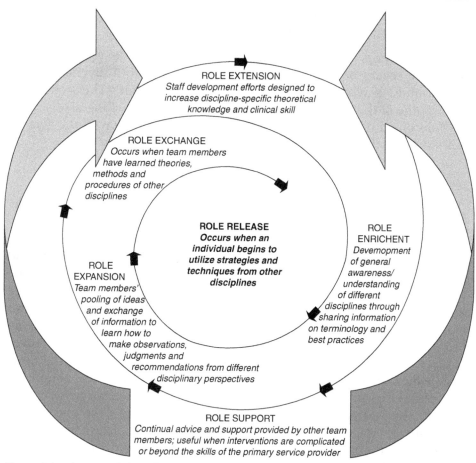

Figure 4.1. Aspects of the role release process. (From King et al. [2009], The Application of a Transdisciplinary model for Early Intervention Services. *Infants and Young Children*, 22[3], pp. 211–23; reprinted by permission.)

own to decipher what to do next. (See Chapter 6 for an example of how to write an assessment report as a transdisciplinary team.) To maximize the benefits of a transdisciplinary team, particularly through the assessment process, members should develop and maintain a set of skills around their role and the role of other team members. Figure 4.1 depicts the cycle, or various aspects, of role release.

While role release, enrichment, expansion, extension, and so forth can be overwhelming and a bit intimidating initially, the underlying notions are that no one team member is more important than another, that one can assess skills and abilities that fall outside one's traditional training (e.g., a physical therapist can help observe and document a child's performance as the child interacts and communicates with familiar adults), and that it is the collective and multiple lenses at which we view a child within the context of their family that provides the most accurate and comprehensive information. Given the complexity of issues and mediating factors that need to be considered when assessing children with diverse abilities, teachers can easily see how having more eyes is better.

GENERAL CONSIDERATIONS FOR
ASSESSING CHILDREN WITH DIVERSE ABILITIES

The next section provides general considerations for assessing children who have severe or multiple disabilities, who are from diverse cultural backgrounds, or who are dual- or multilanguage learners. The section discusses some of the challenges teachers face when conducting assessments for children with diverse abilities and presents an overview of the general issues surrounding the measures teachers have available to them.

Severe or Multiple Disabilities

Children with severe or multiple disabilities are often considered untestable. In fact, a national study of eligibility practices of over 250 preschool psychologists with over 7,000 children found that nearly 60 percent of the children would have been deemed "untestable" if the psychologists had followed standardized procedures (Bagnato & Neisworth, 1995). The extremity of behaviors and skill levels characteristic of children with severe or multiple disabilities can make it difficult for teams to differentiate whether poor performance on an assessment is due to skill deficits or another issue directly related to the child's disability (e.g., lack of functional motor movements, language, attention; Neisworth & Bagnato, 1992). Often, the measures being used contribute to the challenge because they are generally inappropriate for children with severe or multiple disabilities (Neisworth & Bagnato, 2004). Specifically, the mismatch between the child and the assessment can be found within the content, the expected response, or the method for gathering assessment information associated with the measure.

Content of the assessment refers to what the test items are actually measuring. For children with severe or multiple disabilities, items measuring specific sets of skills are often beyond their capabilities (Snow & Van Hemel, 2008). For example, items measuring locomotor skills such as running, skipping, riding a bike, are typically beyond the scope of what a child with a severe motor impairment can or will be able to accomplish. Other early developmental assessments contain items that are beyond the scope of the abilities of a young child with sensory impairments. For example, a child with a visual impairment may have difficulty demonstrating competence on items that require a performance that is heavily dependent on vision (e.g., visually recognizes mother, eye–hand coordination in reaching).

In addition, content often measures specific responses to scripted items that do not exemplify the skills needed for participation in daily routines (McCormick & Nellis, 2004). In other words, assessment content often measures form rather than function. *Form* refers to the specific skill the child is to perform, whereas *function* refers to the purpose of the skill. For example, a test item that examines a child's ability to use a spoon to transfer food from a bowl to his or her mouth is an item that measures a specific skill (i.e., form). The purpose of the skill (i.e., the function) is to feed oneself, not necessarily to use a spoon. In another example, a child

---

BOX 4.1

"What is this item really measuring?"
Examples of assessment content that measures form versus function

Form	Function
Picking up a towel to reveal a hidden object	→ Finding common objects in hidden and/or usual locations
Jumping over an 8-inch hurdle	→ Navigating objects while moving
Saying noun/verb phrases	→ Getting wants and needs met
Lacing a 4 x 6 inch card with five holes	→ Manipulating objects
Walking 10 feet in a straight line	→ Getting from point A to point B
Fastening four buttons on a shirt or jacket	→ Putting on a front-opening garment using any functional means
Walking on a balance beam	→ Displaying balance when mobile
Putting together a four-piece inlaid puzzle	→ Solving problems
Saying name, age, and address	→ Providing personal information
Stringing beads	→ Following a sequence

---

with a hearing impairment may be unable to turn and look at a noise-producing object (i.e., form) but he or she is perfectly capable of attending to environmental stimuli (i.e., function). Formal assessment measures often include content that emphasizes form, and does not allow for examination of true functions of skills or behaviors, making it easy to misinterpret an issue directly related to the child's disability as a skill deficit. (See Box 4.1 for more examples of assessment content that measures form versus function.)

Method refers to the process used to obtain the information about a child's performance and includes the cuing systems used to present test items as well as the response accepted from the child. Generally, standardized cuing systems such as verbal instructions paired with visual stimuli are a barrier for many children with severe or multiple disabilities. For instance, children with visual or hearing impairments will have difficulty seeing or hearing the stimuli being presented. Children with sensory impairments struggle with either hyper- or hyposensitivity to particular test stimuli involving sound, touch, movement, or positioning (Downing & Chen, 2003; Ermer & Dunn, 1998), which often leads to avoidance behaviors such as "shutting down" or running away (Autism Speaks, 2008; Hirstein, Iversen, & Ramachandran, 2001).

Concurrently, standardized responses such as labeling, pointing, and moving objects are barriers for many children with severe or multiple disabilities (Rowland, 2009). For instance, the child with a severe motor delay might have limited capacity for these standardized responses, whereas children with speech or language impairments may be unable to produce linguistic information (e.g., labeling objects) and, therefore, unable to communicate a correct response.

More often than not, it is both the content and the method of an assessment that are mismatches for a child with severe or multiple disabilities. For example, the content and method of traditional intelligence tests are language dependent (Schum, 2004). A child with a language disorder would probably be unable to access a traditional intelligence test for multiple reasons. First, it is likely that the child would be unable to interpret the linguistic information provided within the test questions. Second, even if the child could interpret the test questions, he or she would probably be unable to communicate a response. Finally, even if the child could interpret the linguistics of the question and communicate a response, it is often the case that the information is beyond the scope of the understanding or experience of a preschool age child. The use of measures with nonfunctional items outside the scope of children's capabilities, inflexible cuing systems, and required standardized responses plays an enormous role in the challenge of assessing young children who have severe or multiple disabilities (Schum).

Diverse Cultural Backgrounds and Dual- or Multilanguage Learners

When children from particular racial or ethnic groups are identified as having a disability at a greater or lesser rate than all other students, then that group is said to be *disproportionately* represented in special education (Williams, 2007). When a particular group is represented at a greater rate than the population in general, that group is said to be *overrepresented* (e.g., when a group represents 10% of the population but constitutes 20% of children being served in special education). Children who are from diverse cultural backgrounds or who are dual- or multilanguage learners have historically been, and continue to be, overrepresented in special education placements (Strand & Lindsay, 2009). Many professionals would agree that at least a portion of the overrepresentation of culturally and linguistically diverse children is directly related to errors in the assessment process (Macswan & Rolstad, 2006). According to Espinosa (2010), "If children are assessed in a language they do not fully use or comprehend or with invalid measures, their language skills will be underestimated." She goes on to say, "invalid measures of language will result in over-referral of typical language learners or under-referral of at risk children" (Espinosa, 2010). Children are all too often placed in special education when a cultural or linguistic variation is confused with a skill deficit or a need for special education service.

In reality, the confusion and frequent misinterpretation of results is due, not to professional misunderstanding, but to an overreliance on culturally and linguistically biased assessments (Espinosa, 2005, 2010). In fact, most assessments are culturally or linguistically biased in one way or another (Notari-Syverson, Losardo, & Sook Lim, 2003). Children have different learning styles, experience with materials, family preferences, and ways of approaching adults that are unique to their culture (Guild, 2001). Many assessment items require children to engage in tasks or activities using predetermined sequences or actions (e.g., self-help skills) that they are not expected to engage in, or that they engage in differently, at home. Children also have unique experiences with, and exposures to materials that are dependent on their cultural surroundings. For example, a child may be familiar with real objects rather than pretend or play items, or a child's family may encourage certain toys for boys or for girls. Given that many assessments use picture or object naming as a test of cognition or communication skills, the child's exposure to the testing materials, or lack thereof, contributes to testing bias (Qi, Kaiser, Milan, Yzquierdo, & Hancock, 2003). It may not be that the child's communication skills or cognition are lacking; instead, it may be that the child's performance is simply a product of things experienced within his or her unique family and culture.

The ways in which children approach adults also varies greatly among cultures, presenting yet another barrier to the assessment process. In some cultures, children are told "not to talk until they are spoken to" or perhaps "not to call attention to themselves" (California Department of Education, 2007). The following example illustrates such a difference in approaches: A typical social skill assessment might examine the ways in which children approach their peers and the familiar adults in the preschool setting. Children are expected to look at the teacher when she is talking and respond verbally. It is also assumed that the children will use verbal means of approaching their peers. Philips (1983) conducted a study of classroom participation comparing Anglo-American and Native American students. The Native American children looked at the teacher less often, were less likely to respond to the teacher verbally, and showed attentiveness to peers through physical contact. A Native American child in the scenario might be labeled as displaying inappropriate behavior and assigned a low score on a social skill assessment when, in fact, the child is only acting the way he or she was taught to interact with others at home.

Children who are dual- or multilanguage learners are especially vulnerable to culturally and linguistically biased testing (Snow & Van Hemel, 2008). Dual- or multilanguage learners come from a variety of cultural experiences; moreover, they are expected to access assessment items presented in a language other than their own. Similar to children with language or communication impairments, children who are dual- or multilanguage learners will have varying degrees of capability to understand test instructions and communicate the correct response. In the early childhood setting, children who are dual- or multilanguage learners will be at different stages of the "additional language" learning process (Barone & Xu, 2008). During the first stage of the additional language learning process, often referred to as the "silent stage," a child is observing the environment and using little or no verbal communication (Clarke, 1992; Drury, 2007). During this stage, it is all too easy for a team to misinterpret the child's nonverbal behavior as a language delay or disorder.

In recognition of the obstacles surrounding the assessment of children who are dual- or multilanguage learners, the Individuals with Disabilities Education Improvement Act (IDEA) of 2004 (PL108-446) requires that assessments be provided in a child's native language—unless it is clearly not feasible to do so. For example, if a child speaks Spanish, teachers are expected to administer a Spanish version of the same assessment that is given to all children. The intentionality of IDEA is good; however, most assessments are not readily available in a variety of languages other than English, making it infeasible to offer the assessment in a child's native language (Spinelli, 2008). Furthermore, standardized tests, such as those utilized for statewide mandated assessments, cannot be readily provided in a language other than English, as translation could compromise the validity of the test (Menken, 2000).

SPECIFIC RECOMMENDATIONS

This section provides specific recommendations for assessing children who have severe or multiple disabilities, who are from diverse cultural backgrounds, or who are dual- or multilanguage learners. The section provides specific recommendations regarding *what* and *how* information is gathered across assessment purposes. The recommendations provided will apply to all of the specified populations of children (*children with diverse abilities*) unless otherwise specified by one of the following: *children with multiple or severe disabilities, children from diverse cultural backgrounds,* and *children who are dual- or multilanguage learners.*

What to Assess

When assessing *children with multiple or severe disabilities*, teachers need to gather information about the general effects of the disability on typical development to support their interpretations of test results (i.e., determine whether a documented delay should be considered an area of need or if the delay is within the typical trajectory for same-age peers with the same disability). For most children with multiple or severe disabilities, the course of development is different, not necessarily slower (Ferrell, 1998). For example, research has shown that children with visual impairments learn things in a different sequence and at a different rate than children who are typically developing (see Box 4.2). As a general rule, teachers should avoid comparisons between children who are typically developing and children with a disability and should keep in mind that a disability in one area affects a child's abilities or developmental trajectories in other areas.

Gathering information about the child's use of functional skills is critical when assessing young *children with multiple or severe disabilities* (Browder, 2001). As previously mentioned, teachers should examine function rather than form. For example, an item that measures ability to get from Point A to Point B is a more appropriate assessment of a child's

> **BOX 4.2**
>
> ## Executive summary conclusions about how children with visual impairments learn things in a different sequence at a different rate
>
> Research Question 1: Do children between birth and 5 years of age who are visually impaired attain developmental milestones at ages that differ from those of children who are typically developing?
>
> Results:
>
> - The age of acquisition for 12 milestones was delayed in comparison to typically developing children.
> - For five milestones, median age of acquisition was within the range of attainment for typical children. All five milestones that fell within the range for typically developing children were behaviors that required expressive and receptive communication.
> - Two milestones were acquired earlier by children in this study than by typical children (copying a circle; relating past experiences). Earlier acquisition is somewhat suspect, however, because data are available for less than 10% of the total sample.
>
> Research Question 2: Do children between birth and 5 years of age who are visually impaired attain developmental skills in a sequence that differs from the sequence followed children who are typically developing?
>
> Results:
>
> - Seven milestones were acquired in a different sequence for children in this study than for typically developing children.
> - Searching for a dropped object, feeding self bite-size pieces of food, and moving 3 or more feet by crawling were generally acquired in a later sequence by all children, with and without additional disabilities.
> - Walking without support, controlling bowel movements, and repeating two-digit sequences were acquired in a later sequence for children with additional impairments.
> - Copying a circle occurred earlier in the sequence for children with additional impairments but later in the sequence for children without additional impairments. However, this, too, is suspect because of low numbers of children who had actually acquired the skill.
>
> Adapted from a portion of the executive summary report from *Project PRISM: A Longitudinal Study of Developmental Patterns of Children who are Visually Impaired.*
>
> To access the complete executive summary and/or the full research report, please visit: http://www.unco.edu/ncssd/research/PRISM/default.html

functioning than an item that focuses on specific locomotor skills, such as walking or running. Children may demonstrate the function of the skill by moving around in a wheelchair, crawling, or using a walker. Likewise, an open-ended item that measures a child's ability to communicate his or her wants and needs is more functional than focusing on specific verbal communication skills, such as speaking or pointing. Therefore, teachers should focus on developing comprehensive descriptions of a child's functioning on tasks or skills considered important to the child's present and future performance (Meisels & Atkins-Burnett, 2000).

When assessing children from diverse cultural backgrounds or children who are dual- or multilanguage learners, teachers should gather information about the child's culture and language patterns in the home (Espinosa, 2010; Sandall, Hemmeter, Smith, & McLean, 2005). It would be wise to collect information about the child's learning style and experience with materials, the family's preferences and child-rearing practices, as well as what behaviors and ways of approaching adults are culturally appropriate before conducting screening and assessment (California Department of Education, 2007). Furthermore, teachers should determine who in the child's family speaks or understands which languages and for what purposes (e.g., read the newspaper, watch TV, listen to the radio, talk to friends or socialize). Simply determining the language spoken in the home is not enough. Parent surveys or as recommended by the American Speech-Language-Hearing Association (Westby, Burda, & Mehta, 2003), ethnographic interviewing, can be used for gathering information regarding the language a child is exposed to, how and when they use various languages, and for gaining a better understanding of the family context and preferences.

Gathering information about the language patterns in the home can provide insight about the acculturation of the child and family. The term *acculturation* refers to the process in which members of one cultural group adopt the beliefs, behaviors, language, or cultural traits of another cultural group (Schumann, 1978). Understanding the level of acculturation is important, given that young children who are dual- or multilanguage learners are acquiring not just a new language, but a new culture as well. When children experience culture shock, their academic and social behaviors can appear to mirror those of a student with special needs (Grassi & Barker, 2010). Consider the preschool child who is not expected to feed himself at home. At preschool, food is placed in front of the child with the expectation that he will feed himself. The child might scream, cry, or simply "shut down" out of fear or frustration, not understanding the situation or not being able to perform the task. During the assessment process, teachers might interpret the child's behavior as a number of things that are untrue about the child's abilities (e.g., a fine motor delay, challenging behavior, sensory processing issue). (See Box 4.3 for further examples of

---

BOX 4.3

Behaviors exhibited by dual or multilanguage learners experiencing culture shock

- Constantly asking to go to the bathroom or the school nurse
- Crying or exhibiting signs of depression
- Throwing chairs or books across the room
- Being unable to stay focused on tasks
- Falling asleep during class
- Exhibiting outbursts of anger, violence, frustration, or sadness
- Getting into fights at recess
- Leaving the classroom or asking to go home
- Being out sick from school for many days

From Grassi, E., & Baker, H.B. [2010]. *Culturally and linguistically diverse exceptional students: Strategies for teaching and assessment.* Copyright © 2003 by SAGE Publications. Reprinted by permission of SAGE Publications.

behaviors exhibited by dual- or multilanguage learners experiencing culture shock.)

Finally, when assessing the language skills of children who are dual- or multilanguage learners, it is critical to gather information about the child's language acquisition for each language the child speaks and avoid comparisons with children who are native English speakers (Goodz, 1994). Teachers should determine whether the child who is a dual- or multilanguage learner has an age-appropriate level of vocabulary and syntax in his or her native language in order to evaluate the child's English language acquisition. If there is no communication disorder in the child's native language, then the likelihood is that there is no communication disorder. If possible, another strategy is to compare children who are dual- or multilanguage learners with same-age peers who are also dual- or multilanguage learners. If the child is acquiring English at the same rate as other nonnative English speakers of the same age, then chances are there is no significant communication disorder. In other words, the likelihood of both children exhibiting a communication disorder at the same rate is small. That being said, when making comparisons between children, teachers should consider the length of time each child has been exposed to the new language because children spend a predictable amount of time in each stage of the language acquisition process (Haynes, 2006).

How to Assess

The remainder of the section provides recommendations for *how* transdisciplinary teams should approach the assessment process for children with diverse abilities (i.e., those who have multiple or severe disabilities, who are from diverse cultural backgrounds, or who are dual- or multilanguage learners). Teachers need to consider the influences and biases inherent to the assessment process, integrate and use interchangeable cuing systems and alternative materials, and allow children to provide alternative responses.

Influences and Biases

When assessing young children with diverse abilities, teachers should consider influences and biases created by both the assessment setting or situation and those who are conducting the assessment. Using an authentic assessment approach (i.e., familiar adults in familiar settings) is critical to the success of the assessment process. Research has shown that when conducting assessments of young children who have severe or multiple disabilities, who are from diverse cultural backgrounds, or who are dual- or multilanguage learners in familiar settings, familiar adults are able to elicit better performance and more elaborate responses (Barkley, 1982; Copenhaver-Johnson & Katz, 2009; Fuchs & Fuchs, 1984).

When gathering information for a child who is from a diverse cultural background or who is a dual- or multilanguage learner, teachers should match the child with an examiner who is knowledgeable about the child's culture and who speaks the same language (McLean, 2000). Furthermore, the examiner should understand the language acquisition process. It is important the examiner have a firm understanding of the types of grammatical, phonological, and discourse errors that dual- or multilanguage learners typically make as well as the common errors made in interlanguage (Grassi & Barker, 2010). The term *interlanguage* refers to a made-up linguistic system developed by a child who is learning a second language in which the child uses language transfer, overgeneralization, and simplification to approximate the target language while preserving features of the native language. When conducting the assessment, if it is not possible to find someone who is knowledgeable about the child's culture, who speaks the same language, or who understands the language acquisition process, the team should at the very least, arrange for a one-on-one situation with an interactive adult, caregiver, or teacher. High-context situations, such as a one-on-one interaction, can enhance receptive language abilities as well as increase the likelihood of expressive speech (Copenhaver-Johnson & Katz, 2009).

Interchangeable Cuing Systems

Teachers should also try to incorporate interchangeable cuing systems when assessing children with diverse abilities. Assessments should be administered in the mode of communication most commonly used by the child (Espinosa, 2005). Often, the mode of communication used by children with diverse abilities is nonverbal. Teachers should incorporate the use of picture communication systems, augmentative communication devices, object and tactile cues, and gestures or sign language when appropriate. Nevertheless, teachers should beware of translating standardized verbal tests into any alternative mode of communication. For example, sign language is not a precise equivalent of spoken language, so translation can invalidate the standardization of test procedures (Schum, 2004).

For children who are dual- or multilanguage learners, assessments should be administered in the child's native language. Keep in mind, again, that translation is not always an exact science. Sometimes words or phrases can sound inappropriate and even offensive to another culture (Fabri & Freidel, 2008). If an English language assessment is translated into another language, the assessment should be carefully reviewed for linguistic and cultural appropriateness by someone who understands the language and culture and who is well versed in the complex issues of both assessment and translation (National Association for the Education of Young Children, 2009). When translation is not available, nonverbal cuing systems paired with multiple visual or gestural cues can support the assessment of young children who are dual- or multilanguage learners.

In addition to using interchangeable cuing systems, the manner in which cues are represented should be adjusted to match the needs of the child. For example, children with receptive language deficits will benefit when test questions, instructions, and commands are short, concrete, and repeated (Zentall, 1988). For children with hearing impairments, teachers should ensure the administration of any auditory information is within the child's acuity level. Pairing appropriate cues with reinforcement can help improve motivation and, therefore, test performance for children with behavioral disabilities (Singh, Barto, & Chentanez, 2005). When using reinforcers, teachers should consider the interests and preferences of the child. For example, for children with autism, repetitive stimulation (e.g., strobe light, vibration, rocking) can be more motivating than typical primary reinforcers (e.g., food; Freeman, Frankel, & Ritvo, 1976; Margolies, 1977).

Alternative, Flexible Materials

When assessing young children with diverse abilities, teachers also need to utilize alternative and flexible materials. Choosing materials that are a match for the child's capabilities and that allow for flexibility in the assessment process will give children with diverse abilities multiple ways of accessing the test content. For example, when children have visual impairments, teachers should choose materials that provide tactile information or large, contrasting visual displays. For children with behavior disorders, instruments with more manipulative items and shorter duration of tasks are an appropriate choice (Shaw, 2008).

Specifically for young children who have diverse cultural backgrounds or who are dual- or multilanguage learners, teachers should use materials that align with the child's cultural or linguistic background. The National Association for the Education of Young Children (2005) recommends a systematic, observational assessment process incorporating culturally and linguistically appropriate tools as the primary source of guidance. In other words, when using multiple assessments, teachers should rely more heavily on those which are 1) observation based and 2) culturally and linguistically appropriate for the child (Espinosa, in press). If the transdisciplinary team has enlisted the support of a "cultural guide" who knows and understands the child's language and culture, that person can help determine the appropriateness of assessment tools by examining them for cultural bias. Box 4.4 includes useful resources that teachers can use as a starting place in finding assessments that may be appropriate for children who are dual- or multilanguage learners.

Alternative Responses

When allowing for alternative responses, teachers should consider the strengths of the child and attempt to align the response options with the child's unique set of skills (Neisworth & Bagnato, 2004). For example, instruments that emphasize nonverbal procedures, such as pointing to pictures or signaling choice with an eye gaze are appropriate for children with communication disorders or who are nonverbal. For children with motor impairments, teachers should acknowledge and verify movement responses that are approximations of standard responses and appear to demonstrate

---

BOX 4.4

Support for individuals searching for assessment tools appropriate for children who are dual- or multilanguage learners

The Culturally and Linguistically Appropriate Services (CLAS) Early Childhood Research Institute offers a wide range of online resources and supports for individuals seeking to provide nonbiased services to young children who are from diverse cultural backgrounds or who are dual- or multilanguage learners. The CLAS web site includes literature reviews, technical reports, teacher resources, and articles in both English and Spanish versions.

CLAS web site: http://clas.uiuc.edu

In particular, the *Review Guidelines for Material Selection Checklist for Child Assessment* is a good resource to support the testing material review and adaptation process. The review guidelines are designed to help teachers determine which materials are most appropriate for a given child or population of children.

Review guidelines: http://clas.uiuc.edu/review/ChildAssessment.pdf

The American Speech-Language-Hearing Association (ASHA) also has a valuable web site with a variety of resources for individuals seeking assessments designed for children who are dual- multilanguage learners. For example, they include descriptive information about a bilingual vocabulary assessment measure, a language proficiency questionnaire, a verbal ability test, and a classroom communication profile.

ASHA website: http://www.asha.org

To find the above-mentioned resources, the ASHA web site allows visitors to search an electronic directory of speech-language pathology assessment instruments. The directory includes a filtering system that can help visitors look for assessments in specific languages or for assessments designed for culturally and linguistically diverse populations (or both).

http://www.asha.org/assessments.aspx?type=&lang=

intent (Robinson & Fieber, 1988). Sometimes, incorporating materials that are familiar to the child such as pictures, toys, or objects from the child's home can encourage children who are from diverse cultural backgrounds or who are dual- or multilanguage learners to narrate stories or role-play events to show what they know and can do (Copenhaver-Johnson & Katz, 2009; Hills, 1992). Allowing children to draw their responses is an alternative option. When children produce verbal responses, teachers should focus on the function or content of the response rather than the form. Finally, children with diverse abilities should be given the option of using adaptive equipment, augmentative communication devices, or other supportive technologies to accommodate their responses during the assessment process.

MEASURES

Regardless of a child's ability or the assessment purpose, federal law, state policies, and recommended practice repeatedly call for using measures that are technically sound, multifaceted, and nonbiased. These terms are defined more fully as follows:

- *Technically sound*—supports purposes for which the assessments or measures are valid and reliable; administered by trained and knowledgeable personnel, using only assessment materials that have been validated for the specific purpose for which they are used

- *Multifaceted*—uses more than one procedure or criterion for determining an appropriate educational program for a child; made by a multidisciplinary team or group of persons, including at least one teacher or specialist; develops partnerships with parents and families as essential stakeholders in the assessment process

- *Nonbiased*—administered so as not to be discriminatory on a racial or cultural basis, in the child's native language or other mode of communication, and in the form most likely to yield accurate information; accurately reflects the child's aptitude or achievement level or whatever other factors the test purports to measure, rather than reflecting the child's impaired sensory, manual, or speaking skills; uses assessment methods that are developmentally appropriate, culturally and linguistically responsive; provides individually, culturally, and linguistically appropriate assessment of all children's strengths

Unfortunately, as with many assessments available, used, or mandated in early childhood intervention, there is a dearth of appropriate assessment measures for young children with diverse abilities. Specifically, 1) few assessments have been normed or validated for children with disabilities or children from specific cultural populations, 2) the use of standardized testing procedures or materials creates bias and a lack of fairness, and 3) many assessments were not designed with universality or equity in mind.

As noted in Chapter 5, many assessments lack basic technical adequacy; however, the areas where assessments lack are of greater concern when it comes to children with diverse abilities. Specifically, few standardized assessments include children from diverse cultural, linguistic, socioeconomic, and disability backgrounds in the standardization or normative group (Peña, Spaulding, & Plante, 2006). Further, items, procedures, and interpretations have not been validated for children with various disabilities or with those from different cultures (Johnstone, Thompson, Bottsford-Miller, & Thurlow, 2008). As noted in this chapter and elsewhere (Cole & Mills, 1997; Eisner, 1998; Fuchs, Fuchs, Benowitz, & Barringer, 1987; Neisworth & Bagnato, 1992), many of the prompts, settings, materials, procedures, and even items are biased or otherwise unfair and penalize children with diverse abilities. Rarely are modifications allowed, instructions on how to make appropriate modifications provided, or little, if any, evidence available of the validity and reliability of scores or findings when modifications are made.

In addition, few assessments were designed with *universality* and *equity* in mind (Thurlow, Quenemoen, Thompson, & Lehr, 2001). *Universality* is defined as design procedures or built-in accommodations that enable all children to demonstrate their underlying and often-unrealized functional capabilities (i.e., universality identifies both strengths and limitations). Universality is increasingly being considered from an instructional perspective; however, little attention has been given to the need for universality of assessment measures. At the heart of universality is the notion of equity and leveling the playing field. *Equity* refers to assessment items and procedures, which are designed so that any child can demonstrate

---

BOX 4.5

Characteristics of universally designed assessments

- Are aimed at inclusive assessment populations
- Measure what they intend to measure (precisely defined constructs)
- Contain accessible items with minimal bias
- Have simple, clear, and intuitive instructions and procedures
- Are amenable to accommodations
- Are readable and comprehensible
- Are legible

Sources: Johnstone et al. (2008); Thompson and Thurlow (2002).

---

underlying competence. Equity in this sense emphasizes functional rather than topographical content (form) and adheres to universal design concepts. In other words, equity signifies that assessments are designed for all children, including children with disabilities, without heavy reliance on adaptations or special design; promoting full integration; and acknowledging differences as a part of everyday life (e.g., gets across the room vs. walks 15 feet). Few tests, however, are designed with equity in mind, and assessment items tend to emphasize topographical versus functional content. (See earlier discussion regarding form and function, as well as Box 4.5 for the characteristics of a universally designed assessment according to Johnstone et al., 2008; and Thompson and Thurlow, 2002).

There are some assessments that are not hindered by the measurement issues related to assessing children with diverse abilities. For example, the Adaptive Behavior Assessment System, Second Edition (ABAS-II; Harrison & Oakland, 2003); the Behavior Assessment System for Children, Second Edition (BASC-2; Reynolds & Kamphaus, 2004); and the Pediatric Evaluation of Disability Inventory (PEDI; Haley, Coster, Ludlow, Haltiwanger, & Andrellos, 1992) include children with disabilities in their normative sample. Further, the Assessment, Evaluation, and Programming System for Infants and Young Children, Second Edition (AEPS®; Bricker, 2002); BASC-2; PEDI; and Transdisciplinary Play-Based Assessment, Second Edition (TPBA-II) (Linder, 2008) have been validated for particular populations, including children with disabilities. Lastly, AEPS® and the Desired Results Developmental Profile access (DRDP access) (Desired Results access Project, California Department of Education, Special Education Division, 2007) are examples of assessments that emphasize universality and equity. (See Bagnato et al., 2010, for a complete review of 81 common early childhood intervention assessments.) Table 4.1 includes a summary of assessments that were specifically designed for children with severe or multiple disabilities. While the assessments in Table 4.1 may not meet all recommended practice standards discussed here and throughout the book, they were, at a minimum, designed or validated for children with severe or multiple disabilities. See Box 4.6 for general considerations for selecting assessments when working with children with severe or multiple disabilities.

Table 4.1. Alphabetical listing of assessment measures designed for young children with severe/multiple disabilities

Assessment	Brief assessment description	Target audience	Age span	Contact information (authors, publishers, web site)
The Callier-Azusa Scale (CAS)[a]	Developmental assessment with subscales that evaluate children's visual, auditory, and tactile development	Children that are deafblind, but also useful for any child with multiple or severe disabilities, particularly hearing and/or visual impairments	Children functioning below a developmental age of 6–7 years	**Author(s):** R.D. Stillman **Publisher:** University of Texas at Dallas, Callier Center for Communication Disorders **Web site:** http://www.utdallas.edu/calliercenter/academic/azusa-scale/ Scale G, which assesses children's overall development (latest revision 1978), and Scale H, which assesses children's communicative development (latest revision 1984), can be ordered through the web site.
Central Institute for the Deaf Preschool Performance Scale (CID–PPS)	Intelligence test yielding a Deviation IQ that assesses nonverbal cognition	Children with hearing impairments	Children with a chronological age of 2–6 years	**Author(s):** A.E. Geers & H.S. Lane **Publisher:** Stoelting Co. **Web site:** http://www.stoeltingco.com/stoelting/productlist13c.aspx?catid=1957&home=Psychological
Communication Matrix	Developmental assessment that evaluates communication skills and behavior and that assists users in identifying logical communication goals	Individuals who experience any type or degree of disability, including severe and multiple disabilities, intellectual limitations, and sensory or physical impairments	Individuals of all ages at the earliest stages of communication development; individuals with a communication developmental age of 0–24 months	**Author(s):** C. Rowland **Publisher:** Design to Learn Projects of the Oregon Health & Science University **Web site:** http://www.communicationmatrix.org/Default.aspx and/or http://www.designtolearn.com/products
DRDP access[a]	A criterion-referenced assessment with domains that measure children's self-concept, social and interpersonal skills, self-regulation, language, learning, cognitive competence, math, literacy, motor skills, and safety and health	Young children with disabilities	Children birth to 5 years	**Author(s):** Desired Results access Project, California Department of Education, Special Education Division **Publisher:** California Department of Education, Special Education Division **Web site:** http://draccess.org

79

Table 4.1. (continued)

Assessment	Brief assessment description	Target audience	Age span	Contact information (authors, publishers, web site)
Every Move Counts[a]	Curriculum-based assessment using a functional hierarchy to evaluate sensory-based communication	Children with significant sensorimotor and developmental disabilities, including autism	Children functioning at a developmental age of 18 months or less	**Author(s):** J. Korsten, T. Foss, & L. Berry **Publisher:** EMC, Inc. **Web site:** http://www.everymovecounts.net/program2.html
Infused Skills	Developmental assessment that analyzes social communicative interactions, emotional development, senses/motor skills, basic concepts, and representation and cognition.	Children with visual impairments who may also have cognitive and behavioral challenges	No specific chronological or developmental age indicated; appropriate for children with no verbal skills to those with higher cognitive functioning but still in need of life skills instruction	**Author(s):** Texas School for the Blind and Visually Impaired Texas School for the Blind and Visually Impaired **Web site:** www.ksb.k12.ks.us/deafblind/assessment/infusedSkills.pdf
INSITE[a]	Developmental checklist designed for use by home-based programs and parents	Children with sensory and/or multiple impairments	Children with a chronological age of birth through 6 years	**Author(s):** The SKI-HI Institute; a Division of the College of Education's Department of Communicative Disorders and Deaf Education at Utah State University. **Publisher:** HOPE, Inc. **Web site:** http://www.hopepubl.com/products.php?cat=9 and/or http://www.skihi.org/Research.html
Leiter-R	Nonverbal cognitive (intelligence) assessment that is administered in the manner of a game that assesses reasoning, visualization, memory, and attention	Children with speech impairments, autism, ADHD, hearing, vision, and/or motor impairments, traumatic brain injury, and other types of communication and/or sensory disabilities	Children and individuals with a chronological age of 2–20 years	**Author(s):** G.H. Roid & L.J. Miller **Publisher:** Western Psychological Services (WPS) **Web site:** http://portal.wpspublish.com/portal/page?_pageid=53,114601&_dad=portal&_schema=PORTAL

	Description	Population	Ages	Source
The Language Environment Analysis System (LENA)	Automatic, computerized language assessment that screens and diagnoses verbal language delays and disorders in children and adults	Children, but especially those with or at risk for disabilities, particularly autism	Children with a chronological age of 2–48 months	**Author(s):** T. D. Paul, & J. A. Paul **Publisher:** LENA Foundation **Web site:** http://www.lenafoundation.org/ and/or http://www.lenababy.com/
The Nonspeech Test	Standardized assessment of receptive and expressive language	Children with communication disabilities, but can also be used with older children with multiple disabilities	Children functioning at a developmental age of no more than 48 months	**Author(s):** M.B. Huer **Publisher:** Don Johnston Incorporated (though discontinued as of 02/2007). **Web site:** For reference information, see http://www.abledata.com/abledata.cfm?pageid=19327&top=14158&productid=77903&trail=22,14033&discontinued=1
Oregon Project[a]	Criterion-referenced assessment that measures child performance on cognitive, language, self-help, socializaion, fine motor, and gross motor skills	Children who are blind or visually impaired	Children with a chronological age of birth through 6 years	**Author(s):** S. Anderson, S. Boigon, & K. Davis **Publisher:** Southern Oregon Education Service District **Web site:** http://www.soesd.k12.or.us/sectionindex.asp?sectionid=132
Ski-Hi[a]	Curriculum-based language assessment that assists in developing individualized goals by evaluating receptive and expressive language	Children who are deaf or hard or hearing	Children with a chronological age of birth through 5 years	**Author(s):** S. Watkins **Publisher:** HOPE, Inc. **Web site:** www.hopepubl.com and/or www.skihi.org

(continued)

Table 4.1. *(continued)*

Assessment	Brief assessment description	Target audience	Age span	Contact information (authors, publishers, web site)
School Inventory of Problem Solving Skills/Home Inventory of Problem Solving Skills (SIPSS/HIPSS)	Developmental assessment that gauges object interaction skills, including basic skills, ways to gain access to objects, and ways to use objects	Children who are non-verbal with multiple disabilities, including those with severe mental retardation or sensory impairments such as deafblindness	No specific chronological or developmental age indicated	**Author(s):** Oregon Health and Science University **Publisher:** Design to Learn Projects of the Oregon Health and Science University **Web site:** http://www.designtolearn.com/content/school-inventory-problem-solving-skills-sipss and/or http://www.designtolearn.com/content/home-inventory-problem-solving-skills-hipss
Strategies for Teaching Based on Autism Research (STAR)	Curriculum-based assessment within an applied behavior analysis framework with a focus on receptive language, expressive language, spontaneous language, functional routines, academics, and play and social skills	Children with autism	Individuals of any age; the program and assessment are available at three distinct levels to meet the needs of all learners.	**Author(s):** J. Arick, L. Loos, R. Falco, D. Krug, & J. Gil **Publisher:** STAR Autism Support, LLC **Web site:** www.starautismprogram.com

aIndicates the assessment was reviewed in Bagnato, S.J., Neisworth, J.T., & Pretti-Frontczak, K. (2010). *LINKing authentic assessment and early childhood intervention: Best measures for best practices* (2nd ed.). Baltimore: Paul H. Brookes Publishing Co.

BOX 4.6

Considerations for selecting an assessment instrument for use with children with severe/multiple disabilities

- Do the items describe behaviors that a child with vision and hearing losses and/or motor impairments could be expected to show?
- Are there sufficient items at the early developmental levels to clearly identify a child's current skills and measure progress in small steps?
- Are the items appropriate to the child's chronological age, or do they describe behaviors one would expect to see only in infants and toddlers?
- Are there sufficient examples to clarify the items and to determine how a particular skill might be observed in a child who is deafblind?
- Does the assessment require information derived from observations in natural settings?
- Do the results provide applicable information for program planning, or are they primarily numerical scores?
- Does the instrument provide ideas about the "next step" for the child?
- Are the results in a format that can be easily communicated to, and understood by, families?
- Does the instrument require the user to possess specialized training or professional credentials?
- Is there a parent version that a family member could complete, or a way for parents to provide their input and perspectives?

From Rowland, C. (2009). *Assessing Communication and Learning in Young Children Who are Deafblind or Who Have Multiple Disabilities* (p. 9). Portland, OR: Design to Learn Projects; reprinted by permission.

Assessing the growing number of children who are from diverse cultural backgrounds can be especially challenging given the lack to appropriate tools available to teachers. As a result, some teachers have turned to learning stories as an alternative assessment practice (Williamson, Cullen, & Lepper, 2006). Learning stories are defined as follows:

> A way of documenting the different ways that children learn….a learning story uses a storytelling format rather than a more traditional "observation" report to describe children's learning. The child becomes the subject of the story and his learning journey is captured through a description of what he's doing, as well as what he may be feeling (Ryan, 2006, p. 25).

The stories focus on what the child can do, and in this way they provide insights into children's strengths, interests, and learning dispositions (e.g., taking an interest and being involved). Learning stories may help alleviate concerns with conventional assessment, or even with authentic assessment, that may be biased against culturally and linguistically diverse children and families.

Learning stories allow teachers to focus on children's interests, strengths, and learning within the context of daily activities (Dunn, 2000; Williamson et al., 2006). Such narrations are designed to emphasize what are referred to as *dispositions,* versus specific knowledge and skills (e.g., counting, participating, walking, describing). In other words, developmental information regarding the child's performance is de-emphasized, while what the child is doing, where, and with whom is emphasized from a sociocultural perspective (Dunn). Figure 4.2 provides an example of a learning story regarding Kayleigh's strengths and actions during a circle-time activity (referred to as mat time) and during clean up (referred to as tidy up time). While there are many advantages to using learning stories, the stories are not without fault, limitations, or controversy (Blaiklock,

Kayleigh loves singing at mat time. I know you like to sing the Ka Kite song at the end of the mat session and you look to see if your Mum is waiting for you. Before mat time, the music for tidy-up time is played. I can see you keep yourself busy at this time, Kayleigh. I noticed you stayed out of the way and stopped and looked at the change in movement of your friends. A few seconds after your friends had passed, you took 3 heavy-footed steps followed by tiptoes toward the mat where mat time happens. It is great that you know what happens at this time.

I noticed that you found an item to hold and look at while your teachers and friends tidied up. You sat at the table and studied a picture you had chosen. I think you looked at everyone from time to time as the tidy-up process went on around you. Sometimes your friends got quite close, so you moved from the table to leaning facing into the back of the chair. Did you feel safer in this position?

When Mary came over, you looked very briefly at the item in her hand and then turned away. When she offered you another item, you made the decision to push them both onto the floor. I think maybe you wanted to tell her you were happy on your own. I noticed you got off your chair when your friend hung over it to see what you were looking at. Were you happier lying on the floor face down where everyone could pass by you? As tidy-up time came to an end, you sat up, looked around, and put your arms up toward Jess, who had stopped beside you. Jess noticed you and gave you a hug. Is that what you wanted? You sat alone on the cleared mat with folded arms and legs and waited for every one to arrive.

Do you think the tidy-up-time music is the time to think about going home? Maybe you are not sure about what to do at tidy-up time. Sometimes we just have to do things we don't really want to do. June thinks it is important to tidy up and so does Jess. Mum wants you to tidy up at home as well. It is a busy time, with every one picking up things and putting them away. Perhaps it is all a bit too busy and you feel a bit unsafe and confused. I noticed you looking very closely at the chair and the picture, and I wondered if you were able to block out all that noise, or perhaps it is just something you like to do. I noticed you ignored your friends and teachers and wondered if you couldn't make sense of what we were wanting you to do. I noticed that tidy-up time changes the whole mood of the kindergarten and that things are just not like they have been all morning. I wonder if you like to keep things the same when you are busy at kindergarten.

Figure 4.2. An example of a learning story created during a circle-time activity.

Next time I will warn you that tidy-up time is coming and prepare you for the change by showing you a picture of tidy-up time and saying, "Tidy-up time in 3 minutes." I will make sure I come back and say "2 minutes," and when it is 1 minute, I will show you another picture and say, for example, "Gabriel, tidy-up time, block on shelf." I will either point to the shelf or go with you to the shelf. I will leave you to choose to carry on or come back in a few minutes to repeat the process. I could point in the direction you need to go to put it away. I will keep my words to a minimum so that you can have a clear understanding of what I want. I won't ask you to look at me and listen to me at the same time. I will make sure that you can see me and that my actions are clear. I will try to interpret your actions and words by pausing and waiting for your responses. I will notice when you need time out to just be by yourself. I think next time I will warn you that tidy-up time is coming up before the music comes on.

Katie is going to make up a chart for us all to note how often we remember to support you in all these different ways so that we can see what supports work best. Patricia is going to make sure she has the pictures in her pocket to use at this time, and the teachers are going to have a set by the office door. Mum and Dad are going to have two pictures to use at home for having a bath and then to bed with a book. Together, we will be able to see how each individual has supported you. I think it will be good to see how we are going at tidy-up time next time we read my portfolio.

2008). As with any practice, teachers will need to examine their intentions, the population being serviced, their own ability, and the degree to which the assessment practice meets recommended practices.

SUMMARY

The purpose of this chapter was to promote the use of recommended assessment practices discussed in Chapter 1 as they apply to children with diverse abilities. In the current chapter, children with diverse abilities were described as children with severe or multiple disabilities, children with diverse cultural experiences, and children who are dual- or multilanguage learners. First, the chapter illustrated the need for the teacher to work as a member of a transdisciplinary team when assessing young children with diverse abilities, highlighting the importance of role release. Next, general considerations for assessing young children with diverse abilities were described and an overview of the challenges teachers face was included. Issues surrounding the content and method of traditional assessments were explored and the inherent biases involved in the assessment process were discussed.

Specific recommendations for assessing young children with diverse abilities were provided next, and readers were directed to consider *what* and *how* information should be gathered across purposes within the assessment process. Teachers were encouraged to gather authentic assessment information from families, to focus on functional skills, to consider the influences and biases created during the assessment process, to incorporate interchangeable cuing systems, and to utilize alternative, flexible materials and allow children to provide alternative responses. Finally, issues around the measures available for assessing young children with diverse abilities were discussed and suggestions for selecting an appropriate assessment tool were provided to better serve these unique learners.

REFERENCES

Allen, K.E., & Marotz, L.R. (2010). *Developmental profiles: Pre-birth through twelve*. Belmont, CA: Wadsworth Cengage Learning.

Autism Speaks (2008). *School community tool kit*. Retrieved January 5, 2010 from the Autism Speaks web site: http://www.autismspeaks.org/docs/family_services_docs/sk/School_Community_Tool_Kit.pdf

Bagnato, S.J., & Neisworth, J.T. (1995). A national study of the social and treatment "invalidity" of intelligence testing for early intervention. *School Psychology Quarterly, 9*(2), 81–102.

Bagnato, S.J., Neisworth, J.T., & Pretti-Frontczak, K. (2010). *LINKing authentic assessment and early childhood intervention: Best measures for best practices (2nd ed.)*. Baltimore: Paul H. Brookes Publishing Co.

Bagnato, S.J., & Simeonsson, R.J. (2007). *Authentic assessment for early childhood intervention: Best practices*. New York: The Guilford Press.

Ballantyne, K.G., Sanderman, A.R., & McLaughlin, N. (2008). *Dual-language learners in the early years: Getting ready to succeed in school*. Washington, DC: National Clearinghouse for English Language Acquisition. Retrieved January 1, 2010, from http://www.ncela.gwu.edu/resabout/ecell/earlyyears.pdf

Barkley, R.A. (1982). Specific guidelines for defining hyperactivity in children (Attention Deficit Disorder with Hyperactivity). In B. Lahey & A. Kazdin (Eds.), *Advances in clinical child psychology* (Vol. 5, pp. 137–180). New York: Plenum Press.

Barone, D.M., & Xu, S.H. (2008). *Literacy instruction for English language learners: Pre-K–2*. New York: Guilford Press.

Blaiklock, K.E. (2008). A critique of the use of learning stories to assess the learning dispositions of young children. *NZ research in ECE Journal, 11*, 77–87.

Bricker, D. (2002). *Assessment, evaluation, and programming system for infants and children*. (2nd ed., Vols. 1–4). Baltimore: Paul H. Brookes Publishing Co.

Bronfenbrenner, U. (1977). Toward an experimental ecology of human development. *American Psychologist, 32*, 513–531.

Browder, D.M. (2001). *Curriculum and assessment for students with moderate and severe disabilities*. New York: Guilford Press.

Bruder, M.B., & Bologna, T. (1993). Collaboration and service coordination for effective early intervention. In W. Brown, S.K. Thurman, & L.F. Pearl (Eds.), *Family-centered early intervention with infants and toddlers* (pp. 103–128). Baltimore: Paul H. Brookes Publishing Co.

California Department of Education (2007). *Assessing children with disabilities who are English language learners: Guidance for the DRDP access and the PS DRDP-R for children with IEPs*. Retrieved December 31, 2009, from http://www.draccess.org/pdf/ELGuidance.pdf

Clarke, Priscilla, & F.K.A. Multicultural Resource Centre. (1992). *English as a 2nd language in early childhood*. Free Kindergarten Association, Multicultural Resource Centre, [Richmond, Vic.].

Cole, K., & Mills, P. (1997). Agreement of language intervention triage profiles. *Topics in Early Childhood Special Education, 17*, 119–130.

Copenhaver-Johnson, J., & Katz, L. (2009). *Supporting young English language learners and their families*. A Professional Development Module supported by the Ohio Department of Education. Columbus, OH: Early Childhood Quality Network.

Copple, C., & Bredekamp, S. (Eds.). (2009). *Developmentally appropriate practice in early childhood programs serving children birth through eight: Third edition.* Washington, DC: National Association for the Education of Young Children.

Desired Results Access Project. (2007). *Desired Results Developmental Profile (DRDP).* Rohnert Park, CA: Napa County Office of Education, California Department of Education, Special Education Division.

Downing, J.E., & Chen, D. (2003). Using tactile strategies with students who are blind and have severe disabilities. *Teaching Exceptional Children, 36*(2), 56–60.

Drury, R. (2007). *Young bilingual learners at home and school. Researching multilingual voices.* Stoke-on-Trent Staffordshire: England, Trentham.

Dunn, L.M. (2000). Using "learning stories" to assess and design programs for young children with special needs in New Zealand. *Infants and Young Children, 13*(2), 73–82.

Durand, T.M. (2008). Celebrating diversity in early care and education settings: Moving beyond the margins. *Early Child Development and Care.* doi: 10.1080/03004430802466226

Eisner, E.W. (1998). The enlightened eye: Qualitative inquiry and the enhancement of educational practice. *School Psychology International, 16*(1), 5–7.

Ermer, J., & Dunn, W. (1998). The sensory profile: A discriminant analysis of children with and without disabilities. *The American Journal of Occupational Therapy, 52*(4), 283–290.

Espinosa, L.M. (2005). Curriculum and assessment considerations for young children from culturally, linguistically, and economically diverse backgrounds. *Psychology in the Schools, 42*(8), 837–853.

Espinosa, L.M. (2010). *Getting it RIGHT for young children from diverse backgrounds: Applying research to improve practice.* New York: Pearson.

Espinosa, L.M. (2010, May). *Assessing young dual language learners: Challenges and opportunities.* Presented at the Listening and Learning about Early Learning Tour, Chicago, IL. Available from http://www2.ed.gov/about/inits/ed/earlylearning/espinosadeck.pdf

Espinosa, L. (in press). Second language acquisition in early childhood. In New, R. & Cochran, M. (Eds.). *Early Childhood Education.* Westport, CT: Greenwood Publishing Group.

Etscheidt, S. (2006). Least restrictive and natural environments for young children with disabilities. *Topics in Early Childhood Special Education, 26,* 167–178. doi: 10.1177/02711214060260030401

Fabri, M., & Freidel, D. (2008). Cultural adaptation and translation of assessment instruments for diverse populations: The use of the Harvard Trauma Questionnaire in Rwanda. In L.A. Suzki, J.G. Ponterotto, & P.J. Meller (Eds.), *Handbook of multicultural assessment: Clinical, psychological, and educational implications* (3rd ed.). San Francisco, CA: Jossey-Bass.

Ferrell, K.A. (1998). *Project PRISM: A longitudinal study of developmental patterns of children who are visually impaired.* Greeley: University of Northern Colorado. Retrieved from http://www.unco.edu/ncssd/research/PRISM/ExecSumm.pdf.

Freeman, B.J., Frankel, B.J., & Ritvo, E.J. (1976). Effects of frequency of photic stimulation upon autistic and retarded children. *American Journal of Mental Deficiency, 81,* 32–40.

Fuchs, L.S., & Fuchs, D. (1984) Criterion-referenced assessment without measurement. *Remedial and Special Education, 5*(4), 29–32.

Fuchs, D., Fuchs, L.S., Benowitz, S., & Barringer, K. (1987). Norm-referenced tests: Are they valid for use with handicapped students? *Exceptional Children, 54,* 263–271.

Goodz, N.S. (1994). Interactions between parents and children in bilingual families. In F. Genesee (Ed.), *Educating second language children: The whole child, the whole curriculum, the whole community* (pp. 61–81). New York: Cambridge University Press.

Grassi, E., & Barker, H.B. (2010). *Culturally and linguistically diverse exceptional students: Strategies for teaching and assessment.* Thousand Oaks, CA: Sage Publications, Inc.

Guild, P.B. (2001). *Diversity, learning style and culture.* Retrieved January 5, 2010, from the New Horizons for Learning Web site: http://www.newhorizons.org/strategies/styles/guild.htm#_ftn1

Haley, S.M., Coster, W.J., Ludlow, L.H., Haltiwanger, J.T., & Andrellos, P.J. (1992). *Pediatric Evaluation of Disability Inventory (PEDI).* Boston: New England Medical Center.

Harrison, P.L., & Oakland, T. (2003). *Adaptive Behavior Assessment System®* (2nd ed.). San Antonio, TX: Psychological Corporation.

Haynes, J. (2006). Everything ESL.net. Retrieved January 2, 2010 from http://www.everythingesl.net/inservices/language_stages.php

Hills, T.W. (1992). Reaching potentials through appropriate assessment. In S. Bredekamp & T. Rosegrant (Eds.), *Reaching potentials: Appropriate curriculum and assessment for young children* (pp. 43– 64). Washington, DC: National Association for the Education of Young Children.

Hirstein, W., Iversen P., & Ramachandran, V.S. (2001). Autonomic responses of autistic children to people and objects. *Proceedings of the Royal Society B, 268,* 1883–1888.

Individuals with Disabilities Education Improvement Act (IDEA) of 2004, PL108-446, 20 U.S.C. §§ 1400 *et seq.*

Jackson, S., Pretti-Frontczak, K., Harjusola-Webb, S., Grisham-Brown, J., & Romani, J.M. (2009). Response to intervention: Implications for early childhood professionals. *Language, Speech, and Hearing Services in Schools, 40,* 424–434. doi: 10.1044/0161-1461

Johnstone, C.J., Thompson, S.J., Bottsford-Miller, N.A., & Thurlow, M.L. (2008). Universal design and multimethod approaches to item review. *Educational Measurement: Issues and Practice, 27*(1), 25–36.

King, G., Strachan, D., Tucker, M., Duwyn, B., Desserud, S., & Shillington, M. (2009). The application of a transdisciplinary model for early intervention services. *Infants and Young Children, 22,* 211–223.

Klingner, J.K., Blanchett, W.J., & Harry, B. (2007). Race, culture, and developmental disabilities. In S.L. Odom, R.H. Horner, M.E. Snell, & J. Blacher (Eds.). *Handbook of developmental disabilities.* New York: Guilford Press.

Linder, T. (2008). *Transdisciplinary play-based assessment 2.* Baltimore: Paul H. Brookes Publishing Co.

Macswan, J., & Rolstad, K. (2006). How language proficiency tests mislead us about ability: Implications for English language learner placement in special education. *Teachers College Record, 108*(11), 2304–2328.

Margolies, P.J. (1977). Behavioral approaches to the treatment of early infantile autism: A review. *Psychological Bulletin, 84,* 249–264.

McCormick, K. & Nellis, L. (2004). Assessing cognitive development. In M. McLean, M. Wolery, & B. Bailey Jr. (Eds.). *Assessing infants and preschoolers with special needs* (3rd ed.). Upper Saddle River, NJ: Pearson.

Meisels, S.J., & Atkins-Burnett, S. (2000). The elements of early childhood assessment. In J.P. Shonkoff & S. Meisels (Eds.), *Handbook of early childhood intervention* (2nd ed., pp. 231–257). New York: Cambridge University Press.

McLean, M. (2000). Conducting child assessments. *Culturally and linguistically appropriate services early childhood research institute technical report #2.* Champaign: University of Illinois at Urbana-Champaign.

McLean, M., Wolery, M., & Bailey, D.B. (2004). *Assessing infants and preschoolers with special needs* (3rd ed.). Upper Saddle River, NJ: Pearson Education Inc.

Menken, K. (2000). *What are the critical issues in wide-scale assessment of English language learners?* (Issue Brief No. 6). Washington, DC: National Clearinghouse for Bilingual Education. Retrieved November 4, 2002, from http://www.ncela.gwu.edu/ncbepubs/issuebriefs/ib6.htm

National Association for the Education of Young Children. (2005). *Where we stand on the screening and assessment of young English-language learners.* Retrieved November 28, 2009 from the NAEYC Web site: http://www.naeyc.org/files/naeyc/file/positions/WWSEnglishLanguageLearnersWeb.pdf

National Association for the Education of Young Children. (2009). *Where we stand on assessing young English language learners.* Retrieved January 12, 2010, from http://www.naeyc.org/files/naeyc/file/positions/WWSEnglishLanguageLearners Web.pdf

Neisworth, J.T., & Bagnato, S.J. (1992). The case against intelligence testing in early intervention. *Topics in Early Childhood Special Education, 12,* 1–20.

Neisworth, J.T., & Bagnato, S.J. (2004). The mismeasure of young children the authentic assessment alternative. *Infants and Young Children, 17,* 198–212.

Notari-Syverson, A., Losardo, A., & Sook Lim, Y. (2003). Assessment of young children from culturally diverse backgrounds: A journey in progress. *Assessment for Effective Intervention, 29*(1), 39–51.

Peña, E.D., Spaulding, T.J., & Plante, E. (2006). The comparison of normative groups and diagnostic decision making: Shooting ourselves in the foot. *American Journal of Speech-Language Pathology, 15,* 247–254.

Philips, S.U. (1983). *The invisible culture.* New York: Longman Publishing.

Qi, C.H., Kaiser, A.P., Milan, S.E., Yzquierdo, Z., & Hancock, T.B. (2003). The performance of low income African American children on the Preschool Language Scale-3. *Journal of Speech, Language, and Hearing Research, 46,* 576–590.

Raab, M., & Dunst, C.J. (2004). Early intervention practitioner approaches to natural environment interventions. *Journal of Early Intervention, 27,* 15–26.

Reynolds, C.R., & Kamphaus, R.W. (2004). *Behavior Assessment System for Children* (2nd ed.). Circle Pines, MN: American Guidance Service.

Robinson, C., & Fieber, N. (1988). Cognitive assessment of motorically impaired infants and preschoolers. In T.D. Wachs & R. Sheehan (Eds.), *Assessment of young developmentally disabled children* (pp. 127–152). New York: Plenum Press.

Rowland, C. (Ed.). (2009). *Assessing communication and learning in young children who are deafblind or who have multiple disabilities.* Portland, OR: Oregon Health and Science University.

Ryan, K. (2006). Learning stories. *JiSAW, 31,* 25–26.

Sandall, S., Hemmeter, M.L., Smith, B.J., & McLean, M.E. (2005). *DEC recommended practices: A comprehensive guide for practical application in early intervention/early childhood special education.* Longmont, CO: Sopris West.

Schum, R. (2004). Psychological assessment of children with multiple handicaps who have hearing loss. *The Volta Review, 104,* 237–255.

Schuman, J. (1978). *The pidginization process: A model for second language acquisition.* Rowley, MA: Newbury House.

Shaw, S.R. (2008). An educational programming frame work for a subset of students with diverse learning needs: border line intellectual functioning. *Intervention in School and Clinic, 43*(5), 291–299.

Shonkoff, J.P., & Phillips, D.A. (Eds.). (2000). *From neurons to neighborhoods: The science of early childhood development.* Washington, DC: National Academies Press.

Singh, S., Barto, A.G., & Chentanez, N. (2005). Intrinsically motivated reinforcement learning. In *Advances in Neural Information Processing Systems 17 (NIPS).* Cambridge, MA: MIT Press.

Snow, C.E., & Van Hemel, S.B. (2008). *Early childhood assessment: Why, what, and how?* Washington, DC: National Academies Press.

Spinelli, C.G. (2008). Addressing the issue of cultural and linguistic diversity and assessment: Informal evaluation measures for English language learners. *Reading & Writing Quarterly, 24,* 101–118.

Strand, S., & Lindsay, G. (2009). Evidence of ethnic disproportionality in special education in an English population. *The Journal of Special Education, 43,* 174–190. doi: 10.1177/0022466908320461

Thompson, S., & Thurlow, M. (2002). *Universally designed assessments: Better tests for everyone!* (NCEO Policy Directions No. 14). Minneapolis: National Center on Educational Outcomes, University of Minnesota.

Thurlow, M., Quenemoen, R., Thompson, S., & Lehr, C. (2001). *Principles and characteristics of inclusive assessment and accountability systems* (Synthesis Report 40). Minneapolis, MN: National Center on Educational Outcomes.

U.S. Department of Education. (2006). *Profiles of Part B and Part C programs.* Office of Special Education Programs, data analysis system. Children with disabilities receiving special education under Part B of the Individual-s with Disabilities Education Act. Retrieved November 15, 2008, from https://www.ideadata.org/tables30th/ar_1-1.xls.

Westby, C., Burda, A., & Mehta, Z. (2003). Asking the Right Questions in the Right

Ways: Strategies for Ethnographic Interviewing. Retrieved on May 15, 2007, from www.asha.org/about/publications/leader-online/archives/2003/q2/f030429b.htm.

Williams, P. (2007, January). Disproportionality and overrepresentation (Module 5). *Building the legacy: IDEA 2004 training curriculum.* Washington, DC: National Dissemination Center for Children with Disabilities. Retrieved December 31, 2009, from http://www.nichcy.org/Laws/IDEA/Documents/Training_Curriculum/5-discussionSlides1-9.pdf

Williamson, D., Cullen, J., & Lepper, C. (2006). Checklists to narratives in special education. *Australian Journal of Early Childhood, 31*(2), 20–29.

Woodruff, G., & McGonigel, M.J. (1988). Early intervention team approaches: The transdisciplinary model. In J. Jordan, J. Gallaher, P. Huntinger, & M. Karns (Eds.), *Early childhood special education: Birth to three* (pp. 163–182). Reston, VA: Council for Exceptional Children.

Zentall, S.S. (1988). Production deficiencies in elicited language but not in the spontaneous verbalizations of hyperactive children. *Journal of Abnormal Child Psychology, 16,* 657–673.

CHAPTER 5

Recommended Practices for Determining Technical Adequacy

Kristie Pretti-Frontczak and
Nicole R. Shannon

Ms. Leah has taught early childhood intervention (ECI) for 8 years. Recently she re-located to a new school district in a different state. She is very happy with her new position because she is using her expertise to work with young children in an inclusive setting. However, Ms. Leah is very disturbed by the assessment practices in the school district. One common practice in the district is to administer a norm-referenced test to children suspected of having developmental delays. If the child qualifies for services, the results of that test are used solely to develop the child's individualized education program (IEP). This practice also concerns her because the tests are sometimes inappropriate for the particular children being tested. In addition, Ms. Leah is bothered by the fact that the school district requires every preschool teacher to use a developmental screening instrument twice a year to assess every child in the program. Ms. Leah understands that there are many assessment mandates in ECI, but she is troubled by how her new district meets these requirements. In her former district, the educational team carefully selected instruments for determining eligibility based on each child's characteristics (e.g., blind, hearing impaired, speech impaired). When developing IEPs and demonstrating children's progress from the beginning to the end of the year, the classroom staff utilized curriculum-based assessments. Ms. Leah does not want to cause trouble in her new district but feels she must say something. She recalls discussing using the right tool for the right purpose and making sure that tests are appropriate for the populations being tested in her college assessment course. After a trip to the attic to find her old textbook and research on the topic, she decides to make an appointment with her supervisor and discuss her concerns.

Using the right tool for the job is a logical recommendation for any profession or identified task. For example, if one wants to stir a pot, using a large spoon is helpful, or if one wants to measure a temperature, a thermometer is handy. As highlighted in the chapter vignette, however, ECI teachers face a number of challenges in using assessment instruments for their intended or validated purposes. First, local, state, or federal agencies may develop policies or mandate practices that are impractical, invalid, and, arguably, unethical. For example, many times assessments are used or required, without documented technical adequacy. Further, assessments are often used for purposes other than those intended or scores/procedures validated. Second, ECI teachers may lack the training and ongoing support needed to administer assessments with fidelity and to interpret and use assessment information to better serve young children and their families. In general, providers may find navigating the world of ECI assessment practices frustrating, with many policies conflicting with recommended practice.

The purpose of this chapter is to help providers be critical consumers of assessments and use assessments for the purposes for which they were intended and validated. The chapter is divided into three main sections. First, basic terms related to the technical adequacy of assessments are discussed. Second, the different types or classifications of ECI assessments are reviewed. Third, the skills needed for using conventional assessments are described, including calculating chronological age, adjusting for prematurity, establishing basals and ceilings, and interpreting reports.

TECHNICAL ADEQUACY

Throughout the book, we discuss how teachers use assessments to make a wide array of decisions (e.g., eligibility for services, planning instructional efforts, program evaluation) that often have a significant impact on the lives of young children and their families. Thus, it is imperative that teachers understand how to select and use assessment instruments for their intended purposes (e.g., screening, program evaluation) and populations (e.g., 4-year-olds, children who are at risk).

The first *rule* for selecting and using an assessment instrument (regardless of reason or population) is to ensure its technical adequacy (American Educational Research Council, American Psychological Association, & National Council on Measurement in Education, 1999). Technical adequacy relates to documented evidence of an assessment instrument's unbiased, reliable, and valid scores or procedures that are used in making sound decisions for a given population.

Teachers need to be aware, however, that not all assessment instruments sold, mandated, or selected have established technical adequacy. In fact, since the 1960s, expert and consumer reviews of ECI assessment practices have found a paucity of evidence that scores produced and inferences made, are valid or reliable for the purposes or populations for which they are used. (See Box 5.1.) Thus, numerous ECI assessments are rated as authentic and suggest a strong link to instruction but lack basic evidence of technical adequacy, and most have not been validated for marketed purposes (e.g., progress monitoring) or for use with young children from a variety of backgrounds and with a variety of abilities (Bagnato, Neisworth, & Pretti-Frontczak, 2010; Brown & Hubbell, 2010).

Teachers must have the knowledge and confidence to select and use assessment instruments with established technical adequacy. All too often, individuals in leadership or administrative positions lack a background or

---

BOX 5.1

Examples of reviews documenting how assessment instruments lack technical adequacy

- 1970s—Salvia and Ysseldyke (1978) found that common assessments used by special educators were lacking in technical adequacy and did not meet recommended assessment practices.

- 1980s—Bracken (1987) found that of the hundreds of early childhood intervention assessments, many did not meet any standard set forth regarding technical adequacy. Of the 10 reviewed, all had limitations in the areas of reliability and validity.

- 1990s—Bracken, Keith, and Walker (1998) found that 13 preschool measures of social-emotional functioning lacked or had low reliability and validity, had issues with the standardization samples, as well as issues with item structure as related to basals, ceilings, and gradation.

- 2000s—Macy, Bagnato, Lehman, and Salaway (2007) found no research to support the common assessments used for early intervention eligibility, and Brown and Hubbell (2010) found many common assessments to be lacking in documented technical adequacy and a notable discrepancy between publishers' defined intended uses and research to validate those uses.

expertise in working with young children or are unaware of recommended assessment practices. In such instances, assessment instruments may be used inappropriately for a given purpose or population (e.g., using a screening instrument for reporting accountability data). The next section defines common measurement terms related to technical adequacy and provides suggestions that will allow teachers to serve as critical consumer of assessment instruments (see Box 5.2). Specifically, validity, reliability, and bias are discussed.

BOX 5.2
Consumer tip

Use Rabinowitz and Sato (2006) worksheet to examine the technical adequacy of a given assessment instrument. While the worksheet was developed for examining assessments used for English language learners, it can easily be used to examine assessments for any population, including young children with diverse abilities.

Validity

As defined by the American Educational Research Association, American Psychological Association, and National Council on Measurement in Education, . . . *validity* is "the degree to which evidence and theory support the interpretations of test scores entailed by proposed uses of tests" (1999, p. 9). As stated by McCloskey,

> Validity is not an inherent characteristic; it is a function of how and with whom the scale is used. If a scale is seen as having many uses (e.g., to determine eligibility; plan children's programs), then it must be validated for each use. Also, if the scale is to be used with one or more rater groups, its use must be validated for each rater group. (1990, p. 54)

The basic tenet of validity is that an assessment instrument correctly and accurately measures what it was intended to measure (i.e., the overall degree of justification for test interpretation and use). For instance, a teacher interested in measuring a child's ability to read would use an assessment instrument known to measure characteristics or indicators of reading capabilities (e.g., vocabulary, fluency, picture naming, rhyming). Using a test that measured the child's problem-solving skills or ability to count objects in order would not be a valid way to assess a child's reading ability. Although the preceding example is obvious in terms of validity, it gets at the heart of the matter; that is, if a child is being assessed with an instrument not meant for that purpose, it is difficult to obtain an accurate measure of what the child is truly able to accomplish.

There are many *forms* of validity, but all relate or contribute to the appropriateness, meaningfulness, and usefulness of the specific inferences made from test scores. Some common terms related to validity include *criterion, concurrent, construct, content, convergent, discriminant, face,* and *predictive*. In recent years, the terms *social validity* and *treatment validity* have been increasingly referenced. Table 5.1 defines and lists characteristic of common types of validity. Further, McCloskey (1990) provides teachers with suggestions about how to determine the validity of an assessment's scores or procedures. (See Box 5.3.)

Table 5.1.   Common types of validity and basic definitions and associated characteristics

Type	Definitions/characteristics
Content	"Refers to whether the items on a test represent the domain that the test is supposed to measure" (Sattler, 2001, p. 115) • Consumers should consider the appropriateness and completeness of items (e.g., does the test contain enough items related to the domain of interest) as well as how the items assess the domain of interest (e.g., what is the level of mastery being assessed). • Asks the question as to whether the domain of interest (e.g., reading, expressive communication, motor skills) is actually being assessed • Example: Strong and convincing rationale by test developers in terms of the process by which content was selected and clear evidence that the content is theoretically sound and/or supported by experts for inclusion
Criterion	"Refers to the relationship between test scores and some type of criterion or outcome . . ." (Sattler, 2001, p. 115) • One thing (e.g., test, variable) corresponds to something else. • Two types—*concurrent* and *predictive* • Example: Each item on the Assessment, Evaluation, and Programming system for Infants and Young Children (AEPS®) (Bricker, 2002) includes a criterion to which a child's performance is compared to a judgment being made in terms of whether the child can perform the skill, how well the child performs the skill, how often he or she performs the skill, and so forth. For example, the criterion for the AEPS item of "responds to established social routines" is "When given general verbal and/or contextual cues, the child performs a single response associated with established social routines such as mealtime, toileting, dressing/undressing, bathing/washing, naptime/bedtime, and/or classroom events."
Concurrent	"Refers to whether test scores are related to some currently available criterion measure" (Sattler, 2001, p. 115) • "Extent to which a test correlates with another measure administered close in time to the first" (McLean, Wolery, & Bailey, 2004, p. 39). • Type of *criterion* validity • Example: Findings from administering the gross motor area of the Hawaii Early Learning Profile (Holt, Gilles, Holt, & Davids, 2004) and the gross motor area of The Carolina Curriculum for Preschoolers with Special Needs, Second Edition (Johnson-Martin, Jens, Hacker, & Attermeier, 1991) at similar points in time produce related findings.
Predictive	"Refers to the correlation between test scores and future performance on a relevant criterion" (Sattler, 2001, p. 115) • Answers the following question: Is the score obtained on the test an accurate predictor of future performance on the criterion? • Type of *criterion* validity • Example: A relationship between a child's performance on picture naming and rhyming as measured by Individual Growth and Development Indicators during preschool and the child's future performance in reading as measured by Dynamic Indicators of Basic Early Literacy Skills (DIBELS) during first grade.

(continued)

Table 5.1.   *(continued)*

Type	Definitions/characteristics
Construct	"Refers to how well performances on different measures of the same domain in different formats correlate positively" (Sattler, 2001, p. 116) • Not established in a single study but rather based upon an aggregate of evidence over time • Two types—*convergent* and *discriminant* • Example: Results of a factor analysis confirm that findings are similar for more than one population, that responses by different people are similar, or that test items cluster as expected.
Convergent	"Refers to how well performances on different measures of the same domain in different format . . . correlate positively" (Sattler, 2001, p. 116) • Measures that should be related are in reality related • Form of *construct* validity • Example: Positive correlations are found between a curriculum-based assessment and a parent report regarding a child's current abilities.
Discriminant	Refers to the "extent to which a given scale differs from other scales designed to measure a different conceptual variable" (Eisert, Sturner, & Mabe, 1991, p. 45) • Measures that should not be related are in reality not related (i.e., tests designed to measure unrelated constructs should not correlate). • Form of *construct* validity and sometimes called divergent validity. • Example: A child's social skills as measured by the Battelle Developmental Inventory (Newborg, 2005a) should not correlate with the child's ability to count objects as measured by the Brigance Inventory of Early Development-II (Brigance & Glascoe, 2004).
Face	Refers to "what the test appears to measure, not what it actually does measure" (Sattler, 2001, p. 115) • Is important because if the test does not appear to measure what it is supposed to measure, examinees may become skeptical and not perform adequately • Example: While an assessment's items have been aligned to Office of Special Education Program child outcomes (see Chapter 7 regarding crosswalks), and the assessment appears to measure a child's performance regarding positive social relationships, without at least some sort of expert or social validation, the extent to which the assessment actually measures a child's performance on federal outcomes is not truly known
Social	"Takes into account the perceived usefulness of the scale's items" (McCloskey, 1990, p. 55) • Extent to which assessment procedures and findings are found to be meaningful, useful, and accurate by consumers • Example: Both providers and parents are satisfied with the procedures and findings from a play-based assessment using the Transdisciplinary Play-Based Assessment.
Treatment	"Refers to the degree to which an assessment or assessment process is shown to contribute to beneficial treatment or intervention outcomes" (Meisels & Atkins-Burnett, 2000, p. 252) • Leads to constructive changes and effective interventions • Sometimes called treatment or instructional utility • Example: Documented evidence that by conducting an assessment, more meaningful and relevant individualized family service plans or individualized education programs are developed and that the correct amount/type of instruction is then provided.

BOX 5.3

**Suggestions for examining the validity
of an assessment's scores and procedures**

Users should look for evidence of one or more of the following: (a) content reviews by experts verifying that the items of the scale adequately represent behaviors thought to be associated with the trait, (b) results of practitioner surveys listing behaviors commonly associated with the trait and evidence that survey responses were used to develop the scale items, and (c) references to research studies that identified behaviors common to a trait. (p. 54)

The scale manual should (a) discuss the current knowledge base regarding the nature of the trait being rated (e.g., if the trait is thought to change over time or in certain situations or if the trait is rated differently for males and females) and (b) provide data to substantiate that rating scale scores accurately reflect the trait's nature. (p. 55)

A scale must show evidence of validity for each purpose for which it will be used, and with each group of raters who will be using it. Users also must confirm that validation efforts have been conducted with children similar to those with whom the scale is to be used. (p. 56)

From McCloskey, G. *Topics in Early Childhood Special Education* (10, 3) pp. 39–64, Copyright © 1990 by SAGE Publications. Reprinted by permission of SAGE Publications.

Reliability

Reliability, an issue closely related to validity, refers to the stability and consistency of assessment results (Sattler, 2001). Within the assessment process, some form of error is anticipated; however, the higher the reliability of an assessment's scores or procedures, the more confidence users can have in its accuracy. Reliability results are reported most often in the form of correlation coefficients (e.g., $r = .80$, $r = .93$). Reliability correlation coefficients range from -1.00 to $+1.00$. A negative correlation means there is an inverse relationship: As one score or attribute goes up, the other goes down. A positive correlation means that, as one score or attribute goes up, the other goes up, or as one goes down, the other goes down. Stated differently, a correlation of 0 indicates no consistency and a correlation of $+1.00$ or -1.00 indicates perfect consistency (i.e., a perfect positive linear relationship or a perfect decreasing linear relationship exists). Scores from well-constructed assessments with many items should produce correlations in the .80 to .95 range, while the scores of assessments with fewer items or fewer scoring options are typically in the .70 to .85 range. Correlations for questionnaires often fall around .5.

Generally speaking, higher correlation coefficients indicate more reliable assessment instruments. Further, the higher the stakes in terms of the decisions made from the assessment, the higher the correlations should be. For example, when making decisions about whether a child is eligible for special education (a high-stakes decision), reliability correlations should be .80 and higher.

There are two main forms of reliability: test–retest and interrater reliability. *Test–retest reliability* indicates how stable or consistent scores are when the tests are administered to the same group of individuals at least (indeed, generally) twice and within a short span of time (Sattler, 2001).

The basic idea behind test–retest reliability is to make sure that the scores that are calculated at the end of the assessment are accurate and do not fluctuate greatly. For example, if a child scores 85 out of 100 and 2 weeks later scores 90 on the same assessment, then the assessment could be considered reliable. Conversely, a test that produced a score of 85 the first time and then 1 week later a 65 would be considered less reliable. The basic aim is that even though a score from administration to administration may change, that scores are within the stated or accepted confidence interval.

A *confidence interval* is a range of scores that indicates where a child's *true* score would fall, if there were no error in the administration. However, there is always error in assessment administration. For example, extraneous variables that the examiner is unable to control or may not even think about may affect the child's performance. Therefore, confidence intervals were created to give an idea of where the child's true score would be, and test–retest reliability provides a gauge of the child's ability in a given area. If, after several administrations of a test within a short period, the scores fall outside the confidence interval, then there is little reliable information to be gained. If a test, however, produces the same information about a child after multiple assessments conducted within the relatively same period of time, then there is a better understanding of the child's abilities.

The second aspect of reliability is *interrater reliability*. Interrater reliability, unlike test–retest reliability, usually applies to observation, as would be used in assessing a child's behavior. The purpose of interrater reliability, however, remains that of ensuring that the assessment score is an accurate representation of the child. Because a child's behavior can vary from one day to the next, interrater reliability is conducted by having two or more (usually two) individuals observe the child at the exact same time, using the same metric. Once the observation is complete, the ratings of the observers are compared. The more similar the ratings, the higher the reliability is between the observers. Higher reliability indicates that the assessment is a more reliable gauge of the child's behavior.

Bias

Various empirical processes can be used to determine whether a particular assessment is biased (meaning that systematic differences are obtained) on the basis of children's membership in a particular group. Fairness, a related issue, "is a value judgment about the appropriateness of decisions or actions based on test scores" (Thorndike & Thorndike-Christ, 2010, p.193). Bias and fairness affect all types of assessments; however, norm-referenced assessments (discussed in the next section in greater detail) are particularly susceptible. Assessments with a normative sample or group allow for comparisons between a child and other children of the same age, gender, race, ethnicity, ability, geographic location, economic status, and so forth and provide a basis for interpreting tests (Kritikos, 2010). The composition of the normative group will likely affect team interpretations and should be examined before an assessment instrument is selected and used. Thus, when using norm-referenced assessments (described subsequently), teachers should consider the year the norms were established (e.g., norms from 20 years ago may not provide accurate comparisons), characteristics of the normative sample (e.g., representation, size), and whether the sample is relevant to the target population and includes children with disabilities.

The idea behind *representativeness* is that the normative sample should "match as closely as possible the major demographic characteristics of the population as a whole" (Sattler, 2001, p. 96). In other words, representativeness can be made up of multiple factors, such as age, grade, gender, geographic location, ethnicity, and socioeconomic status (SES), and should relate to and be a relatively accurate depiction of the population. The manual that accompanies the assessment will often have information about many, if not all, of these factors. When examining norms for an assessment instrument, a teacher must take into consideration the specific child being assessed and how closely he or she resembles the norm. The more a child resembles a normative group for an assessment instrument, the more valuable the results of the assessment can be (Kidsource Online, 2009).

Although it is unlikely for an assessment instrument to have perfect representation of a population, information such as the U.S. census, or the equivalent, can help in determining whether the assessment instrument is appropriate or beneficial. It is important, however, to examine the date (year) in which the normative information was taken—the older it is, the greater is the likelihood that it is not truly representative of children today (Kidsource Online, 2009). Another factor to examine is the idea that results for some assessments may appear skewed for a particular gender, ethnicity, or SES group. Skewed in this sense means that the information is not representative or is biased. Knowing whether the information is skewed is just as important as finding out how the normative sample compares against the general population and can help teachers determine whether they should use the instrument for a child from an affected group. Finally, teachers should look for deficiencies in the sample (e.g., geographic area, age, gender). Although a deficiency will not indicate which children should not be assessed by a particular instrument, a sample that is not representative should signal caution. Deficiencies, if indicated, are sometimes stated in a sentence or two that can be easily overlooked. When information regarding the population that is supposed to represent the child is lacking, teachers should be cautious about using the assessment instrument. It is important to note that lack of information about a particular population does not necessarily mean that the instrument is *faulty* or that the population was not represented; there simply may have been nothing to report. Either way, professional judgment may be necessary to determine the appropriateness of the instrument.

The *size* of a sample is very important. In general, the sample should be large enough to ensure accurate representation (Sattler, 2001). In addition, subgroups within the population should be represented within the sample. Typically, when reviewing information about size, the more individuals in the norm group, the more stable the group. A general rule of thumb for actual size is at least 100 participants per group (e.g., per age grouping, per gender, per SES categorization). Often, the size of the sample will be abbreviated as *N* or *n*. Big *N*, as it is sometimes referred to, depicts the number of the whole population or the whole sample of the normative group (e.g., a total of 2,000 participants in the normative sample). Little *n* refers to the number of individuals in the sample or of a particular group (e.g., 24 boys or 600 4-year-olds within the whole sample of 2,000).

A final aspect of normative samples is the issue of *relevance*, which also refers to scoring accuracy. Without having an appropriate scale to measure a child's performance, results do not have much meaning. Oftentimes, the assessment instruments that are used are based upon national norms. National norms are beneficial when information regarding the child's performance compared to peers outside of their immediate locale is warranted (Sattler, 2001). Generally, the information about what type of norm (national vs. local) is contained in an assessment instrument's administration manual. Typically, national norms are found in mass-published assessments, like the Battelle Developmental Inventory–II (BDI-II). Local norms, however, may be employed as well, particularly when information is needed to rank the child with individuals from the local population (Sattler, 2001), and can be beneficial in terms of monitoring progress and comparing children with their peers. This is a technique that is common when schools benchmark using DIBELS or a similar instrument.

Also related to relevance is the group or sample to which a child is being compared. For example, comparing a 3-year-old child's ability to identify 5 out of 20 numbers with a 5-year-old child's ability to identify 20 out of 20 does not provide valuable assessment information about the 3-year-old. However, comparing the 3-year-old child with other 3-year-old children in respect of their ability to identify numbers would be an appropriate group comparison.

Relevance is also affected by whether children with disabilities were included in the normative sample. According to McLean, Wolery, and Bailey (2004), children with disabilities are rarely incorporated into the normative sample. The rationale for excluding children with disabilities is that usually the comparative tests were designed to accurately represent typical development, so including children with disabilities would be unfair. The contrary viewpoint holds that children with disabilities should be included in the normative sample, and assessment instruments do exist that contain normative information about children with disabilities that would, for example, "compar[e] the development of a child with a hearing impairment . . . with that of a hearing child" (McLean et al., p. 28). (See Box 4.4 for examples.)

BOX 5.4

Examples of normative samples from common ECI norm-referenced assessments

Adaptive Behavior Assessment System, Second Edition (ABAS II; Harrison & Oakland, 2003)

- Individuals with intellectual disability, learning difficulties, ADD/ADHD, or other impairments
- $n \geq 2,500$ in national norms for preschool ages.

Battelle Developmental Inventory, Second Edition (Newborg, 2005a)

- Sample is nationally representative in the areas of age, gender, ethnicity, geographic location, and SES (based upon the 2001 U.S. Census)
- $n = 2,500$ children ages birth through 7 years, 11 months

Bayley Scales of Infant Development, Second Edition (Bayley, 1993)

- Sample is based on age, gender, region, race/ethnicity, and parent education
- $n = 1,700$ children 1 to 42 months

Behavior Assessment System for Children, Second Edition (BASC-2; Reynolds & Kamphaus, 2004)

- Multiple norms are available for each scale, including norm groups of the general population, all clinical conditions, LD, ADHD, male only, female only, and clinical 19–21 years still in high school
- Preschool norm group sizes range from 125 to 1,200.

Devereux Early Childhood Assessment (DECA; LeBuffe & Naglieri, 1999)

- DECA-I/T: $n = 2,183$
- DECA: $n = 2,000$

McCarthy Scales of Children's Abilities (McCarthy, 1972)

- Sample is based on race, geographic region, father's occupational status, in accordance with the 1970 U.S. census
- $n = 1,032$ children 2.5–.5 years old

Pediatric Evaluation of Disability Inventory (PEDI; Haley et al., 1992)

- Sample of children with neuro-physiological concerns and/or combined physical and cognitive deficits
- $n = 402$ children 2–7.5 years old

Key: ADD, attention-deficit disorder; ADHD, attention-deficit/hyperactivity disorder; LD, learning disabilities; SES, socioeconomic status.

The technical adequacy terms defined and described here, fall under a larger measurement model referred to as Classical Test Theory (CTT) or True Score Theory. (See Crocker & Algina, 1986.) Increasingly, however, ECI assessments are being developed and their scores or procedures validated under a modern measurement approach: the Item Response Theory (IRT), otherwise known as Latent Trait Models (see Hambleton & Swaminathan, 2001). For example, the developers of the Assessment, Evaluation, and Programming System for Infants and Young Children (Bricker et al. 2008; Bricker, Yovanoff, Capt, & Allen, 2003), the Desired Results Developmental Profile access (Desired Results access Project, California Department of Education, Special Education Division, 2007), and the Galileo Preschool (Bergan, Burnham, Feld, & Bergan, 2009) have used IRT to describe and track children's performance on a developmental path versus their relative standing compared to a normative group. Many believe that IRT is more flexible than

CTT, is sophisticated, and provides more information for a researcher to improve the reliability of an assessment instrument. Another possible advantage of IRT is its focus on items versus scores—in other words, the latent trait (e.g., gross motor ability) of interest versus the test. IRT analyses use the difficulty of items in an effort to differentiate between children with low and high ability. Meisels (2007) and others have recommended using IRT to develop ECI assessments, particularly for assessing the efficacy and quality of instructional efforts, which are by nature complex and multidimensional.

CLASSIFICATION OF MEASURES

As previously discussed, assessment instruments are used for a wide variety of purposes, and most were developed for a single or dedicated purpose. As the demands for more testing and accountability have increased, so too has the use of assessment instruments for purposes for which they were not designed or validated. To better understand which instruments might be right for the job, it is important to first understand the broad classifications of assessment instruments. In ECI, instruments can roughly be classified as *criterion referenced, curriculum-based assessments, curriculum-based measures,* and *norm referenced.* Table 5.2 includes common ECI assessment classifications, common uses, and examples of instruments that fall within a given classification. Readers may also be interested in Huitt's (1996) table that compares criterion-referenced and norm-referenced tests. While most assessment instruments are of a particular type, some are hybrids. For example, some assessment instruments 1) may have a normative sample but do not require any standardized administration of all items or 2) may be normed and criterion referenced. The BDI-II (Newborg, 2005a), the Vineland Adaptive Behavior Scales (VABS); Second Edition (Sparrow, Cicchetti, Balla, & Doll, 2005), the Brigance Inventory of Early Development-II (IED-II; Brigance & Glascoe, 2004), and the Vulpe Assessment Battery-Revised (Vulpe, 1994) are all examples of normed and curriculum-referenced assessment instruments.

While Table 5.2 may be useful in helping providers know which assessments fall under which category and might in turn guide selection and use, critical consumers should also understand that very few assessments have been validated for the population or purposes for which they were designed (Bagnato et al., 2010). Specifically, in a review of 11 common ECI assessments, Brown and Hubbell (2010) found that nine had no validation studies for at least one of the instruments' intended purpose. In their review, Brown and Hubbell defined intended purposes as the *use* advertised by the publisher. For example, the Work Sampling System (Meisels, Jablon, Dichtelmiller, Marsden, & Dorfman, 2001) is marked for use as an assessment of progress monitoring and for Office of Special Education Programs (OSEP) accountability reporting. In their review, no evidence that the system has been validated for these purposes, however, was found. Of the 11 assessments examined, only the Pediatric Evaluation of Disability

Table 5.2. Alphabetical listing use long form assessment types, definitions, common uses, and examples

Type	Definition(s)	Common uses	Example(s)
Criterion-referenced	"CRTs determine what test takers can do and what they know, not how they compare to others" (Anastasi, 1988, p. 102). "Typically have nonstandardized item administration procedures and, as a result, items can be administered in various contexts using a variety of methods (e.g., direct observation, caregiver report)" (Andersson, 2004, p. 59) "A criterion-referenced test is one which scores are available that compare student performance to a criterion for mastery. Standards for mastery can be developed for any test. The term is sometimes applied to tests which were developed to show instructional progress rather than to compare students to each other. Thus, test questions would be selected for the test to measure important learning outcomes, regardless of whether or not they spread students out in terms of achievement" (Arter, 1988, p. 9). "Compare the individual's performance to some predetermined standard (i.e., pass/fail)" (Hart & Shaughnessy, 2006, p. 50). "Measure mastery of specific objectives defined by predetermined standards of criteria" (Losardo & Notari-Syverson, 2001, p. 16).	• Establish current skill level of individual children as compared to a criterion of mastery • Measure a child's own progress over time	• The Assessment of Basic Language and Learning Skills-Revised (ABLLS-R; Partington, 2006) • Behavioral Characteristics Progression (BCP; Holt et al., 1997) • Functional Emotional Assessment Scale (FEAS; Greenspan, DeGangi, & Wieder, 2001) • School Function Assessment (SFA; Coster, Deeney, Haltiwanger, & Haley, 1998)
Curriculum-based assessment (CBA)	"A form of criterion-referenced measurement wherein curricular objectives act as the criteria for the identification of instructional targets and for the assessment of status and progress" (Bagnato, 2009, p. 119). "Measurement that uses direct observation and recording of a student's performance in the local curriculum as a basis for gathering information to make instructional decisions" (Deno, 1987, p. 41). "Curriculum-based assessment incorporates three key features: Test stimuli are drawn from students' curricula; repeated testings occur across time; and the assessment information is used to formulate instructional decisions" (Fuchs & Deno, 1991, p. 488).	• Plan and revise instructional efforts • Develop IFSPs/IEPs • Monitor ongoing progress • Some CBAs provide a direct link to a "curriculum" or what should be taught (i.e., they are embedded); others can be used across various curricular objectives (i.e., they are referenced)	Direct link to a specific educational program: • Assessment, Evaluation, and Programming System for Infants and Young Children (AEPS®; Bricker, 2002) • The Carolina Curriculum for Preschoolers with Special Needs, Second Edition (Johnson-Martin, Jens, Hacker, & Attermeier, 1991) • The Creative Curriculum® for Preschool: Developmental Continuum, Fourth Edition (Dodge, Colker, & Heroman, 2002) • High/Scope Child Observation Record (High/Scope Educational Research Foundation, 2002)

(continued)

Table 5.2. *(continued)*

Type	Definition(s)	Common uses	Example(s)
	"A curriculum-based assessment (CBA) is a criterion-referenced test that is teacher constructed and designed to reflect curriculum content" (Idol, Nevin, & Paolucci-Whitcomb, 1996, p. 1). "Direct application of criterion-referenced assessment strategies to educational content" (Losardo & Notari-Syverson, 2001, p. 17) "Curriculum-based assessment includes any approach that uses direct observation and recording of a student's performance in the school curriculum as a basis for obtaining information to make instructional decisions" (Mercer, 1997, p. 530).		• The SCERTS® Model (Prizant, Wetherby, Rubin, Laurent, & Rydell, 2005) Compatible with most educational programs: • Adaptive Behavior Assessment System, Second Edition (ABAS II; Harrison & Oakland, 2003) • Functional Assessment and Curriculum for Teaching Everyday Routines (FACTER; Arick, Nave, Hoffman, & Krug, 2004) • The New Portage Guide Birth to Six (Larson et al., 2003) • Partners in Play (PIP; Ensher et al., 2007)
Curriculum-based measurement (CBM)	CBM is one type of CBA and most often involves standardized procedures for measuring student performance in reading, math, and writing (Hosp, Hosp, & Howell, 2007). CBM are used to assess instructional interventions and generally consist of standardized, short tests (i.e., 1–5 minutes) (Shinn, 1989, 1998, 2008). "Curriculum-based measurement encompasses an assessment methodology that can be used to develop goals, benchmarks, or short-term objectives for individualized educational programs for students with disabilities. Teachers also use curriculum-based measurement as a means for monitoring student progress across the year" (Stecker, 2007, p. 1). "CBM is a reliable and valid assessment system for monitoring student progress in basic academic skill areas, such as reading, writing, spelling and mathematics" (Stecker, 2007, p. 1).	• Track basic growth trends/patterns using a standard set of procedures • Measure progress over time	• Dynamic Indicators of Basic Early Literacy Skills (DIBELS) • AIMSweb • Individual Growth and Development Indicators for Young Children (e.g., Greenwood, Carta, & Walker, 2004)

"CBM is an alternative assessment system that also borrows some features from standardized, norm-referenced assessment. The CBM procedures, including test administration, scoring and interpretation, are standardized; that is, tests are given and scored in the same way each time. The content of the CBM tests may be drawn from a specific curriculum or may represent generalized outcomes for a student at that grade level. In either case, CBM test content represents important, global outcomes for the year and not just an individual objective or series of objectives representing current instructional lessons" (Stecker, 2007, p. 1).

"CBM data reflect generalized outcome performance, producing trend data that can be used to make within- and between-child comparisons. Additionally, CBM data form the basis for meaningful normative and bench-mark comparisons" (Vanderhey-den, 2005, p. 32).

Norm-referenced

Provides ability to compare an individual child to a reference group by indicating corresponding location within a normal distribution (Anderson, 2004; Salvia & Ysseldyke, 2004)

"A norm-referenced test is one in which scores are available that compare student performance to that of other similar students. . . . The term is sometimes used to refer to standardized, published tests, but most tests can be normed" (Arter, 1988, p. 9).

"Allow the individual's performance to be compared to performance of other individuals with similar characteristics (e.g., age, gender, location, etc.). Norm-referenced tests typically report percentiles or standardized scores to help in assessing the individual's performance" (Hart & Shaughnessy, 2006, p. 50).

"Provide information on how a child is developing in relation to a larger group of children of the same chronological age" (Losardo & Notari-Syverson, 2001, p. 16).

"In norm-referenced measurement, we compare an examinee's performance with the performance of a specific group of subjects. A norm provides an indication of the average, or typical, performance of a specified group and the spread of scores above and below the average" (Stattler, 2001, p. 124).

• Compare a child's performance with that of a group of children of the same age, often to make decisions regarding eligibility for EI/ECSE services

• Behavior Assessment System for Children, 2nd edition (Reynolds & Kamphaus, 2004)
• Behavior Rating Inventory of Executive Function-Preschool Version (BRIEF-P; Gioia, Espy, & Isquith, 2002)
• Bayley Scales of Infant Development (Bayley, 1993)
• Devereux Early Childhood Assessment (LeBuffe & Naglieri, 1999)
• Infant–Toddler Social and Emotional Assessment (Carter & Briggs-Gowan, 2006)
• McCarthy Scales of Children's Abilities (McCarthy, 1972)
• Stanford-Binet Intelligence Scales, Fifth edition (Roid, 2003)

Inventory (Haley, Coster, Ludlow, Haltiwanger, & Andrellos, 1992) and the Developmental Observation Checklist System (Hresko, Miguel, Sherbenou, & Burton, 1994) had research to support the validity of all its publisher-defined intended uses.

COMMON PRACTICES RELATED TO CONVENTIONAL ASSESSMENT

Despite concerns about their efficacy, conventional assessments (see to Chapter 2) are commonly used in ECI, particularly given state rules regarding eligibility for special services. For example, providers are often required to use conventional assessments as they screen children and determine whether they qualify for early intervention/early childhood special education services. (See Chapter 6 for more information on screening and eligibility.) Further, while neither necessary nor federally required, many states have chosen to use conventional assessments for program evaluation and accountability purposes. Thus, as critical consumers, ECI providers need to have basic skills to correctly administer conventional assessment including calculating chronological age (CA), establishing basals and ceilings, and interpreting reports.

Calculating Chronological Age

CA is the exact age of the child on the date of the test (typically represented in years, months, and days). A child's CA is calculated by subtracting the child's date of birth from the date of the test. Figure 5.1 provides three examples of how a child's CA is typically calculated.

As highlighted in Figure 5.1, an issue that arises in determining CA is the fact that the months of the year have different numbers of total days (i.e., some have 30, 31, or even 28 days). In general, most assessments consider all months to have 30 days for CA calculation. It is good practice, however, to double-check the manual to determine how CA is calculated for each particular assessment, in case there are any differences from the general rule. Also noted in Figure 5.1, there are rules for rounding children's ages. Again, the assessment manual should be consulted to determine when (i.e., on what day) one should round up to the next month, for example.

A helpful trick for calculating CA is using online calculators. An Internet search will result in a variety of CA calculators, some of which can be downloaded onto a computer or handheld device. The following is a site that professionals have used when making calculations or double-checking a calculation performed by hand: http://www.pearsonassessments.com/calc/AgeCalculator.html. Providers should be cautious because CA calculators have different orders in which test date and birth date are entered and may not disclose the algorithm being used to round. The Pearson calculation device, however, does go by the guideline of 30 days per month.

Example 1: March 2, 2005, as the child's date of birth and the assessment date of June 10, 2009:

	Year	Month	Day
Test date	*2009*	*06*	*10*
Date of birth	*2004*	*03*	*02*
Age	**5**	**3**	**8**

This child's chronological age is 5 years 3 months (this can also be written as 5-3). The following two examples will help guide these calculations:

Example 2: September 8, 2007, as the child's date of birth and the assessment data of December 14, 2009:

	Year	Month	Day
Test Date	*2009*	*12*	*14*
Date of Birth	*2007*	*09*	*08*
Age	**2**	**3**	**6**

In this example, the child's CA is 2 years 3 months, or 25 months. Because 15 or fewer days have passed into his 25th month (in this case, 6 days), the child's CA is rounded downward.

Example 3: November 24, 2004, as the child's date of birth and the assessment date of February 10, 2008:

	Year	Month	Day
Test Date	*2008*	*02*	*10*
Date of Birth	*2004*	*11*	*24*
Age	**3**	**2**	**16**

In the third example, the child's CA is 3 years 3 months (9 months). On February 10th, the test date, 16 days have passed since the 15th of the previous month. Therefore, even though he has not yet reached 39 months, because more than 15 days have passed into his 39th month, his age is rounded upward to 39 months.

For the third example, you may have noticed that the date of birth was larger than the testing date. When this occurs, there are a few steps that can be taken to make this calculation. When the birthday is larger than the day of testing, borrow 30 days (no matter how many days are actually in the month). Be sure to adjust the month column to reflect the change of a month to days. It would look something like this for the third example:

	Year	Month	Day
Test Date	*2008*	*01*	*40*
Date of Birth	*2004*	*11*	*24*
			16

The next step is to subtract the birth month from the test month. However, we run across the same issue of the birth number being larger than the test number. This time we borrow from the year column (remembering to adjust for the year) and adding 12 to the month column. This step is displayed as follows:

	Year	Month	Day
Test Date	*2007*	*13*	*40*
Date of Birth	*2004*	*11*	*24*
		2	**16**

Now the calculation can be completed by subtracting the birth year from the test year:

	Year	Month	Day
Test Date	*2007*	*13*	*40*
Date of Birth	*2004*	*12*	*24*
Age	**3**	**2**	**16**

Figure 5.1. Example of how to calculate chronological ages. (Source: From Bricker, D., Pretti-Frontczak, K., Johnson, J.J., & Straka, E. [2002]. *Assessment, Evaluation, and Programming System for Infants and Children (AEPS), Second Edition: Volume I. AEPS Administration guide.* Baltimore: Paul H. Brookes Publishing Co.; reprinted by permission.)

Establishing Basals and Ceiling

When administering conventional assessments, providers need to know when to start and stop testing. The technique of establishing and using basals and ceilings will help guide providers in administering conventional assessments appropriately. The basic premise is that basals and ceilings serve as indicators of where to begin and end an assessment. Before starting the assessment, however, providers should familiarize themselves with the instrument's protocol or testing sheet. (For the purposes of this chapter, the testing sheet will be referred to as the examiner's record, although it may be called by different names, depending on the assessment instrument being used.) In general, the examiner's record is used as the item sheet on which the test administrator keeps scores and tallies of the skills being assessed or the questions the child answers (either correctly or incorrectly).

The examiner's record also will likely have a cover sheet or page. On the cover page of the examiner's record, general information about the child is noted, typically including name, gender, grade, school, examiner, date of birth (DOB), and CA. Also depending upon the assessment instrument, the results of the assessment may be placed on the cover page. (Information about results is recorded only after completion of the assessment and scoring of items). In terms of conventional assessments, there are often multiple components that focus on different skills or developmental areas; these are generally referred to as subtests or subdomains. The cover sheet may provide a place to record the child's performance across each of the subdomains. Figure 5.2 contains a cover page of the examiner's record from the BDI-II (Newborg, 2005a).

Once general information about the child has been recorded, an administrator is ready to begin the assessment (i.e., to establish a basal). The starting point is often based upon the child's CA. Using the BDI-II as an example; one can see how the subtests have age indicators for groups of questions. For example, if a child is 2 years and 4 months (2-4) old, a teacher would begin the assessment at the 2-year-old mark, starting with Question 11, and work through the rest of the assessment.

If a child is unable to perform Question 11 (i.e., help dress him- or herself by holding out arms and legs), it would be marked as a 0. Receiving scores of 0 on several other items within the 2-year-old portion of the assessment suggests that the child did not meet basal for the self-care subtest. The basal for self-care is "a score of 2 on three consecutive lowest-numbered items administered or the first item in the subdomain is a basal cannot be established" (Newborg, 2005b, p. 3). The basal rule indicates that if a child does not get a score of 2 on the first three questions within the age range, the assessment administrator needs to reverse the order of questions being asked—instead of continuing to Question 12, the administrator will go back to question 10. The action of moving to an earlier question (e.g., moving to Question 10 instead of 12) is called a

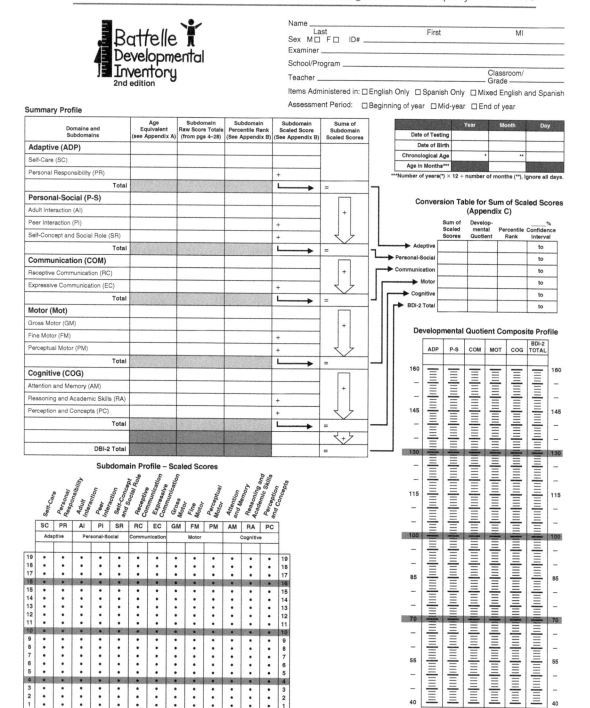

Figure 5.2. Cover sheet from the BDI–II (From Newborg, J. [2005]. *Battelle Developmental Inventory examiner's manual* [2nd ed., p.3]. Itasca, IL: Riverside Publishing; reprinted by permission.)

reversal or following the reversal *rule*. An administrator then continues to move in reverse order until the child has met the basal of three consecutive questions receiving a score of 2 or the first question of the subdomain is reached.

If a child is known to have a developmental age that is not commensurate with their chronological age or a delay is suspected, it is permissible for the team to start the testing at a lower age range than the actual age of the child. There will be times when an assessment administrator will need to engage in the reversal rule (in order to establish basal), but the possibility of having to use the reversal rule is not a reason to start every child at an earlier set. For most children, beginning the subtest at an earlier starting point will just add more questions or criteria to the testing procedure than is necessary.

As an assessment administrator proceeds through the subtest, the questions or criteria become harder or more advanced, the child's performance will likely begin to decline. It is important to note that an assessment should *not* be stopped when the end of an age bracket is met. However, there are instances where the age bracket is the end of a test. As such, starting and stopping instructions should be verified by consulting the assessment instrument's manual. For example, the assessment of the child in the 2-year-old range should not end with question 16 where the age bracket ends. It is important to end only when the assessment indicates that testing should be completed. Typically, the ending point will come in the form of a ceiling rule. The ceiling rule is the reverse of the basal—it tells you when to stop. According to the ceiling for the self-care subtest, testing should continue until "a score of 0 on *three consecutive* highest-numbered items administered or the last item in the subdomain if the ceiling cannot be established" (Newborg, 2005a, p. 3). In other words, an assessment administrator will continue the subtest until the child receives a score on three consecutive questions or the administrator runs out of questions to ask, due to the completion of the subtest. As can be viewed on the example examiner's record, even though the child had to have questions below the age-2 starting point to get a basal, the ceiling for the child is in the 3-year-old range.

Determining basals and ceilings can be difficult, particularly if a child has to go through several reversals to get the basal or has several close calls in reaching a ceiling (e.g., getting two consecutive questions wrong and then getting the third correct). For the administrator, it can be difficult to watch the child thinking and struggling to answer a question she does not fully comprehend several times in a row, only to have to do it all over again because she answered one question correctly. The important thing to remember is that the purpose of an assessment is to better understand what the child knows or is able to do. Basals and ceilings make the testing procedure more efficient (i.e., spending less time asking unnecessary questions, avoiding frustrating the child by asking questions that are clearly too easy or too difficult).

Adjusting for Prematurity

Adjusting for prematurity may be an important consideration when a child was born 1 or more months preterm. Use of the actual date of birth during the first 2 years of life for preterm infants may lead to inappropriate developmental expectations. Adjustment for prematurity allows more accurate determinations of the child's developmental skills (or maturity) based on his or her expected date of birth rather than the actual date of birth. When adjusting for prematurity, subtract the months a child is preterm from his or her CA. For example, a child whose CA is 18 months but was 2 months premature would have an adjusted age of 16 months.

Historically, it was believed that if age was not corrected for during the first 2 years of life, there was an increased risk of a child being misdiagnosed as having a cognitive deficit (Wilson & Cradock, 2004). The practice of adjusting for prematurity has not changed much since the 1930s. Today, it is often left to the clinician to determine, on a case-by-case basis, how and when age should be adjusted. There are, however, issues related to adjusting for prematurity. First, given that adjustment for prematurity is performed on a case-by-case basis, not everyone may adjust for a given child, leading to inconsistent and incomparable scores. Second, agreement has not been reached as to when teams should stop adjusting. Some individuals believe that correction should be made up to 2 years of age, while other individuals believe it should only be the first year. Last, agreement has not been reached regarding what is considered full term (e.g., *full term* may mean "anytime from 37 to 40 weeks"; Aylward, 1994).

While there is no definitive set of rules for how and when to adjust for prematurity, there are suggestions that may help. Wilson and Cradock (2004) suggested that infants who were born 3–5 weeks premature might need to have their age adjusted only for the first year. Research has shown that children who were 3–5 weeks premature tend to catch up with their full-term peers. For children that were born before 28 weeks, however, adjustment may be needed for up to 2 years.

Interpreting Reports

Interpreting the results from a conventional assessment can be intimidating, given the use of jargon and the need to convert scores and notes to other types of information. Understanding the reports that come from the test results can be even more difficult if an individual is unfamiliar with the assessment instrument. As a first step, the team should review the assessment instrument's manual as a refresher about the types of scores that will be generated. The jargon that is used to describe conventional assessment results are based on a great deal of statistical background. Therefore, an understanding of the basic statistics referenced in reports may aide in interpreting and using the results to make sound decisions.

First, there are two types of scores generally created through conventional assessment. The first is what is called a raw score. A *raw score* is simply the score the child receives on a particular test or subtest. There is, however, no real meaning behind a raw score—it is just a number. It would be like giving a picture-naming test to a child but not having a scale (like the classmates' performance on picture naming) with which to measure it. Reports should not include raw scores, as they are considered uninterpretable. The second type of score generated from conventional assessments are *standard scores*, which are derived from a child's raw score. A standard score allows for comparisons to be made among children and across different tests by having a set mean and standard deviation. A *mean* is defined as the sum of all the scores, divided by the number of scores (Howell, 2002). In other words, the mean is the average. *Standard deviation* (SD) is defined as "a statistic that measures a distribution's amount of dispersion" (Woodrich, 1997, pp. 6–7). Means and SDs for standard scores can be placed onto a normal curve for help with visual interpretation. The SD can help determine how much a child's score differs from the mean (Woodrich). A *normal curve* is defined as "a representation of scores based on the population" (Kritikos, 2010, p. 37). A normal curve is often referred to as a bell curve and sometimes a normal distribution. (See Figure 5.3 for an illustration of a normal curve.)

Underneath the normal curve, and in the top row of Figure 5.3, is an indication of where the mean score would be (indicated with the 0 and sometimes with the word Mean) and how the normal curve is divided into plus (+) and minus (−) SDs. The ±1 indicates that the child's performance is within one SD of the mean performance for the normative group, with ±2 SDs being well above or below average. The SD area of ±1 is the largest group from a sample, with 68% of the total represented. The further away from average (i.e., the mean) a score is, the smaller the percentage of children from the sample. In other words, there are fewer people who have that score.

As stated previously, to understand or compare a child's performance on a conventional assessment, his or her raw score is converted to a derived or standard score, often either a developmental quotient or a percentile rank. A *developmental quotient* (DQ) is a score that is calculated by dividing a child's developmental age by his or her CA and multiplying the results by 100 (McLean et al., 2004). A *percentile rank* simply indicates where a child's score falls in a grouping of 100 possible data points. The percentile may be easier for team members to understand because it allows

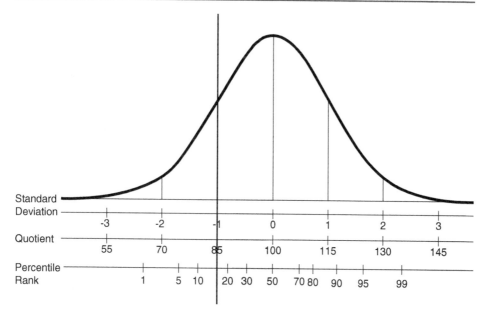

Figure 5.3. Illustration of a normal curve with means of 0 and 100 with associated standard deviations (SDs) and percentile rank indices.

for a child's score to be compared to their peers. As standard scores, both DQ and percentile rank show or compare a child's performance against the mean. As noted on Figure 5.3, a child who receives a DQ of 85 is in the 16th percentile and is −1 SD from the mean of the normative group. All three pieces of information (i.e., a DQ, a percentile rank, and an indication of how many SDs the child is from the mean) give a teacher the same information regarding a child's performance compared with the normative sample (i.e., how close or far the child is from the mean). Any score within 1 SD of the mean is considered acceptable; even −1.3 SDs is considered to represent how children who are typical would perform. It is not until the child's performance reaches −1.5 that concerns are raised or special services considered.

In general, teachers should not be fearful or confused by the numbers and scores provided in reports from conventional assessments. Rather, teachers should take the opportunity to engage in role release as described in Chapter 4 and ask school psychologists, therapists, or others with training in conventional assessment to explain what the numbers mean from a developmental and instructional perspective. Readers are also encouraged to review the caveats with generating age equivalencies, which are also often found in reports from conventional assessments. (See Chapter 6.) Having a better understanding of what means, SDs, DQs, percentile ranks, and age equivalencies do and do not mean will help all team members make sound decisions.

SUMMARY

This chapter has offered suggestions and strategies for using the right assessment tool for the job at hand. Assessment instruments are often used with little consideration for their technical adequacy or appropriateness for a given purpose or population. Terms related to technical adequacy were defined and standards and examples provided. Specifically, validity, reliability, and bias were addressed. The chapter also provided a summary of how ECI assessments are classified and included definitions or the various classifications as well as examples of corresponding assessment instruments. Having information regarding an instrument's technical adequacy and classification should serve teachers in selecting and using the right tool for each job.

The chapter also provided descriptions of the skills needed for using conventional assessments. Specifically, strategies and suggestions for calculating chronological age, when and why teams adjust for prematurity, and how to establish basals and ceilings were provided. Lastly, key statistical terms (e.g., mean, standard deviation, percentile rank) were defined and illustrated. Teachers need confidence in interpreting such terms given their prevalence when reports are generated from conventional assessments.

REFERENCES

American Educational Research Association, American Psychological Association, & National Council on Measurement in Education. (1999). *Standards for educational and psychological testing.* Washington, DC: American Educational Research Association.

Anastasi, A. (1988). *Psychological testing.* New York: MacMillan Publishing Company.

Andersson, L. (2004) Appropriate and inappropriate interpretation and use of test scores in early intervention. *Journal of Early Intervention, 27*(1), 55–68.

Arick, J.R., Nave, G., Hoffman, T., & Krug, D.A. (2004). *Functional Assessment and Curriculum for Teaching Everyday Routines (FACTER).* Austin, TX: Pro-Ed.

Arter, J.A. (1988). *Curriculum-referenced test development workshop series: Workshops one through three.* Retrieved December 22, 2009, from http://www.eric.ed.gov/ERICWebPortal/custom/portlets/recordDetails/detailmini.jsp?_nfpb=true&_&ERICExtSearch_SearchValue_0=ED303486&ERICExtSearch_SearchType_0=no&accno=ED303486

Aylward, G.P. (1994). *Practitioner's guide to developmental and psychological testing.* New York: Plenum Medical Book Company.

Bagnato, S. (2009). *Authentic assessment for early childhood intervention: Best practices.* New York: Guilford Press.

Bagnato, S.J., Neisworth, J.T., & Pretti-Frontczak, K. (2010). *LINKing authentic assessment and early childhood intervention: Best measures for best practices.* Baltimore: Paul H. Brookes Publishing Co.

Bayley, N. (1993). *Bayley scales of infant development.* 2nd ed. San Antonio, TX: Psychological Corp.

Bergan, J.R., Burnham, C.G., Feld, J.K., & Bergan, J.R. (2009). The Galileo pre-k online system for the electronic management of learning. Retrieved January 10, 2010, from Assessment Technology, Incorporated: http://www.ati-online.com/pdfs/researchPreschool/GalileoTechManual.pdf

Bracken, B.A. (1987). Limitations of preschool instruments and standards for minimal levels of technical adequacy. *Journal of Psychoeducational Assessment, 5,* 313–326.

Bracken, B.A., Keith, L.K., & Walker, K.C. (1998). Assessment of preschool behavior and social–emotional functioning: A review of thirteen third-party instruments. *Journal of Psychoeducational Assessment, 16*(2), 153–169.

Bricker, D., Pretti-Frontczak, K., Johnson, J., & Straka, E. (with Capt, B., Slentz, K., & Waddell, M.). (2002). Assessment, Evaluation, and Programming System for Infants and Children (AEPS®). Vol. 1: Administration guide (2nd ed.).

Bricker, D., Yovanoff, P., Capt, B., & Allen, D. (2003). Use of a curriculum-based measure to corroborate eligibility decisions. *Journal of Early Intervention, 26,* 20–30.

Bricker, D., Clifford, J., Yovanoff, P., Pretti-Frontczak, K., Waddell, M., Allen, D., & Hoselton, R. (2008). Eligibility determination using a curriculum-based assessment: A further examination. *Journal of Early Intervention, 31,* 3–21.

Brigance, A.H., & Glascoe, F.P. (2004). *Brigance Diagnostic Inventory of Early Development—Second Edition (IED-II).* North Billerica, MA: Curriculum Associates.

Brown, T., & Hubbell, S.P. (January, 2010). *Evidence-base of commonly-used assessments in early childhood special education.* Center for Excellence in Early Childhood Research and Training, Kent State University, Kent, OH. Retrieved January 10, 2010, from http://www.ehhs.kent.edu/ceecrt/

California Department of Education, Special Education Division. (2008). *Reliability and validity of the Desired Results Developmental Profile access (DRDP access): Results of the 2005–2006 calibration study.* Retrieved January 10, 2010, from http://www.draccess.org/assessors/ReliabilityAndValidity.html

Carter, A.S., & Briggs-Gowan, M.J. (2006). *Manual for the infant–toddler social & emotional assessment (ITSEA)—Version 2.* San Antonio, TX: Psychological Corporation.

Coster, W., Deeney, T., Haltiwanger, J., Haley, S. (1998). *School function assessment.* San Antonio, TX: Psychological Corporation.

Crocker, L., & Algina, J. (1986). *Introduction to classical and modern test theory.* New York: Harcourt Brace Jovanovich College Publishers.

Deno, S.L. (1987). Curriculum-based measurement, program development, graphing performance, and increasing efficiency. *Teaching Exceptional Children, 20,* 41–47.

Dodge, D.T., Colker, L.J., & Heroman, C. (2002). *The creative curriculum for preschool* (4th ed.). Washington, DC: Teaching Strategies.

Eisert, D.C., Sturner, R.A., & Mabe, P.A. (1991). Questionnaires in behavioral pediatrics: Guidelines for selection and use. *Developmental and Behavioral Pediatrics, 12*(1), 42–50.

Ensher, G., Bobish, T.P., Gardner, E., Reinson, C.L., Bryden, D.A., & Foertsch, D.J. (2007). *Partners in play: Assessing infants and toddlers in natural contexts (PIP).* Clifton Park, NY: Thomson Delmar.

Fuchs, L.S., & Deno, S.L. (1991). Paradigmatic distinctions between instructionally relevant measurement models. *Exceptional Children, 57,* 488–501.

Gioia, G.A., Espy, K.A., & Isquith, P.K. (2002). *Behavior Rating Inventory of Executive Function, Preschool Version (BRIEF-P).* Odessa, FL: Psychological Assessment Resources.

Greenspan, S., DeGangi, G., & Wieder, S. (2001). *The Functional Emotional Assessment Scale (FEAS) for Infancy and Early Childhood.* Bethesda, Maryland: The Interdisciplinary Council on Developmental and Learning Disorders.

Greenwood, C.R., Carta, J.J., & Walker, D. (2004). Individual growth and development indicators (IGDIs): Tools for assessing intervention results for infants and toddlers. In W. Heward, T.E. Heron, N.A. Neef, S.M. Person, D.M. Saninato, G.Y., Carledge, R. Gardner, L.D. Peterson, S.B. Hersh, and J.C. Dardig (Eds.), *Focus on behavior analysis in education: Achievements, challenges, and opportunities* (pp. 103–124). Columbus, OH: Pearson/Prentice-Hall.

Haley, S.M., Coster, W.J., Ludlow, L.H., Haltiwanger, J.T., & Andrellos, P.J. (1992). *Pediatric Evaluation of Disability Inventory (PEDI).* Boston: New England Medical Center Hospitals.

Hambleton, R.K., & Swaminathan, H. (2001). *Item response theory: Principles and applications.* New York: H. Paul Jeffers.

Hart, M.A., & Shaughnessy, M.F. (2006). Assessment of the psychomotor skills and physical fitness. In R. Davidson, E. Laman, & M.F. Shaughnessy (Eds.), *Accessing the general physical education curriculum for students with sensory deficits* (pp. 45–59). New York: Nova Science Publishers, Inc.

Harrison, P.L., & Oakland T. (2003). *Adaptive Behavior Assessment System, Second Edition (ABAS-II).* San Antonio, TX: Harcourt Assessment.

High/Scope Educational Research Foundation. (2002). *High Scope child observation record.* Ypsilanti, MI: High Scope Press.

Holt, T., Gilles, J., Holt, A., & Davids, V. (2004). *HELP for preschoolers.* Palo Alto, CA: Vort Corporation.

Holt, T., Gilles, J., Holt, K., Holt, A., Mooney, J., & Teaford, P. (1997). *Behavioral characteristics progression.* Palo Alto, CA: Vort.

Hosp, M.K., Hosp, J.L., & Howell, K.W. (2007). *The ABCs of CBM: A practical guide to curriculum-based measurement.* New York: Guilford Press.

Howell, D.C. (2002). *Statistical methods for psychology* (5th ed.). Pacific Grove, CA: Duxbury.

Hresko, W., Miguel, S., Sherbenou, R., & Burton, S. (1994). *Developmental observation checklist system.* Austin, TX: Pro-Ed.

Huitt, W. (1996). Measurement and evaluation: Criterion- versus norm-referenced testing. *Educational Psychology Interactive.* Valdosta, GA: Valdosta State University. Retrieved January 9, 2010, from http://chiron.valdosta.edu/whuitt/col/measeval/crnmref.html

Idol, L., Nevin, A., & Paolucci-Whitcomb, P. (1996). *Models of curriculum-based assessment* (2nd ed.). Rockville, MD: Aspen.

Johnson-Martin, N., Jens, K.G., Hacker, B.J., & Attermeier, S.M., (1991). *The Carolina curriculum for preschoolers with special needs* (2nd ed.). Baltimore: Paul H. Brookes Publishing Co.

Kidsource Online (2009). Assessing children for the presence of a disability: Methods of gathering information. Retrieved January 11, 2010, from http://www.kidsource.com/NICHCY/assessing.2.html

Kritikos, E.P. (2010). *Special education assessment: Issues and strategies affecting today's classroom.* Upper Saddle River, NJ: Merrill.

Larson, N., Herqig, J., Wollenburg, K., Olsen, E., Bowe, W., Chvojicek, & Copa, A. (2003). *The new Portage guide birth to six.* Portage, WI: Cooperative Educational Service Agency 5, Portage Project.

LeBuffe, P.A., & Naglieri,, J.A. (1999). *Devereux early childhood assessment.* Lewisville: Kaplan.

Losardo, A., & Notari-Syverson, A. (2001). *Alternative approach to assessing young children.* Baltimore: Paul H. Brookes Publishing Co.

Macy, M., Bagnato, S.J., Lehman, C., & Salaway, J. (2007). Research foundations of conventional tests and testing to ensure accurate and representative early intervention eligibility. Pittsburgh: Early Childhood Partnerships.

McCarthy, D. (1972). *McCarthy Scales of Children's Abilities.* San Antonio, TX: Psychological Corp.

McCloskey, G. (1990). Selecting and using early childhood rating scales. *Topics in Early Childhood Special Education, 10*(3), 39–64.

McLean, M., Wolery, M., & Bailey, D. (2004). *Assessing infants and preschoolers with special needs* (3rd ed). Columbus, OH: Pearson.

Meisels, S. (2007). Accountability in early childhood: No easy answers. In R.C. Pianta, M.J. Cox, & K. Snow (Eds.), *Schools readiness and the transition to kindergarten in the era of accountability* (pp. 31–47). Baltimore: Paul H. Brookes Publishing Co.

Meisels, S.J., & Atkins-Burnett, S. (2000). The elements of early childhood assessment. In J.P. Shonkoff, & S.J. Meisels (Eds.), *Handbook of early childhood intervention* (2nd ed., pp. 231–257). New York: Cambridge University Press.

Meisels, S.J., Jablon, J.R., Dichtelmiller, M.K., Marsden, D.B., & Dorfman, A.B. (2001). *The work sampling system* (4th ed.). San Antonio, TX: Pearson.

Mercer, C. (1997). *Students with learning disabilities* (5th ed.). Upper Saddle River, NJ: Merrill (Prentice-Hall).

Newborg, J. (2005a). *Battelle Developmental Inventory,* (2nd ed.). Itasca, IL: Riverside Publishing.

Newborg, J. (2005b). *Battelle Developmental Inventory, 2nd edition, examiner's manual.* Itasca, IL: Riverside Publishing.

Partington, J. (2006). *Assessment of basic language and learning skills—Revised.* Pleasant Hill, CA: Behavior Analysts.

Prizant, B.M., Wetherby, A.M., Rubin, E., Laurent, A.C., & Rydell, P.J. (2005). *The*

SCERTS® Model: A comprehensive educational approach for children with autism spectrum disorders. Baltimore: Paul H. Brookes Publishing Co.

Rabinowitz, S.N., & Sato, E. (2006). *The technical adequacy of assessment for alternate student populations: Guidelines for consumers and developers.* San Francisco: WestEd. Retrieved January 5, 2010, from http://www.aacompcenter.org/pdf/taasp.pdf

Reynolds, C.R., & Kamphaus, R.W. (2004). *Behavior assessment system for children, second edition.* Circle Pines, MN: American Guidance Services.

Roid, G.H. (2003). *Stanford-Binet intelligence scales* (5th ed.). Itasca, IL: Riverside.

Salvia, J., & Ysseldyke, J.E. (1978). *Assessment in special and remedial education.* Boston: Houghton Mifflin.

Sattler, J.M. (2001). *Assessment of children: Cognitive applications* (4th ed). Austin, TX: PRO-ED, Inc.

Shinn, M.R. (1989). *Curriculum-based measurement: Assessing special children.* New York: Guilford Press.

Shinn, M.R. (1998). *Advanced applications of curriculum-based measurement.* New York: Guilford Press.

Shinn, M.R. (2008). Best practices in using curriculum-based measurement in a problem-solving model. In A. Thomas & J. Grimes (Eds.), *Best practices in school psychology* (5th ed., Vol. 2, pp. 243–262). Bethesda, MD: National Association of School Psychologists.

Sparrow, S.S., Cicchetti, D.V., Balla, D.A., & Doll, E.A. (2005). *Vineland adaptive behavior Scales, second edition.* Minneapolis, MN: Pearson Assessments.

Stecker, P. (2007). Monitoring student progress in individualized educational programs using curriculum-based measurement. Retrieved December 22, 2009, from http://www.studentprogress.org/library/monitoring_student_progress_in_individualized_educational_programs_using_cbm.pdf

Thorndike, R.M., & Thorndike-Christ, T. (2010). Qualities desired in any measurement procedure: Validity. In *Measurement and evaluation in psychology and education* (8th ed., pp. 154–198). San Antonio, TX: Pearson.

Vanderheyden, A.M. (2005). Intervention-driven assessment practices in early childhood/early intervention: Measuring what is possible rather than what is present. *Journal of Early Intervention, 28,* 28–33.

Vulpe, S.G. (1994). *The Vulpe assessment battery-revised.* Aurora, NY: Slosson Educational Publishers.

Wilson, S.L., & Cradock, M.M. (2004). Review: Accounting for prematurity in developmental assessment and the use of age-adjusted scores. *Journal of Pediatric Psychology, 29,* 641–649.

Woodrich, D.L. (1997). *A guide for nonpsychologists: Children's psychological testing* (3rd ed.). Baltimore: Paul H. Brookes Publishing Co.

Reasons for Conducting Assessment

CHAPTER 6

Recommended Practices in Identifying Children for Special Services

Jennifer Grisham-Brown,
Kristie Pretti-Frontczak, and
Sophia Hubbell

Mr. Marcus is the lead teacher in a preschool classroom at the Hope for Tomorrow Learning Center. There are 19 children in his all-day program. Three of the children in the program have diagnosed disabilities. He receives assistance from the local school district to support the children with disabilities. Recently, however, Mr. Marcus has grown concerned about Edwin, a 4-year-old in his classroom. Edwin lives with his maternal grandmother because his mother has had difficulty with drugs and alcohol. Edwin's grandmother values education and wanted her grandson to participate in a high-quality preschool program while she works. She asked Mr. Marcus to keep an eye on Edwin because she is concerned that her grandson received little attention while living with his mother. When Edwin was enrolled, Mr. Marcus noticed that he talked very little to other children or to the teachers. When he talked, Edwin's speech was sometimes difficult to understand, resulting in the other children ignoring him. Recently, Edwin seems to have become very frustrated when he cannot get others to understand him. As a result, he has started throwing materials and screaming when he wants something.

Mr. Marcus suspects that Edwin may have speech delays and is concerned that if not addressed quickly, he will begin to develop serious behavior problems. He plans to share his concerns with Edwin's grandmother at an upcoming parent–teacher conference. However, he wants to provide Edwin's grandmother with ideas about what can be done to address his suspicions. While Mr. Marcus has children with diagnosed disabilities in his classroom, he has never been involved at the beginning of the special education process and does not know what he needs to do to get the ball rolling so that Edwin can get evaluated and receive services if he needs them.

The scenario described in the vignette is one that commonly occurs in blended classrooms. In blended classrooms, there are children with identified disabilities, children without disabilities, and children who are at risk for disabilities. Frequently, after children have attended a preschool program for a certain length of time, classroom staff begin to develop concerns regarding some children who do *not* have diagnosed disabilities and begin to suspect that there are potential developmental problems. Such situations require that teachers understand how children are identified for special services.

Identifying children for special services is a multistep process. Due to the risk of over identification or under identification for special education services, it is essential that the proper steps be followed for 1) locating children who may have developmental delays, 2) screening children who may have developmental delays to determine whether there is reason for concern, and 3) validating the existence of a developmental delay and making decisions about how to address the need. Teachers in blended classrooms need to understand the Child Find, screening, and eligibility evaluation processes and a teacher's role in ensuring that children get special services if they need them.

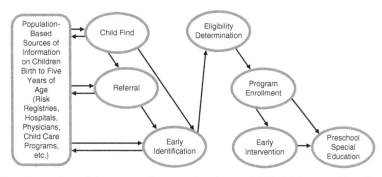

Figure 6.1. Illustration of the process for ensuring that entitled children are identified for special services. (From Tracking, Referral, and Assessment Center for Excellence web site, http://tracecenter.info/model.php. Copyright © 2006–2009 Orelena Hawks Puckett Institute. Reprinted by permission.)

The Individuals with Disabilities Improvement Education Act of 2004 (IDEA 2004; PL 108-446) is the legislation that provides federal funding for special education services for children with disabilities from birth to age 21. In addition, IDEA provides federal regulations about how services can be delivered, who can receive services, and who can deliver services. IDEA includes three major components that will be discussed throughout this chapter. The first is Part B, which describes regulations that affect children ages 3 to 21. Part B is sometimes referred to as the school-age component of IDEA. Within Part B is Section 619, which describes specific regulations for preschool special education programs. Finally, Part C describes regulations that apply only to programs that serve infants and toddlers. Part C is also called the early intervention component.

The purpose of the chapter is to describe the steps associated with identifying children for special services under IDEA and is divided in to three sections. The first section describes the purpose and requirements of Child Find, as well as common Child Find activities and associated recommended practices. The second section provides an overview of traditional and contemporary screening approaches, types of screening instruments, ways of conducting screenings, and recommended practices for implementing screenings. The third, and last, section explains the legal requirements for conducting eligibility assessments and determining eligibility, along with a model for conducting eligibility assessments while adhering to recommended assessment practices. Figure 6.1 shows the entire process for ensuring that children are identified for special services. All key elements (i.e., Child Find, screening, and eligibility determination) are described in this chapter.

CHILD FIND

The first step toward getting young children special services is to *find* children who may need such services. The following section explains the purpose and requirements for conducting Child Find activities. As well, common activities for implementing Child Find efforts and associated recommended practices are summarized.

Purpose and Requirements

Child Find is considered a set of activities for locating children potentially eligible for early intervention or preschool special education services by making families aware of the availability of screening (Meisels & Atkins-Barnett, 2005). Child Find activities "include outreach, initial screening, tracking, and referral" (Pavri & Fowler, 2001, p. 1). IDEA requires that lead agencies of states provide services to children under Part C (Infants and Toddlers) to ensure that

> All infants and toddlers with disabilities in the State who are eligible for services are identified, located, and evaluated including Indian infants and toddlers with disabilities residing on reservations (in coordination with tribes, tribal organizations and consortia) and infants and toddlers with disabilities who are homeless, in foster care and are wards of the state. (Shaw, 2007, p.11)

Similarly, in Part B of IDEA, state education agencies are directed to ensure that

> All children with disabilities residing in the State, including children with disabilities who are homeless children or are wards of the State, and children with disabilities attending private schools, regardless of the severity of their disability, and who are in need of special education and related services, are identified, located, and evaluated; and child find also must include highly mobile children, including migrant children. (Shaw, 2007, p. 12)

The intent of Child Find is to ensure that young children receive special services as early as possible. The agency responsible for delivering Part C (i.e., early intervention) and Section 619 (preschool special education) services is responsible for coordinating and conducting Child Find activities. Important features of Child Find are 1) the activities and coordinating partners and 2) the referral process.

Further, IDEA requires agencies responsible for delivering special education services to young children to coordinate Child Find efforts with other statewide agencies that provide services to young children including, but not limited to, Maternal and Child Health programs under Title V, Child Protection Programs, and The Office of Coordination of Education of Homeless Children and Youth under the McKinney-Vento Homeless Assistance Act. In addition, local agencies work with community-based programs that serve young children, such as child care or Head Start, to make families aware of availability of special services and solicit referrals. In addition to traditional early childhood intervention programs, local agencies coordinate Child Find efforts with local pediatrician offices, hospitals, and health departments who frequently see young children. Other community services that should be aware of the availability of special services for young children are social service agencies, recreation services (e.g., YMCA), and houses of faith.

Common Activities and Recommended Practices

Key components of Child Find activities are public awareness and referrals made by anyone who knows a child whom they suspect has a developmental delay. Agencies use a variety of methods for letting the community know of the availability of services for children who have special needs, including flyers, electronic notices, public service announcements, web sites, printed materials, and even billboard messages (Dunst & Clow, 2007). Referrals are likely to be made by physicians, family members, child care providers, and hospital staff. As it relates to teachers, the period between post-toddlerhood and prekindergarten is one of the most critical in terms of making referrals, a responsibility that often falls to teachers working in blended programs.

Unfortunately, in a review of the literature, Dunst and Clow found that even though states used 630 different public awareness and Child Find activities, most were in the form of nontargeted print materials, such as brochures. In all, they concluded that public awareness activities used by Part C programs "were not consistent with research evidence on practices found effective for child find purposes" (2007, p. 5). In other words, the largest percentage of these activities used by states involved practices that generally were found ineffective for either changing people's help-seeking behavior or influencing referrals from primary sources. Recommendations to the field, including more active and direct contact with primary referral sources (e.g., pediatricians) and targeted activities (such as working directly with visiting nurses), are more effective in changing referral patterns and rates. To meet the requirement to reach populations that have traditionally not been involved in early intervention services, agencies need to do even more. For example, agencies need to make materials available in a variety of languages, provide alternative ways to contact persons and agencies, make Child Find materials accessible, and ensure that the delivery of culturally and linguistically appropriate activities does not conflict with the assumptions, values, or beliefs of those intended to be reached (Pavri & Fowler, 2001).

As with public awareness, there are key attributes to ensuring a referral system is effective. When a child is believed to have a developmental delay, the person making the referral contacts someone in his or her community who oversees Child Find efforts. As mentioned previously, the local education agency (LEA) is responsible for such efforts. Most early intervention systems, however, have a process by which referrals can be made when a child has a suspected delay. (See Box 6.1 for information on how to design an effective referral process.)

BOX 6.1

Information on how to design an effective referral process

Examination of available research evidence, with a focus on the characteristics of the practices that are associated with referrals, indicates that four sets of factors are most important if outreach to primary referral sources is to be successful:

1. Building rapport and establishing credibility with primary referral sources

2. Highlighting and repeating a focused message about the benefits of making a referral to both the primary referral source and the child being referred

3. Using concise, graphic written materials that describe the services, the primary referral source, and the child being referred will receive from program

4. Making follow-up visits to reinforce primary referral source referrals, answer questions, and provide additional information as needed

From Dunst, C.J. (2006). Improving outreach to primary referral sources. *Trace Practice Guide, 1*(2), 1–2; reprinted by permission.

SCREENING

After a child is referred as potentially being in need of special services, the next step in the identification process is screening. Meisels and Atkins-Burnet define screening as a process of identifying "children who may have developmental or learning problems or disabilities" (2005, p. 7). The following section describes traditional and contemporary screening approaches, types of screeners, formats for conducting screening, and recommended screening practices.

Traditional and Contemporary Screening Approaches

Traditionally, screening has been viewed as a process that answers the assessment question *Does the child need further assessment?* Figure 6.2 demonstrates what normally happens following screening. The figure shows that screening results in putting children into two categories: *at risk* (meaning that the results of the screener indicate that the child should be further evaluated) or *not at risk* (meaning that the results of the screener indicate that the child should not be further evaluated). Children who are not at risk are enrolled in the regular classroom with no further assessment. Children who are found to be at risk are then further evaluated to determine whether they are in need of special services.

Recently, referral and screening in preschool have been reconceptualized in some states to mirror practices in K–12 special education. The IDEA 2004 establishes measures to prevent overidentification of children for special education by ensuring that intervention is provided before formal referral to special education is made. Steps to prevent overidentification are now being made in early childhood intervention and affect traditional referral and screening procedures. Rather than children being referred, screened, and evaluated if they are found to be at risk by the screener, some states are now requiring agencies to provide *tiered interventions* prior to the occurrence of formal evaluation. While each state, and sometimes each agency within a state, may approach the process differently,

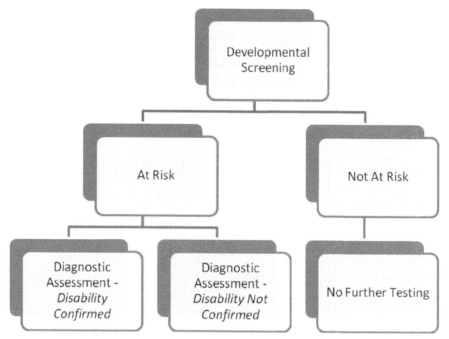

Figure 6.2. Common developmental screening process (adapted from Meisels & Atkins-Burnett, 2005).

the procedures are similar to those found in Figure 6.2. In the more contemporary scenario (see Figure 6.3), children are screened and placed into one of three categories: delay suspected, at risk due to socioeconomic reasons, or typically developing. For children who are *typically developing*, nothing else is done. Children who are *at risk due to economic factors* are enrolled in a preschool on the basis of being economically disadvantaged. Children who have a *suspected delay* are first provided access to a developmentally appropriate curriculum in a preschool classroom (Tier 1 intervention). Data are collected on children's suspected areas of delay while in that class to determine whether exposure to high-quality early childhood intervention positively affects the area of suspected delay. If exposure alone does not improve the child's functioning in the area of the suspected delay, interventions that are more intentional (i.e., Tier 2) are provided and data are collected to determine the impact of the interventions on the suspected delay. If progress is made (see Chapter 8 for a discussion of performance-monitoring efforts), the referral process stops and no further testing occurs. If no progress is made after intentional interventions are provided, a formal referral for evaluation for special education services is made. Again, the intent of providing interventions to children before they are formally tested for special education is to determine whether less-intrusive services will improve the child's functioning in the area of the suspected delay so that the child will not be diagnosed and labeled unnecessarily.

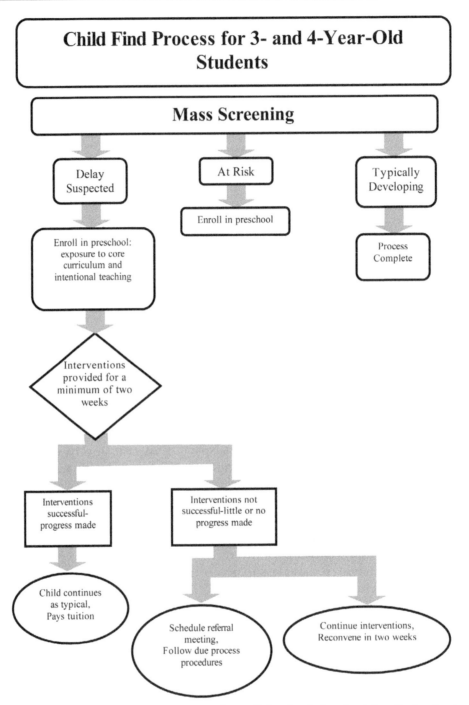

Figure 6.3. Contemporary Screening Process (From Christy Brock, Preschool Coordinator, Franklin County Public Schools, Frankfort, KY; adapted by permission.)

Screening Types and Formats

There are a variety of types and formats of screenings. All serve the purpose of determining a child's need for further evaluation. Universal, sensory, and developmental screeners are common types. Also, screenings can be conducted in a variety of formats. Both types and formats are discussed in the next section.

Screening Types

First, *universal newborn* screening is one of the first types of screenings that young children might experience. Universal newborn screening implies that all newborns are screened. Universal or comprehensive newborn screening is designed to ensure that health or mental conditions are detected early so that children can receive needed intervention and prevent associated problems (Save Babies Through Screening Foundation, 2008). Some universal newborn screenings are associated with health conditions. For example, the heel prick test, or PKU (phenylketonuria) test, is conducted within the first 24–48 hours of a baby's life to determine whether the child has a metabolic condition that can be treated if detected early. While there are no federal requirements that states screen newborns for any conditions, the National Institutes of Health recommend screenings on three conditions: sickle cell diseases, PKU, and congenital hypothyroidism (U.S. General Accounting Office, 2003).

Second, *sensory screening* should be conducted on young children. Early identification of vision and hearing difficulties and appropriate follow-up are essential to children's overall well-being and development. According to Meisels and Atkins-Barnett, indicators of vision and hearing problems include "rubbing eyes, bringing reading materials close to face, turning head to hear something, or not following directions" (2005, p. 11). Visual impairments are associated with delays in other areas of development, particularly gross motor development (Celeste, 2002) and literacy development, especially in the area of letter identification (Gonpel, van Bon, & Schreuder, 2004). Hearing impairments are associated with delays in communication development, behavior, psychosocial well-being, and educational development (U.S. Preventive Services Task Force, 2008).

Recommended strategies for screening young children's vision include 1) observing children's visual behaviors (e.g., Are the child's eyes working together? Does the child tilt his or her head to see?), 2) examining children's distance vision by having the child read letters or pictures at a distance of 20 feet, and 3) photoscreening for nonverbal children where a photograph is taken of the children's eyes and the pictures are examined to look for signs of vision problems (Prevent Blindness America, 2009). In some states, hearing screening is actually part of universal newborn screening. In other states, hearing screening is regularly conducted as part of preschool screening events. Box 6.2 describes hearing screening tests commonly used with young children.

Finally, the most common type of screeners conducted on preschoolers is *developmental screeners*. Developmental screeners can be administered in a relatively short period of time (e.g., 15–30) minutes. Most developmental screeners are used to find delays in all developmental areas (i.e., adaptive, language, cognitive, motor, and social), although some screen for potential delays in only one developmental area (e.g., social). For example, given the

---

BOX 6.2
Commonly used hearing screening tests

Visual reinforcement audiometry (VRA) is the method of choice for children between 6 months and 2 years of age. With VRA, the child is trained to look toward (localize) a sound source. When the child gives a correct response (e.g., looking toward a source of sound when it is presented), the child is rewarded through a visual reinforcement such as a toy that moves or a flashing light.

Conditioned play audiometry (CPA) can be used as the child matures and is widely used for children 2–3 years of age. In CPA, the child is trained to perform an activity each time a sound is heard. The activity may be putting a block in a box, placing pegs in a hole, putting a ring on a cone, etc. The child is taught to wait, listen, and respond.

Tympanometry introduces air pressure into the ear canal making the eardrum move back and forth. A special machine then measures the mobility of the eardrum. Tympanograms, or graphs, are produced that show stiffness, floppiness, or normal eardrum movement.

Acoustic reflex measures the response of a tiny ear muscle that contracts when a loud sound occurs. The loudness level at which the acoustic reflex occurs and/or the absence of the acoustic reflex give important diagnostic information.

Static acoustic measures estimate the physical volume of air in the ear canal. This test is useful in identifying a perforated eardrum or whether ear ventilation tubes are still open.

From American Speech-Language-Hearing Association web site, http://www.asha.org/public/hearing/testing; reprinted by permission.)

---

importance of children's social-emotional well-being and the increasing number of children who are at risk for social-emotional disorders, teachers can administer screening instruments such as the Ages and Stages Questionnaires: Social Emotional (Squires, Bricker, & Twombly, 2002) or Temperament and Atypical Behavior Scale (Bagnato, Neisworth, Salvia, & Hunt, 1999) to determine whether social-emotional concerns are warranted and whether a child should be referred for additional evaluation in the social-emotional area. Rather than evaluating the child's performance in motor skills or cognition, which are not concerns in this example, the teacher can target her screening to the specific area of concern, in this case social-emotional.

In general, developmental screeners yield comparative information between children taking the test and those who were part of the normative sample on whom the test was developed. Information from developmental screeners is typically expressed in some type of standard score. As discussed in Chapter 5, a standard score allows for comparisons to be made among children and across different tests by having a set mean and standard deviation. Scores representing children's performance on a screening instrument help teachers determine whether further evaluation is warranted (i.e., further evaluation is warranted when the child performs significantly lower than the mean of the normative sample). Information on commonly used developmental screeners includes the publisher, cost, developmental areas covered, age range, type of score produced, length of administration, administration methods, and qualifications of administrators.

Screening Formats

Screening instruments are completed using a variety of formats depending on the screening purpose. A primary format is to complete screening instruments during *mass community setting round ups*. For example, an agency may set up stations at a local library, at a YMCA, or even during kindergarten registration where other children (e.g., kindergarteners' younger siblings) are screened in the areas of motor, language, and cognition. Screening instruments can also be administered in a format that is part of a *larger surveillance or monitoring system.* Sometimes referred to as *tracking,* surveillance efforts are broad in scope, are flexible, and include observations of children in routine settings across time. (For instance, pediatricians observe and discuss a child's health and development during well-child checkup, or a child care provider completes a monitoring questionnaire every 3 months for children who are at risk due to socioeconomic reasons.) Lastly, professional or family members of the team can complete screening instruments. For example, the Ages and Stages Questionnaires (ASQ-3, Squires & Bricker, 2009) is a developmental screening questionnaire completed by a parent then scored by a professional. While some have questioned the use of parent-completed screening instruments, considerable evidence can be cited recognizing that such instruments have sound psychometric properties (McLean & Crais, 2004; Puckett & Black, 2008).

Recommended Screening Practices

Meisels and Atkins-Burnett (2005), along with Puckett and Black (2008), provide several recommendations for screening practices. As with other assessment purposes, screening instruments and practices should be sensitive to the child's cultural background, administered in the child's primary language, and based upon multiple sources of information (inclusive of families). In addition, the screener should be administered by trained personal particularly when standardized screening instruments are used. Further, screening instruments should have adequate normative samples (see Chapter 5 for a discussion on adequacy of normative samples), be inexpensive, and be easily administered.

As discussed in Chapter 5, the screening instrument's scores and procedures should have documented technical adequacy. In other words, a screener should be valid (measure what it is intended to measure) and reliable (produce the same results if used on the same population multiple times, by different administrators, or with different forms of the test). In addition to the traditional standards regarding technical adequacy, *sensitivity*, *specificity*, *positive predictive value*, and *negative predictive value* are four indices relative to the quality of a screening instrument. *Sensitivity* (or true positive rate) refers to the ability of a screening instrument to correctly identify children in need of further evaluation (Squires, 2000). *Specificity* (or true negative rate) refers to the ability of a screening instrument to accurately exclude children who do not need further evaluation (Squires). A *positive predictive value* refers to the proportion of children who *do not pass* a screening and were later identified as needing special services (i.e., screening results correctly determined the proportion of children needing further evaluation due to needing special services). A *negative predictive value* refers to the proportion of children who *pass* a screening and were not later identified as needing special services (i.e., proportion of children who were correctly identified as not needing further evaluation due to not needing special services).

	The child *did* need to be tested further because he or she *needed* special services	The child did *not* need to be tested further because he or she did *not* need special services	
Screener indicated child should be tested further (i.e., the child failed the screener)	A True Positive	B False Positive	Leads to index of positive predictive value (precision) $\dfrac{a}{a+b}$
Screener indicated child should *not* be tested further (i.e., the child passed the screener)	C False Negative	D True Negative	Leads to index of negative predictive value $\dfrac{d}{d+c}$
	Leads to index of sensitivity $\dfrac{a}{a+c}$	Leads to index of specificity $\dfrac{d}{d+b}$	

Figure 6.4. Illustration of the relationship among indices related to the technical adequacy of screening instruments.

In addition to the four indices, teachers will hear the terms *true positives* (meaning that the children identified as needing additional evaluation were correctly identified as needing special services), *true negatives/correct rejection* (meaning that the children identified as needing additional evaluation were later determined not to need special services), *false positives/false alarms* (meaning that the children referred for evaluation based on the results of a screening were later found not to be in need of special services), and *false negatives/with miss* (meaning that the children who passed the screening and are not referred for evaluation are later identified as needing special services). Figure 6.4 is designed to illustrate the relationship between indices such as sensitivity and specificity.

While the terms can be confusing, it is critical that teachers are able to interpret the effectiveness of various screening instruments. For example, if sensitivity were reported at 100%, it would mean that the screening instrument identifies all actual positives resulting in low type II errors, or false negatives. If specificity were reported at 100%, it would mean that the screening instrument identifies all actual negatives resulting in low type I errors, or false positives. False negatives can lead to underidentification of children, which can have serious consequences for the children who might have benefited from special services but did not receive the services due to errors (e.g., a lack of technical adequacy). False positives can lead to over identification of children, which can cause undo anxiety for families and unnecessary expenses for agencies. False positives, however, are often preferred over false negatives. Some suggest that the positive predictive value is the most critical index for screeners (Glover & Albers, 2007), but the index is dependent upon the prevalence of children needing further evaluation. For example, a screening instrument can have low precision (i.e., a low positive predictive value) and high specificity if there are far more true negatives than true positives. Thus, others have suggested that screening instruments should be evaluated in terms of sensitivity, specificity, *and* positive predictive values, all of which should be above 70–75% (sometimes noted as a decimal such as .70 or .75). In general, the higher the stakes, the higher the index percentages will be that teachers should look for (Meisels & Atkins-Burnett, 2005).

As a guide to help teachers be critical consumers of screening instruments, Jackson, Korey-Hirko, Goss, and LaVogue (2008) created a rating rubric to guide in selecting, implementing, and using high-quality developmental screening instruments. The rubric allows teachers to rate various developmental screening instruments across 17 critical elements, including cost, multiple means of expression, representative norm sample, training, and usefulness of follow-up information. In addition to employing the rubric, teachers can use reviews of screening instruments to guide their decision making. (See Box 6.3 for a brief summary of screening instrument compendia and reviews.)

Recommended practice repeatedly indicates that any assessment instrument should be used for the purposes for which it was intended and validated. Increasingly, however, practitioners and researchers have expressed interest in "stretching" the uses of screening tools for assessment and evaluation purposes beyond the typical scope of screening (Bricker, Squires, & Clifford, 2010). For example, professionals are asking whether they can use a screening instrument to develop goals, evaluate progress,

---

BOX 6.3

Screening instrument reviews

Drotar, D., Stancin, T., & Dworkin, P. (2008, February 26). *Pediatric developmental screening: understanding and selecting screening instruments.* Retrieved from The Commonwealth Fund web site: http://www.commonwealthfund.org/~/ media/Files/ Publications/Fund%20Manual/ 2008/Feb/Pediatric%20Developmental%20Screening%20% 20Understanding%20and% 20Selecting%20Screening%20Instruments/ Pediatric_Developmental_Screening%20pdf.pdf

First Signs. (2009). *Recommended screening tools.* Retrieved from First Signs web site: http:// www.firstsigns.org/screening/tools/rec.htm#dev_screens

Ghazvini, A.S. (Ed.). (2005). *Birth to three screening and assessment resource guide.* Retrieved from the Florida Institute of Education web site: http://www.unf.edu/dept/fie/ PDF%20Folder/resource.pdf

Minnesota Department of Health. (2009). *Developmental and social–emotional screening of young children in Minnesota: All instruments at a glance.* Retrieved from Minnesota Department of Health web site: http://www.health.state.mn.us/divs/fh/mch/devscrn/ glance.html

Printz, P.H., Borg, A., & Demaree, M.A. (2003). *A look at social, emotional, and behavioral screening tools for Head Start and Early Head Start.* Retrieved from the Center for Children and Families Education Development Center web site: http://ccf.edc.org/PDF/ screentools.pdf

measure developmental changes and thereby establish eligibility for special services, and meet federal accountability mandates. As stated by
Bricker et al.,

> Screening measures such as the ASQ were not designed to develop in-
> tervention goals and content or to [monitor] child progress over time
> and currently no empirical base exists to suggest how well or how poorly
> a screening measure may contribute to these assessment/evaluation
> purposes. (2010, p. 19)

Thus, teachers need to recognize that screening instruments should not be
used to diagnose children, write individualized goals, plan instruction,
monitor children's performance over time as a response to instruction, or
evaluate a program; nor should they be used for state or federal accountability purposes (Meisels & Atkins-Burnett, 2005). Screening instruments
"can only alert teachers and families to areas of concern for further evaluation and consultation" (Printz, Borg, & Demaree, 2003, p. 4).

DETERMINING ELIGIBILITY FOR SERVICES

Public funding (under IDEA) is available to support the educational needs
of children with disabilities through federal grants to states that choose to
participate. In order to qualify for the grant, a state must abide by the relevant federal laws and regulations. The grant covers only a portion of the
cost of educating children with disabilities. State education agencies
(SEAs) and LEAs are responsible for covering the remaining portion of the
costs. It is important to understand the basic funding structure that supports the educational needs of children with disabilities because it directly
affects who receives services, what services children receive, and how services are delivered. The next section describes federal regulations and state
variations related to determining eligibility for services.

Federal Regulations

In addition to stating regulations related to funding, IDEA lists several general requirements for completing eligibility determination. *Eligibility determination* is the process by which a child meets the federal and state definitions of a child with a disability. (See Box 6.4 for the federal definition of a
child with a disability.) Once a child is determined to be eligible, he or she
is entitled to receive special education services under IDEA funding. IDEA
describes essential characteristics of assessments used for eligibility and
regulations about assessment administration, which apply to children from
birth through age 21. IDEA regulations can be grouped into five minimum
standards for eligibility measures and procedures as follows.

BOX 6.4

IDEA definition of child with a disability

PUBLIC LAW 108–446—DEC. 3, 2004 118 STAT. 2653

(3) CHILD WITH A DISABILITY—

  (A) IN GENERAL—The term "child with a disability" means a child—

    (i) with mental retardation, hearing impairments (including deafness), speech or language impairments, visual impairments (including blindness), serious emotional disturbance (referred to in this title as 'emotional disturbance'), orthopedic impairments, autism, traumatic brain injury, other health impairments, or specific learning disabilities; and

    (ii) who, by reason thereof, needs special education and related services.

  (B) CHILD AGED 3 THROUGH 9—The term "child with a disability" for a child aged 3 through 9 (or any subset of that age range, including ages 3 through 5), may, at the discretion of the State and the local educational agency, include a child—

    (i) experiencing developmental delays, as defined by the State and as measured by appropriate diagnostic instruments and procedures, in 1 or more of the following areas: physical development; cognitive development; communication development; social or emotional development; or adaptive development; and

    (ii) who, by reason thereof, needs special education and related services.

Source: The Individuals with Disabilities Education Improvement Act of 2004, PL 108-446.

First, when assessing a child for eligibility, no one procedure can be used as the sole criterion for determining eligibility; a variety of tools and strategies should be employed (Evaluation Procedures, 2005). For example, though a child clearly presents with a speech impairment, it is unacceptable to find the child eligible solely on the basis of a speech therapist's report. Even if the child has an expressive language score on a norm-referenced assessment that is two standard deviations below the mean, additional data must be used to determine the child's eligibility. Anecdotal information about how the child communicates his or her wants and needs during an observation in child care and parent reports of the child's functional language skills at home and in other familiar environments should be used to support the speech therapist's conventional assessment results for eligibility determination.

Second, the eligibility determination process, including all measures, should be free of racial and cultural bias (Evaluation Procedures, 2005). It is nearly impossible to find an early childhood assessment instrument that is free from cultural bias because many typical early childhood skills are linked to culture preferences. For example, dressing oneself independently is a skill linked to cultural beliefs about developing independence. In a culture that places a high value on children developing independence from their parents or caregivers at an early age, it may be typical for a 3-year-old to dress himself independently. In another culture that values community and family over independent expression, it may be typical for a 5-year-old to be dressed by his mother on a daily basis. When selecting and administering developmental assessment instruments, teachers can address issues of item-embedded racial or cultural bias by being aware of such biases, not relying solely on the results of one measure for eligibility, and gaining an understanding of each child's racial and cultural background through observations and parent interviews.

Third, any test given as part of the eligibility process to children with sensory impairments must be selected and administered such that the results adequately represent the children's abilities and aptitude (Evaluation Procedures, 2005). For example, it would be clearly inappropriate to use a picture naming test to identify the vocabulary of a child who has a vision impairment. When a child has a significant sensory impairment, such as blindness (in the previous example), it may seem obvious that certain tests would be inappropriate. When a child demonstrates some functional vision, however, the necessity for using an alternative test instrument for the child to demonstrate his or her true abilities and aptitude may not be as clear.

Fourth, the measure (or measures) used for eligibility must cover all areas related to the *suspected disability* and be sufficiently comprehensive to determine the needed educational supports including related services (Evaluation Procedures, 2005). The suspected disability is the eligibility category that the LEA determines is most appropriate for the child on the basis of the referral and/or results of a screening. The category of suspected disability drives the types of data collected about a child during the eligibility process.

Fifth, any standardized assessment used in the eligibility process must be administered according to the published instructions by an individual with knowledge and training related to its administration (Evaluation Procedures, 2005). This guideline emphasizes the necessity for LEAs to administer tests as the publishers intended. In order for the test results to be reliable and valid, all accompanying instructions must be followed, including any publisher-specified training or credentials required of the test administrators.

Federal Categories

IDEA describes 14 categories under which children ages 3–21 can be found eligible. While brief definitions of each category are provided in IDEA, SEAs are responsible for determining the specific criteria that children in their state must meet in order to qualify under each specific category. Two federal eligibility categories contain more in-depth descriptions in the federal law: *specific learning disability* and *developmental delay*. Specific learning disability is the only eligibility category for which detailed federal eligibility criteria are given. The specific learning disability category, however, is rarely, if ever, used to identify preschool-age children. On the other hand, developmental delay is widely used in the preschool-age group and so deserves special attention.

Developmental Delay

Developmental delay is the only optional federal category and the only category with federally imposed age restrictions. IDEA (2004) permits states to use the term to identify children ages birth through 9 years for special services eligibility. The developmental delay category, however, was introduced in federal special education law in the 1986 Education for All Handicapped Children Act with the advent of special services for infants and toddlers with disabilities. The 1991 authorization of IDEA permitted states to use developmental delay as an eligibility category for children ages 3–5 years, as well as for infants and toddlers. The current age range (birth to 9 years) has been in effect since IDEA 1997.

The phrase *developmental delay*, when used as a category of eligibility, characterizes a condition in which a delay in one or more areas of development is likely to interfere with a child's future educational performance unless it is addressed with special services (McLean, Smith, McCormick, Schakel, & McEvoy, 1991). Beginning at age 3, children must meet criteria under a category defined by the features of their disabilities in order to be eligible for special education services. Any child who is transitioning from Part C services to Part B services will have some type of non categorical label, such as *infant or toddler with a disability* or *child at risk of developmental delay*. While some states use other terms in place of developmental delay for preschool eligibility, such as preschool *child with a disability*, *noncategorical*, or *preschool special needs*, all states have some general category for preschool eligibility with a range of definitional variations (Danaher, 2005).

The Division for Early Childhood (DEC, 2009) recommends using the developmental delay category for children from birth through age 8 and supports its use through age 9. Further, the use of categories other than developmental delay for children ages birth to 8 is generally not recommended by the DEC because such classifications may be inaccurate. The use of developmental delay can allow children to be found eligible for services even if they do not meet the criteria for eligibility under any of the school-age categories. Therefore, the use of the developmental delay category helps to catch children early who may otherwise not be identified until their disabilities present a significant detrimental impact on their performance in school. Children with some types of disabilities, such as specific learning disabilities, mild cognitive disabilities, or social–emotional disabilities that are difficult to diagnose at early ages, may benefit most from the use of the developmental delay eligibility category in early childhood. For example, to meet the federal qualifications under the category of specific learning disability, a child must either demonstrate a significant discrepancy between his academic performance and intellectual ability or demonstrate an inability to make adequate progress in the general curriculum with research-based instruction and interventions. Further, it must be demonstrated that the reason the child met either condition listed was not from lack of appropriate instruction. A preschool-age child who has no school experience prior to referral for special education cannot meet the criteria for a child with a specific learning disability because there is no evidence of prior appropriate instruction.

In a longitudinal study of over 2,000 children who received preschool special education services under the developmental delay category in Florida, Delgado, Vagi, and Scott (2006) found that about one fourth of the children exited special education by third grade. Of the remaining three fourths, more than half were served under the *specific learning disability* or *educable mentally handicapped* (a term for mild cognitive disability) categories in third grade. The results of the Delgado et al. study illustrate the importance of using a non categorical option, such as developmental delay, to identify children with mild disabilities or disabilities with complicated or unknown etiologies, so that young children can receive necessary intervention at an early age.

While there are many positive aspects of using the developmental delay category, one drawback is that it is commonly documented through the use of percent delay. Box 6.5 provides more detailed information on the topic of percent delay in relation to the early childhood eligibility process. In addition, there are a few situations in which use of eligibility categories other than developmental delay in early childhood is essential for children to access appropriate services including specific therapies and adaptive equipment. Special programs, and sometimes funding, are available for children who have been identified under specific eligibility categories such as autism, deaf or hard of hearing, and visually impaired. Therefore, DEC recommends that young children with multiple disabilities, sensory impairments, and autism be identified under their specific eligibility categories rather than using the developmental delay category.

State Variations

Several regulations in IDEA allow flexibility for states, which ultimately affects children's eligibility for services and the services children receive. One state variation that can affect the services children receive is whether states choose to serve 3- to 5-year-olds under Part B or Part C. According to IDEA, children who turn 2 years old during the school year and who

---

BOX 6.5

Issues related to percent delay

Percent delay is defined as the difference between a child's chronological age and developmental age expressed as a percent of the chronological age. Percent delay is often used to determine a child's eligibility for services particularly in early intervention (birth to 3/Part C). Examples of state criteria using percent delay include:

- 25% delay in one or more areas
- 50% delay or equivalent standard deviation
- 33.33% delay in one or more areas prior to 24 months and 50% in one area or a continued 33.33% in two or more areas after 24 months
- 25% delay or 1.5 standard deviations in one or more developmental areas
- 25% (or 1.3 standard deviations below the mean) in one or more areas of development

To calculate the percent delay, teams are to determine "the discrepancy between the child's chronological age and the developmental score the child receives on tests administered during the evaluation" (Andersson, 2004, p. 63). When using percent delay as a criterion, there is a positive emphasis on natural environments, parent report, and informed clinical opinion throughout the assessment process. There are, however, a number of concerns with using percent delay as a criterion for eligibility or measure of a child's performance. See Andersson for a more thorough discussion of the issues, which are outlined as follows:

- First, unlike the scaled or standard scores described earlier in the chapter, percent delay is calculated differently from assessment to assessment, team to team, and state to state. Further, percent delay calculations are not equitable to particular SDs, thus confusing the issue when state criteria use them interchangeably or suggest an equivalency exists.

- Second, percent delay is based upon the notion of age equivalencies. Age equivalencies are problematic for at least two reasons: 1) For many tests, the age associated with a given item is not determined empirically; rather the item is assigned an age based on how ages are assigned in other tests or generally agreed upon developmental milestones. 2) Age equivalencies do not inform teams about a child's strengths, emerging skills, or needs, which a team is responsible for assessing.

- Third, having chronological ages assigned to items may lead interventionists and caregivers to select intervention targets based on the age level of an item rather than selecting items that address children's individual developmental needs.

- Fourth, a 25% delay in one particular area of development (e.g., motor skills) may have greater or lesser implications than a 25% delay in another area of development (e.g., language skills) at a given period in development.

- Fifth, many tests commonly used for determining eligibility, particularly for Part C, indicate that providers cannot generate percent delay from the tool being used. Yet, providers do so on a daily basis. For example, the HELP utility from VORT Corporation indicates on its web site that it "is not standardized or normed. As such, it is *not* intended to be used to calculate a child's single-age equivalent (score or % delay)" (http://www.vort.com/faq0-6.html).

- Sixth, many of the assessments used for eligibility do not have systematic procedures for generating percent delay and leave it up to the provider or team. However, some states and/or authors/publishers have provided guidance in the calculation of percent delay. (See the examples that follow.) Generally speaking, however, comparing age equivalencies to chronological age generates percent delay.

Examples:

- Sample of guidance from an ECI provider: Our team calculates 25% by taking the child's chronological age (CA), multiplying it by .25, and subtracting the months from the CA. So, a 24-month-old child with a 25% delay would have an age equivalency of 18 months or less, and a 14-month-old with a 25% delay would be performing only at an age equivalency of 10–11 months.

- In Virginia, teams are given the formula of CA − DA/CA = percent delay. For example, if the child's CA was 38 and developmental age (DA) was 24, the team would subtract 24 from 38, divide the difference by 38, and round up to 37%.

- The authors of Partners in Play (a curriculum-based assessment, Eshner et al., 2007) instruct teams to determine the child's CA to the nearest month, divide by the number of items a child passed by the number possible for the age, subtract 1, and multiply by 100 to obtain the percent delay. Thus, a 7-month-old child who passes 10 items out of 26 in the neuromotor domain would be considered 61% delayed according to the formula of $[(10/26) - 1] \times 100$.

- Suffolk County Department of Health Services, Bureau of Services for Children with Disabilities provides a step-by-step infant development center percentage delay conversion chart (see http://www.stepbystepny.com/TherapistResources/Percentage%20Delay%20Conversion%20Chart.pdf).

- West Virginia Department of Health and Human Resources provides a birth to three percentage conversion chart to assist providers in determining percent delay for eligibility under the developmental delay category (see www.wvdhhr.org/Birth23/files/WVBTT_PercConvChartInst3409.pdf).

qualify for special services can be served under either Part B or Part C. This regulation affects primarily children who will transition from Part C to Part B services because children who receive services under Part C must be evaluated for Part B eligibility when they age-out of Part C eligibility. Children who are being evaluated for services for the first time close to their third birthdays, however, could also be affected by this regulation. For example, in Ohio, children cannot be served under Part B until their third birthday. In New York, parents can choose to keep their 3-year-olds in Part C services until September 1 or January 2 whichever comes sooner after the child's third birthday. In Maryland, children with disabilities can be served under Part C until they are age-eligible for kindergarten.

Eligibility criteria can vary from state to state and category to category. In order to understand the variations among state eligibility criteria, it is important to understand how states define such criteria. There are three general types of data that states use to define eligibility criteria: diagnosis by a licensed professional, test scores, and informed clinical opinion.

Diagnosis by a licensed professional occurs when a child has been evaluated by a physician, psychologist, audiologist, or other therapist and meets diagnostic criteria for a specific condition or disease. Diagnoses are most commonly included in the eligibility process for sensory impairments and other biologically based impairments with clear etiology such as Down syndrome or spina bifida. Diagnoses are helpful for initial identification of children who are eligible for services and provide general guidance as to the services that a child may require. However, diagnoses rarely provide information sufficient for determining the precise educational needs of a child and, therefore, cannot be used as a sole eligibility factor. For instance, in the Down syndrome example, the diagnosis suggests that the child is likely to have a language delay, a mild to moderate cognitive delay, motor delay, and health complications due to heart defects. However, the diagnosis of Down syndrome does not provide information about the extent of the delays nor does it give any information about the child's functional abilities. A child with Down syndrome may or may not qualify for occupational or physical therapy due to motor delays, depending on his or her functional motor abilities.

Test scores are the most prevalent sources of data used to determine eligibility. Different types of tests result in different types of scores. (See Chapter 5 for more information about different types of tests and their uses in early childhood.) Conventional assessments are the primary type of test used in the eligibility process. As described in Chapter 5, conventional assessments generate standard scores, percentile ranks, and age equivalencies. Standard scores can be used to determine the distance in number of standard deviations (SD) that a child's score falls from the mean. The number of SDs below the mean for an area of development is a pervasive requirement for eligibility across categories and states. The following examples illustrate state SD requirements for preschool eligibility under the developmental delay or similar category:

- The most common quantitative criterion for preschool eligibility (representing 36 states) is two SDs below the mean in one developmental domain or one and one half SDs below the mean in two domains (Danaher, 2007).

- States range from qualifying children who score as little as one SD below the mean in one domain to requiring score as much as three SDs below the mean in one domain (Danaher, 2007).

Some states use age-equivalent scores expressed as *percent delay* to determine eligibility. Box 6.5 defines percent delay in detail, describes how to calculate percent delay, and lists issues related to using percent delay. While test scores tend to provide more detailed information about children's strengths and weaknesses than diagnoses, like diagnoses, test scores offer limited information about children's functional skills. Therefore, test scores should not be used as the sole criterion for determining eligibility.

The final type of data used to determine eligibility is *qualitative*. Qualitative data include descriptive or anecdotal information gathered through interviews and observations and provide the most detailed information about children's functional abilities, compared with other types of data. Qualitative data are often "measured" or reported using *informed clinical opinion*, or *clinical judgment*. Bagnato (2007) identifies five practices that are necessary for accurate decision making based on clinical judgment. First, the assessment team should create operational definitions of attributes of the constructs or functional domains that will be examined. For example, if clinical judgment will be used to identify a child as eligible for services due to a language impairment, the team must define the functional language skills that they consider typical, at risk, and delayed. The second essential practice is to use structured rating formats to record informed opinions. Using the previous example, the team would create a checklist and/or rating scale to record the child's functional language skills. Next, the team should gather data from multiple sources. The fourth essential practice is to establish a consensus decision-making process for the team to use. Clearly defining a decision-making process facilitates the resolution of disagreements among team members and results in more accurate eligibility decisions. The fifth, and final, essential practice is to provide training to facilitate reliable ratings.

Often, states require specific types of data to determine eligibility. For example, to qualify under the autism category, several states require a diagnosis from a licensed physician, while some states permit diagnosis by school psychologists and other states do not require a diagnosis at all. A few states list specific team members who must be included (e.g., a speech language clinician, school social worker, psychiatrist) in order to determine eligibility under the autism category. Some states require an observation of the child, while others define specific tests that must be used, as well as specific test scores that must be met for eligibility (Muller & Markowitz, 2004). (For further information about state-specific special education laws and policies refer to Box 6.6.)

BOX 6.6

State-specific special education law and policy resources

IDEA regulations are minimum federal requirements. States always have the option of creating state laws and policies that exceed the minimum requirements described in the federal law. Therefore, it is important to know about related state laws and policies in addition to understanding the federal laws. Here are some resources for finding state-specific information on special education laws and policies:

- The National Early Childhood Technical Assistance Center
  http://www.nectac.org/default.asp
- National Dissemination Center for Children with Disabilities
  http://www.nichcy.org/Pages/StateSpecificInfo.aspx
- Regional Resource Center Program
  http://www.rrfcnetwork.org/

RECOMMENDED PRACTICES FOR ELIGIBILITY DETERMINATION

Understanding federal and state laws, regulations, and common practices is an important step toward understanding the eligibility determination process. The next step is to incorporate recommended practices in early childhood intervention assessment with federal and state requirements to create the ideal eligibility determination process. The recommendations that follow represent ideal practices that programs should strive to implement as much as possible, while recognizing that time demands, financial resources, scheduling conflicts, and personal preferences may dictate deviations from these practices.

Transdisciplinary Teaming During Eligibility

When conducting eligibility assessment, teams of professionals are often involved in the process. Teams can be structured in one of four ways: unidisciplinary, multidisciplinary, interdisciplinary, and transdisciplinary. Each of these structures is explained in Box 6.7. The transdisciplinary team structure, as described in Chapter 4 in terms of its value for assessment of children with diverse abilities, is the recommended structure for preschool special education eligibility assessment (Sandall, Hemmeter, Smith, & McLean, 2005). Grisham-Brown (2000) describes a process of conducting a trandisciplinary assessment with young children who may have disabilities. The first step of the transdisciplinary assessment process is for the individual coordinating the assessment (e.g., school psychologist) to gather information from the child's family and other familiar caregivers. The information collected should focus on not only what the child can do, but also any priorities and concerns families have about the child's development. As well, the assessment coordinator needs to collect information about the child's preferences (e.g., activities, materials). (See Chapter 3 for information on methods of gathering information from families.) If applicable, the assessment coordinator should request any prior school records, including Individual Family Service Plans (IFSPs) or Individual Education

---

BOX 6.7

Team structure variations

Unidisciplinary	• Each team member completes his or her discipline-specific evaluation of the child individually, including the related report. • Team members do not communicate with each other about any aspect of the assessment process or intervention. • Parents are not included in the team.
Multidisciplinary	• Each team member completes his or her discipline-specific evaluation of the child individually, including the related report. • Team members share their results and recommendations with each other. • Each team member implements his or her intervention independently. • Parents are not included in the team.
Interdisciplinary	• Each team member completes his or her discipline-specific evaluation of the child either individually or simultaneously with other team members. • Team members combine their results to create one report and make recommendations together as a team with the child's parents. • Team members may collaborate minimally to implement interventions.
Transdisciplinary	• Team members collaborate on every aspect of the assessment and intervention processes, including report writing. • Parents are essential members of the team throughout the assessment process and intervention. • Each team member contributes to assessment and intervention across all disciplines.

Programs (IEPs), health information, and reports from previous related-service providers. While meeting with the family, the assessment coordinator explains the assessment process to the family.

Once information is gathered from the child's family and previous records, the assessment coordinator determines who should comprise the assessment team (e.g., speech therapist, occupational therapist, physical therapist, vision or hearing specialist, assistive technology specialist). The team reviews the assessment information, gathered by the assessment coordinator, and plans the assessment. Based on information from the family, the assessment team identifies activities in which they will conduct the assessment. As well, they select appropriate assessment instruments to use while conducting the evaluation. If the team works in a state where the use of a conventional assessment instrument is required as part of the state's eligibility criteria, the team should also rely on a curriculum-based assessment instrument to assist in gathering functional assessment data.

During the assessment, one team member is selected to facilitate the assessment. This individual can be anyone on the team, including a member of the child's family. The facilitator engages the child in activities that have been planned by the team as opportunities to observe developmental skills in the areas in which the child was referred. For example, if the child was referred for potential speech/language and fine motor delays, the team might plan a snack activity in which its members can observe the child's use of speech/language skills to request, describe, and comment on the snack. The team might also provide open containers, a sandwich spread, and liquids for the child to pour. (Chapter 7 gives further information on how to create assessment activities.) The assessment facilitator creates opportunities for the observing team members to see the child demonstrate behaviors that might indicate delay. For example, the facilitator might not give the child a spoon to eat his or her yogurt, in order to determine whether the child will request a spoon. Similarly, the facilitator might leave the top on the cream cheese container to see if the child can independently use both hands together to remove the top. Observations are documented by team members and noted on test-scoring protocols. The goal of a transdisciplinary eligibility assessment is to conduct as much of the assessment through observation as possible. In situations where the use of conventional assessment instruments is required, the team should abide by the following guidelines: 1) Most conventional assessments allow for some flexibility in scoring some of the items. (If an item can be scored through observations, then the team member should score while observing.) 2) If the administration guidelines of the assessment disallow the collection of data through observation or the team member does not observe the child demonstrate the behavior, the team member should wait until after the observation period and then complete any direct testing that is required.

After the assessment is complete, the team meets (including the family) to debrief about the assessment. Each member shares the data she collected about the child with the team. The team then sorts the data to determine the child's strengths, weaknesses, and primary educational needs (i.e., priorities). The team structures the discussion around the child's primary educational needs that emerged during the assessment. For each of those priorities (e.g., making requests), the team brainstorms 1) sample activities in which the child might learn the skill, 2) adaptations and modifications that the child needs in order to learn the skill, and 3) supports the child needs in order to learn the skill (i.e., people). Figure 6.5 shows an example of a grid that can be used to capture information about each priority. After determining the child's priority educational needs, the final step in the transdisciplinary assessment process is to summarize the team's findings in a written report.

Report Writing

The purpose of an assessment report is to merge all the information from pertinent sources into one document to generate a complete picture of the child. Kritikos (2010) indicated that there are five main areas to report writing: background/history, assessment tools used, informal information, results, and interpretations and recommendations. Because the middle three sections (assessment tools used, informal information, and results)

Team Meeting Grid	
Skills	**Activities**
Communication • Express wants and needs (hungry, tired, belly hurts, drink, sick)	• Across all activities (home, school, community) • Teach through role play with dolls or puppets during dramatic play or story time • Activities that she enjoys (movement, water)
Supports	**Adaptations**
• Parents • Interpreter • Therapists • Vision services • Functional vision assessment • Other school personnel • Peers	• Use a combination of Big Mac and Speakeasy communication devices. • Some messages ("My belly hurts") need to be with her at all times. • Expand switches (3 or 4) on the Speakeasy so that the number of choices can be expanded. • Try placing one switch on her tray and one on her foot plate. • If switchs remain on her tray, change their angle to vertical, instead of horizontal, as they are now. • Provide stable position in her wheelchair so that she can use her upper extremities better to touch the switches on the communication device.

Figure 6.5. *Example of a grid used to capture information about priorities.* From Grisham-Brown, J. (2000). Transdisciplinary activity assessment for young children with multiple disabilities: A program planning approach. *Young Exceptional Children*, 3(3), 3–10; reprinted by permission.

often overlap with or have relevant data, they will be discussed primarily as a whole, rather than as individual parts.

The background or history section provides basic information about the child's age, grade, dates of assessments, and so forth. The background should include any pertinent information about the pregnancy, birth, and early development. Medical information (e.g., allergies, hospitalizations, surgeries, disorders or impairments), academic information, and information about the child's social history would also be located in the history.

The next section involves the assessment instruments and procedures used. There are many different assessments and assessment types (speech and language, cognitive, achievement, etc.) that can be included in a single report. The assessment section should list all of the tools that were used to gather information. For instance, if cognitive, achievement, and sensory assessments were given to a child, all three of the assessments would be listed in assessments-used section. The full name, with the edition or version, should be given, along with any abbreviations.

A description of the assessment purpose can serve as an introductory paragraph into the results of the assessment. The overall score of the test should be given along with the results of each of the subtests administered. In terms of standardized tests, a standard score and percentile are reported. Using two different ways of reporting the score (standard score and percentile) helps to explain the test more effectively than just reporting the standard score.

Along with the reporting of scores, information about what the scores mean should also be given here. It is appropriate to describe what a particular score implies for the child. Information to guide score interpretations can often be found within the manual that accompanies the assessment tool. A report is most informative when it provides implications, based upon the child's score, rather than just restating the standard score and percentile (Wodrich, 1997).

Qualitative information can include all of the observations made during the assessment procedures. Observations about the child's willingness to participate, attitude, and so forth, are all important variables that should be noted. In addition, information about the assessment itself and the environment should be noted. Aspects such as testing location, number of breaks needed or given, interruptions (fire drill), and other factors that could affect the results should be mentioned. Most importantly, team members should provide information on the child's demonstrated functional behaviors during each of the assessment activities.

The final section, interpretation and recommendation, focuses on the identified priorities. Each team member contributes recommendations related to his or her area of expertise for how to teach each priority. In the example in Figure 6.5, the priority is requesting. In the report, the speech therapist would provide suggestions on the type of assistive technology for the child to use. The occupational therapist might contribute ideas about how to position the communication device for optimal fine motor use. The physical therapist would suggest how to position the child so that her fine motor functioning is maximized. The teacher would supply suggestions of motivating activities for teaching the prioritized skill. By including suggestions from each team member related to the identified priorities, the report exemplifies true transdisciplinary service delivery in which shared goals are identified and role-release is intimated (Cloniger, 2004).

SUMMARY

This chapter has described the process used to identify children who are eligible for federally funded special services including Child Find, screening, and assessment for eligibility determination. In addition, the chapter has identified areas of weakness within current practices related to each component of the process and identified recommended practices for improvement.

Overall, the process of identifying children for special services should be viewed as a process with dual purposes: to identify whether a child qualifies for federally funded special services and to identify educational needs and appropriate services. Therefore, even when conventional testing or other non recommended practices (such as diagnosis by a single professional) are required for eligibility, it is important to consider what additional assessment activities are necessary to fully understand the child's educational needs.

The eligibility determination process should utilize authentic assessment measures, particularly with young children. LEAs are often burdened by state and federally mandated timelines, poor interagency cooperation during transitions, scheduling issues with families, and scheduling issues with team members. Conventional testing, as described in Chapter 2, certainly speeds up the eligibility determination process and may be necessary at times. However, LEAs should strive to use a system that is truly authentic, uses multiple methods, and relies on a transdisciplinary team. Further, assessment should focus on a child's educational needs and functioning rather than his deficits and test scores.

REFERENCES

Andersson, L.L. (2004). Appropriate and inappropriate interpretation and use of test scores in early intervention. *Journal of Early Intervention, 27*, 55–68.

Bagnato, S. J. (2007). *Authentic assessment for early childhood intervention: Best practices.* New York: Guilford.

Bagnato, S.J., Neisworth, J.T., Salvia, J.J., & Hunt, F.M. (1999). *Temperament and atypical behavior scale.* Baltimore: Paul H. Brookes Publishing Co.

Bricker, D., Squires, J., & Clifford, J. (2010). Developmental screening measures: Stretching the use of the ASQ for other assessment purposes. *Infants and Young Children, 23*(1), 14–22.

Celeste, M. (2002). A survey of motor development for infants and young children with visual impairments. *Journal of Visual Impairments and Blindness, 96*(3), 169–175.

Cloninger, C.J. (2004). Designing collaborative educational services. In F.P. Orelove, D. Sobsey, & R.K. Silberman *Educating children with multiple disabilities: A collaborative approach* (4th ed.) (pp. 1–30). Baltimore: Paul H. Brookes Publishing Co.

Danaher, J. (2005). Eligibility policies and practices for young children under Part B of IDEA. *NECTAC Notes, 15*, 1–18. Chapel Hill, NC: National Early Childhood Technical Assistance Center.

Danaher, J. (2007). Eligibility policies and practices for young children under Part B of IDEA. *NECTAC Notes, 24.* Chapel Hill, NC: National Early Childhood Technical Assistance Center.

Delgado,C.E.F., Vagi, S.J., & Scott, K.G. (2006). Tracking preschool children with developmental delay: Third grade outcomes. *American Journal on Mental Retardation, 111*, 299–306.

Division for Early Childhood, The. (2009, April). *Developmental delay as an eligibility category.* Missoula, MT: author.

Dunst, C.J., & Clow, P.W. (2007). Public awareness and child find activities in Part C early intervention programs. *Cornerstones, 3*(1), 1–7. Retrieved January 29, 2008, from http://www.tracecenter.info/cornerstones/cornerstones_vol3_no1.pdf

Education for All Handicapped Children Act of 1986. PL 99-457.

Ensher, G., Bobish, T.P., Gardner, E., Reinson, C.L., Bryden, D.A., & Foertsch, D.J. (2007). *Partners in Play: Assessing infants and toddlers in natural contexts.* Clifton Park, NY: Thomson Delmar.

Evaluation Procedures. (2005). 34 CFR 300.532.

Glover, T., & Albers, C. (2007). Considerations for evaluating universal screening assessments. *Journal of School Psychology, 45*(2), 117–135.

Gonpel, M., van Bon, W.H.J., & Schreuder, R. (2004). Word reading and processing of the identity and order of letters by children with low vision and sighted children. *Journal of Visual Impairments and Blindness, 98*(12), 757–772.

Grisham-Brown, J.L. (2000). Transdisciplinary activity-based assessment for young children with multiple disabilities: A program planning approach. *Young Exceptional Children, 3*, 3–10.

Individuals with Disabilities Education Act Amendments of 1991, PL 102-119, 20 U.S.C. §§ 1400 *et seq.*

Individuals with Disabilities Education Act Amendments (IDEA) of 1997, PL 105-17, 20 U.S.C. §§ 1400 *et seq.*

Individuals with Disabilities Education Improvement Act (IDEA) of 2004, PL 108-446, 20 U.S.C. §§ 1400 *et seq.*

Jackson, S., Korey-Hirko, S., Goss, S., & LaVogue, C. (2008). *Developmental screening rating rubric.* Akron, OH: Ohio State Support Team Region 8 and Kent State University.

Kritikos, E.P. (2010). *Special education assessment: Issues and strategies affecting today's classroom.* Upper Saddle River, NJ: Merrill.

McLean, M., & Crais, E. (2004). Procedural considerations in assessing infants and preschoolers with disabilities. In M. McLean, M. Wolery, & D.B. Bailey (Eds.), *Assessing infants and preschoolers with special needs* (pp. 45–70). Upper Saddle River, NJ: Pearson Merrill Prentice Hall.

McLean, M., Smith, B., McCormick, K., Schakel, J., & McEvoy, M. (1991). *Developmental delay: Establishing parameters for a preschool category of exceptionality.* Position statement of the Division for Early Childhood, Council for Exceptional Children. Washington, DC: Council for Exceptional Children.

Meisels, S.J., & Atkins-Burnett, S. (2005). *Developmental screening in early childhood: A guide* (5th ed.). Washington, DC: National Association for the Education of Young Children.

Muller, E., & Markowitz, J. (2004). *Disability categories: State terminology, definitions & eligibility criteria.* Washington, DC: National Association of State Directors of Special Education, Project FORUM.

Pavri, S., & Fowler, S.A. (2001). *Child Find, screening, and tracking: Serving culturally and linguistically diverse children and families* (Technical report). Champaign, IL: CLAS Early Childhood Research Institute.

Prevent Blindness America. (2009). *Children's vision screening.* Retrieved December 29, 2009, from Prevent Blindness America website: http://www.preventblindness.org/vision_screening/ childrens_vision_screening.html

Printz, P.H., Borg, A., & Demaree, M.A. (2003). *A look at social, emotional, and behavioral screening tools for head start and early head start.* Retrieved December ber 27, 2009, from http://ccf.edc.org/PDF/screentools.pdf

Puckett, M.B., & Black, J.K. (2008). *Meaningful assessments of the young child: Celebrating development and learning* (3rd ed.). Upper Saddle River, NJ: Pearson Education, Inc.

Sandall, S., Hemmeter, M.L., Smith, B.J., & McLean, M. (2005). *DEC recommended practice: A comprehensive guide for practical application in early intervention/early childhood special education.* Missoula, MT: DEC.

Save Babies Through Screening Foundation. (2008). *Answers to frequently asked questions.* Cincinnati, OH: author. Retrieved December 27, 2009, from http://www.savebabies.org/faqs.html

Shaw, E.F. (2007, June 21). *Improving early identification for young children with disabilities.* Presented at the National Conversation: Developmental Screening and Referral: "Promising Practice for Coordination of Services." Retrieved December 27, 2009, from the Waisman Center's National Medical Home Autism Initiative website: http://www.waisman.wisc.edu/nmhai/Nat_Con2007.htm

Squires, J. (2000). Identifying social/emotional and behavioral problems in infants and toddlers. *Infant/Toddler Intervention, 10*(2). 107–119.

Squires, J., & Bricker, D. (2009) *Ages and Stages Questionnaires: A parent-completed child-monitoring system* (3rd ed.). Baltimore: Paul H. Brookes Publishing Co.

Squires, J., Bricker, D., & Twombly, E. (2002). *Ages and stages questionnaires: Social emotional.* Baltimore: Paul H. Brookes Publishing Co.

U.S. General Accounting Office. (2003, March). *Newborn screening: Characteristics of state programs* (Report no. GAO-03-449). Washington, DC: author. Retrieved January 31, 2010, from http://www.gao.gov/new.items/d03449.pdf

U.S. Preventive Services Task Force (2008). Universal screening for hearing loss in newborns: U.S. Preventive Services Task Force Recommendations Statement. *Pediatrics, 122,* 143–148.

Wodrich, D.L. (1997). *Children's psychological testing.* Baltimore: Paul H. Brookes Publishing Co.

CHAPTER 7

Assessment for Program Planning Purposes

*Sarah R. Hawkins, Kristie Pretti-Frontczak,
Jennifer Grisham-Brown, Teresa L. Brown,
and Lydia Moore*

Mr. Jason teaches in a rural public preschool program in Appalachia. He teaches 4 days a week to two groups of children: one group that attends in the morning and another that attends in the afternoon. The children in his program attend for one of three reasons. Some 4-year-old children are placed in his classroom because they are considered to be at risk, which is defined by Mr. Jason's state as being socioeconomically disadvantaged. A second group of children attends his program because they have diagnosed disabilities and are 3 or 4 years of age. In addition, the school district for which Mr. Jason works contracts with Head Start, so some children in his classroom are eligible for that program.

The school district has chosen a curriculum-based assessment (CBA) called Help Children Grow and Learn to be used for planning instruction. Mr. Jason must administer the assessment to all the children in both his morning and afternoon preschool classrooms (18 and 16 children, respectively) within the first 45 days of the school year, beginning in August. Mr. Jason finds the idea of giving this test to so many children in a short amount of time overwhelming. In addition to being concerned about collecting all of the data, he's a bit concerned about the instrument itself. Mr. Jason was taught that a high-quality CBA should allow for the use of authentic assessment practices. However, the Help Children Grow and Learn CBA requires him to use direct testing as the primary way of collecting data on the children in his classroom. In addition, Mr. Jason is having difficulty determining how the CBA will help him plan instruction. The items on the Help Children Grow and Learn don't seem very functional to him. For example, there are items related to tasks such as stringing beads and putting puzzles together. Another of his concerns is that some of the children in his program are 3 or 4 years old but function developmentally at a much younger age. The Help Children Grow and Learn CBA was designed for children who are 3 to 5 years of age. Mr. Jason fears that the assessment will not yield any useful programming information for children who have developmental delays. With his concerns about the usefulness and sensitivity of the assessment in mind, Mr. Jason decides to approach the preschool director before school starts and seek guidance about selecting another assessment, as well as help on efficiently collecting and meaningfully using all of the data.

The situation described in the vignette highlights the difficulties that early childhood intervention teachers face when they conduct *assessments that promote development and learning* for program planning purposes. Program planning assessment can be defined simply as the process of determining *what, where,* and *how* to teach children. In order for high-quality program planning assessment to occur, programs need to utilize assessment tools that link assessment with instruction. In other words, the items on the assessment instrument must be items that teachers want their children to learn as part of the curriculum.

As described in Chapter 5, assessment tools are developed for particular purposes. Unfortunately, programs frequently utilize assessment instruments for programming that were intended for another purpose (e.g., screening, diagnosis, accountability). When assessment instruments that were not intended for programming are used for that purpose, teachers feel frustrated because there is no obvious link between what the assessment tells them about the children in their program and what they need to teach.

The purpose of this chapter is to describe recommended practices for program planning for individual children and groups. The chapter is divided into four sections. Section 1 defines and discusses assessment for program planning purposes. Section 2 provides information on selecting and administering a CBA for program planning purposes and discusses administration issues. Section 3 provides information on using information from CBAs to plan programs for individual children and groups, including how to summarize, analyze, and interpret results of the CBA. Lastly, Section 4 provides suggestions and strategies for making decisions around the needs of individual children and groups, setting priorities, and matching needs to instruction.

DEFINITION AND PURPOSES
OF ASSESSMENT FOR PROGRAM PLANNING

In Chapter 1, a curriculum framework was defined as a way of conceptualizing the practices in which early childhood intervention teachers engage to plan for, implement, and evaluate instruction. A curriculum framework includes four elements: assessment, scope and sequence, activities and instruction, and performance monitoring. The assessment element of the curriculum framework is for the purpose of program planning. Program planning is intended to guide instruction. Information gained from the assessment process for programming purposes serves as the baseline that allows educators to make appropriate instructional decisions. High-quality program planning is *comprehensive* in nature (meaning that information is assessed on all areas of development and content), and practices are *authentic* (meaning that information is gathered from multiple worthwhile, significant, and meaningful sources).

High-quality program planning assessment yields information on children's developmental status, their preferences, and the priorities and concerns of their families. In order to design effective instruction for all young children, educators need information about each of these factors. Table 7.1 summarizes the purposes for conducting program planning assessment and the specific types of information gained for each purpose.

In blended classrooms, the purposes for conducting assessment for program planning apply to both individual children and the group. Information on each child's developmental status can be used in combination with information gathered from the child's family to determine individualized outcomes for each child in the class. Information on each child's preferences, in combination with knowledge about routines that they enjoy, can be useful in individualizing instruction for children. For example, if a teacher finds out that a child likes to take baths and play in

Table 7.1. Purposes of Program Planning Assessment and Information Gained

Assessment Purposes	Information Gained
Developmental Status	• Children's performance across all areas of development (e.g., motor, adaptive, cognitive, communication, social)
	• Children's performance across all subject areas (e.g., Language Arts, Science, Social Studies, Math, Technology, Health)
	• Interrelatedness of development
	• Children's strengths, emerging skills, and needs
Interests and Preferences	• What motivates children
	• Children's preferred activities, toys/materials, people, and actions
	• What sustains children's interest, participation, and engagement
Priorities and Concerns	• Family and other familiar caregiver's perspective regarding a child's participation in daily routines and events
	• Priorities for families and other familiar caregivers

water, the teacher may consider using water play as an activity for teaching a high-priority skill such as sharing materials with peers. Furthermore, a child's preferences can assist teachers in selecting instructional strategies. If a child prefers instruction from certain teachers, support in a particular format (e.g., physical, verbal), or small-group versus large-group activities, teachers must consider these preferences when designing individualized instruction for the child.

Teachers also need to consider what program planning assessment data tell them collectively about the children in their classroom. As teachers examine assessment data, they should look for trends that provide guidance in designing curricular goals for the group of children with whom they are working during a given year. The assessment data will help them determine appropriate materials and activities to use with the children, based on the children's preferences. For example, a teacher may have a group of young 3-year-olds who have difficulty with basic social skills (e.g., sharing materials) and adaptive skills (e.g., opening their milk carton, washing their hands). The assessment data help the teacher design curricular activities that focus on social and adaptive outcomes for the children. The assessment might also assist the teacher in determining the interests of the children in order to teach relevant content. For example, if the teacher notices, while gathering assessment data, that the children really enjoy playing "grocery store," he or she might design activities focused on food, where it comes from, and how it is sold. Also, in any given school year, there may be priorities that children's families share. Perhaps a teacher has a group of children who will be entering kindergarten the following year. Those children's families might desire the curriculum to focus on early literacy skills that children need as they approach kindergarten.

CONDUCTING PROGRAM PLANNING ASSESSMENTS

A primary strategy for assessing all young children for program planning is to administer a CBA. As discussed in Chapter 5, a primary purpose of CBAs is to serve as a direct link between assessment and instructional efforts (i.e., to ensure that what is assessed is taught and vice versa). CBAs may also guide teachers in looking at children's overall development and interests and preferences during daily activities, as well as providing direct and indirect opportunities for families to discuss priorities and concerns. The National Early Childhood Technical Assistance Center (NECTAC) investigated the pros and cons of using CBAs. Some of the pros included yielding valid results due to the use of authentic assessment measures, being useful for ongoing intervention planning, providing accountability and progress monitoring, and being individualized in nature where accommodations are built into the environment. An unfortunate con of using CBAs for program planning is that often the whole system must change in order to promote full implementation (NECTAC, 2005). On the basis of their purpose and associated pros, CBAs are viable options in helping teachers gain needed information to plan and subsequently revise instruction. (See Chapter 8 on using a CBA to monitor children's performance over time and revise instruction.) The next section provides strategies and supports for selecting a CBA, reviews how to use a CBA Rating Rubric, and explains how to administer CBAs.

Selecting a CBA for Program Planning

Many different CBAs are available. For example, some CBAs have age expectations or "cutoff" scores, whereas others do not include such information. The absence of cutoff scores can make it difficult to establish developmental level if the assessor does not have a strong knowledge of child development. Some CBAs also require the assessor to have extensive training in order for the results to be reliable (NECTAC, 2005). Table 7.2 provides an overview of commonly used CBAs. The table's description of the assessment instrument includes skill areas covered, age ranges, uses, technology components, and advantages and disadvantages. Not all CBAs, however, help teachers plan intervention or instruction, Unfortunately, as mentioned in Chapter 5, many CBAs lack technical adequacy, are not sensitive to small changes in performance, do not provide strategies to involve families, fail to support family involvement (Bagnato, Neisworth, & Pretti-Frontczak, 2010; Brown & Hubbell, 2010).

CBA Rating Rubric

Pretti-Frontczak, Vilardo, and Kenneley (2005) created a rating rubric to guide teachers in selecting, implementing, and using high-quality CBAs for program planning purposes. The rubric allows teachers to rate the critical elements of various CBAs, including technical adequacy (i.e., reliability,

Table 7.2. Overview of commonly used early childhood intervention curriculum-based assessments

Name of Assessment	Description	Advantages	Disadvantages
Assessment, Evaluation, and Programming System for Infants and Young Children (AEPS), Second Edition Bricker et al. (2002)	• Assesses fine motor, gross motor, adaptive, cognitive, social-communication, and social areas of development. • Available in two age levels: birth–3, and 3–6. • Part of a linked system that utilizes the transdisciplinary team. • Includes curricular guides that provide ideas for how to teach each assessment item within classroom and home activities. • Technology features include a web based management system called the AEPS Interactive (http://apesinteractive.com).	• Can be used with children who are typically developing, those who are at-risk, and those with developmental delays. • Targets functional skills; child can use alternate behavior forms to demonstrate mastery of the skills. • Allows for adaptations for children with disabilities. • Data are collected using authentic assessment methods. • Has strong research bases to validate its use for specific and varied purposes.	• Given the comprehensive nature of the system, can be overwhelming, particularly for those without a strong background in child development. • Large number of components. • Requires a time investment.
The Carolina Curriculum for Preschoolers with Special Needs- CCPSN (2nd ed.) Johnson-Martin, Jens, Hacker, & Attermeier (2004)	• Assessment used for gaining information on a child's mastery level in 6 developmental domains including personal-social, cognition, communication, fine motor, and gross motor. • Assessment is divided into two age levels: 0–24 months and 24–60 months. • System directly links assessment items to curricular activities for children with special needs. • Provides special attention for children with atypical developmental pathways and serious impairments. • Technology features include assessment logs and developmental progress charts available on CD-Rom or online in PDF format.	• Produces information that is useful when developing goals/objectives. • Provides information on skills child has mastered, those that are emerging, and those the child has not yet developed. • Allows for adaptations for children with specific disabilities. • The latest revision of the Carolina made assessment items and related interventions continuous from birth to age 5 to meet the needs of preschool children developmentally functioning below 36 months in one or more domains.	• No specific component for family involvement. • Age scores are not validated. • Lacks research to demonstrate the reliability, validity, and utility of scores and inferences made.

154

Table 7.2   (continued)

Name of Assessment	Description	Advantages	Disadvantages
Creative Curriculum Developmental Continuum Assessment for Ages 3–5 Dodge, Colker, & Heroman (2002) Note: The included information is based on the *Creative Curriculum Developmental Continuum*. The revised assessment, *Teaching Strategies GOLD*, is replacing the Creative Curriculum. See www.teachingstrategies.com for more information.	• 10 goals and 50 objectives across social/ emotional, physical, cognitive, and language development domains. • Designed for children 3–5 years old. • Also has an infant/toddler version. • Includes curricular suggestions tied to each assessment item. • Technology features include a data management system (http://CreativeCurriculum.net).	• Can be used by a wide range of early childhood professionals, particularly those without a strong foundation in development and/or developmentally appropriate practices. • Uses authentic assessment methods.	• Limited evidence or research to support the use for program planning, analyzing and documenting child progress, or use for reporting OSEP outcomes. • Nature of the objectives without accommodations may make the assessment less appropriate for children with special needs.
HELP for Preschoolers Holt, Gilles, Holt, & Davids (2004)	• Covers cognitive, language, gross motor, fine motor, social, and self-help skills. • Comprised of two separate age levels: birth–3, and 3–6. • Includes materials for how to address each assessment item at home. • Technology features include a free score calculator for generating accountability reports. (http://lvort.com/osep).	• Can be used with different populations (children with disabilities, typically developing children, or children who are at-risk). • Can assist in determining child's present levels of performance. • Data can be collected using authentic assessment methods.	• Many items, so therefore large time investment. • Age scores are not validated and lacks research to demonstrate the reliability, validity, and utility of scores and inferences made.
HighScope Preschool Child Observation Record HighScope Educational Research Foundation (2002)	• Assesses 32 dimensions of learning (i.e., key experiences) in 6 categories including social relationships, creative representation, movement and music, language and literacy, mathematics, and science. • Assessment is comprised of two age levels: ages 6 weeks–3 years, and 3–5. • Curricular guidelines for each key experience. • Technology features include an online data management system (http://onlinecor.net).	• Looks broadly at all key areas of development, using a strength-based approach. • Process of gathering data takes place over a number of weeks, or months and requires no change in the child's daily routine. • Allows child to express self using alternative forms of expression.	• Users need a strong foundation in child development and the ability to document children's performance using narrative methods. • Lacks research to validate the *COR* for reporting OSEP outcomes. • Users might find that the *COR* is not sensitive enough to detect small increments of change in development.

(continued)

155

Table 7.2 (continued)

Name of Assessment	Description	Advantages	Disadvantages
The Ounce Scale Meisels, Marsden, Dombro, Weston, Jewkes (2003)	• Observational method used to assess a young child's growth and development in six developmental areas: personal connections, feelings about self, relationships with other children, understanding and communicating, exploration and problem solving, and movements and coordination. • Designed for children who are birth to 42 months. • Consists of three elements: the observational record, the family album, and the developmental profile. • Technology features include web-based data entry and electronic scoring (ounceonline.com).	• Family oriented tool that promotes collaboration among parents and professionals. • Gives "well-rounded" perspective on the child's development. • Can be used to meet IDEA Part C early intervention eligibility criteria.	• Scoring procedure may lend itself to subjectivity. • Additional research is needed to validate use for eligibility and accountability, particularly with children with disabilities.
Transdisciplinary Play Based Assessment, 2nd ed. *(TPBA-2)* Linder (2008)	• Used to gain a comprehensive look regarding a child's cognitive, social emotional, communication and language, and sensori-motor development through observation of play, and observation/interaction with a teacher or peer. • Technology features include a CD-ROM with forms and OSEP Reporting tool.	• Parents can serve as play facilitators, so the process is less intimidating for children. • Emphasis on transdisciplinary teaming. • Easy to use and does not require the use of a standard set of toys or materials. • Includes specific assessment items for children who use American Sign Language.	• Time consuming—total of 386 items which take 1–2 hours to administer. • Lacks sufficient research to support all intended and promoted purposes (e.g., identifying intervention targets, eligibility determination, and OSEP reporting).
Work Sampling System *(WSS)* Meisels, Jablon, Marsden, Dichtelmiller, & Dorfman (2004)	• Based on national and state standards and covers the following domains: personal and social, language and literacy, mathematical thinking, scientific thinking, social studies, the arts, and the physical development. • Can be used with children in pre-kindergarten through fifth grade. • Technology features include a data management system, online scoring, Summary Report completion, design lesson plans and class profiles (worksamplingonline.com).	• Several studies have validated its use as an effective curriculum-embedded assessment. • Incorporates different types of information to assist the teacher in deciphering the child's strengths and planning appropriate instruction. • Promotes collaboration among parents and professionals in sensible and friendly ways.	• Scoring procedure may lend itself to subjectivity. • Lacks evidence of validity and reliability for OSEP child outcome reporting.

validity), degree of family involvement, and appropriateness for children with diverse abilities. Appendix A contains a revised rubric that teachers can use as they review various CBAs to ensure that they are high quality and will meet their needs given the specific population of children they serve. The rubric in Appendix A was adapted from the work of Pretti-Frontczak et al. The revisions were based on a review of current research and recommendations of professional organizations (i.e., DEC, NAEYC) and include new elements regarding professional development, technology, and sensitivity. The rubric is composed of 12 elements: 1) alignment with federal/state/agency standards and/or outcomes, 2) collaboration, 3) comprehensive coverage, 4) equitable design, 5) family involvement, 6) multifactors, 7) professional development, 8) reliability, 9) sensitivity, 10) technology, 11) usefulness for intervention, and 12) validity. (See Appendix A for complete definitions of each element.)

The rubric is to be completed by a team of stakeholders that may include teachers, administrators, related service providers, and parents. Some aspects of the rubric (e.g., reliability, validity) may need to be completed by a member of the team who understands how to interpret psychometric properties. To use the rubric, the team selects a CBA to review, compares the assessment instrument with the stated criteria on the rubric, and decides which rating best describes the CBA. The 12 elements are rated using a Likert scale in which 0 = Unsatisfactory, 1 = Basic, 2 = Satisfactory, and 3 = Excellent. The team circles the rating directly on the rubric. A total score can also be calculated for each CBA that the team reviews. When the team is comparing CBAs in order to select one, it can focus on the assessments that received higher overall ratings. The team may want to consider which elements are most important and must achieve at least a Satisfactory rating. For example, a team may feel that, in order to be useful, a CBA must receive a Satisfactory rating for the criteria of validity, family involvement, and sensitivity to children with diverse abilities.

Given the current educational climate, which includes high expectations for quality instruction and children's readiness for kindergarten, teachers need to consider using an assessment instrument that is efficient and leads to meaningful instruction. Three elements may be of particular interest to teachers who are working in blended programs: alignment with federal/state/agency standards and/or outcomes, family involvement, and technology.

Alignment with Federal/State/Agency Standards and/or Outcomes

Increasingly, teachers are expected to generate data and reports for accountability purposes (see Chapter 9). In particular, accountability mandates in ECI center on producing data regarding children's performance toward agency (e.g., Head Start), state, and federal outcomes. One strategy that is designed to help teachers is to align assessment practices with targeted outcomes. Alignment considers the degree to which the assessment documents children's performance toward targeted outcomes. Alignment, also referred to as crosswalking, is the process of linking curriculum, assessment, classroom instruction, and learning to a set of standards that describes what children should know and be able to do. Some CBAs have been crosswalked with state standards. For example, Kentucky's Early Childhood State Standards have been crosswalked or aligned with 13 CBAs, including

- Assessment, Evaluation, and Programming System for Infants and Young Children (AEPS), Second Edition

- BRIGANCE (2004) Inventory of Early Development-II,

- The Carolina Curriculum for Preschoolers with Special Needs,

- The Creative Curriculum Developmental Continuum Assessment for Ages 3–5

- Hawaii Early Learning Profile

- Transdisciplinary Play-Based Assessment, Second Edition

Educational workgroups were formed to align the assessment items within each of the 13 CBAs with each Early Childhood Standard. In many instances, multiple assessment items were aligned with a single state standard. For example, the Creative Expression Standard 1 ("Demonstrates interest and participates in various forms of creative expression") and its Benchmark 1.1 ("Enjoys and engages in visual arts is aligned with two assessment items [i.e., shows an awareness of pictures and print (Steps 1–3), and experiments with drawing and writing (Steps 1–5)]") were found in the Creative Curriculum Developmental Continuum Assessment for Ages 3–5. In some cases, however, assessment items did not align with a particular state standard. For example, The Creative Curriculum Developmental Continuum Assessment for Ages 3–5 did not have items that aligned Benchmark 1.2 ("Enjoys and engages in music") or Benchmark 1.3 ("Enjoys and engages in movement and dance"), which both fall under the Creative Expression Standard 1 ("Demonstrates interest and participates in various forms of creative expression"). Teachers in Kentucky may choose one of the 13 CBAs to administer to each child in the classroom. Using information from the CBA and corresponding alignments, the teacher can begin to determine whether the child has met specific state standards (Rous & Townley, 2006). Box 7.1 provides examples and links to crosswalks that have been completed between assessment instruments and state, federal, and/or agency outcomes and standards.

Family Involvement

A child's family plays an important role in the assessment process. (Refer to Chapter 3.) Family members are the individuals who know the child best and have additional information to contribute to the CBA. Families also should have the ability to make decisions for their children regarding

---

BOX 7.1

Examples of crosswalks between assessment instruments and state, federal, and/or agency outcomes/standards

The Early Childhood Outcomes (ECO) Center has created assessment instrument crosswalks between the early childhood outcomes and the assessment items for the measures that are most commonly requested by states (e.g., Brigance IED-II, Creative Curriculum Developmental Continuum for Ages 3–5, HELP, WSS). http://www.fpg.unc.edu/~eco/pages/crosswalks.cfm#Crosswalks

The Creative Curriculum for Preschool and the Creative Curriculum Developmental Continuum for Ages 3–5 have been aligned with the Head Start Child Outcomes Framework and many states' early learning standards. http://www.teachingstrategies.com/page/CCPS_AlignStand.cfm

The Assessment, Evaluation, and Programming System (AEPS) has been aligned to many states' early learning standards and Office of Special Education Programs outcomes. http://www.aepsinteractive.com/state_standards.htm

---

program planning. Numerous tools can aid the teacher in gathering information about children from their families. Some examples are the *AEPS Family Report* (2nd ed.) (Bricker, Pretti-Frontczak, Johnson, & Straka, 2002), *Choosing Outcomes and Accommodations for Children (COACH): A Guide to Educational Planning for Students with Disabilities* (2nd ed.) (Giangreco, Cloninger, & Iverson, 1998), and *Reach for the Stars* (Haynes & Grisham-Brown, in press). Each tool can be used to gather specific information such as home routines, priorities for learning, and the child's developmental status from the family's perspective.

Technology

Technology is becoming integral to CBAs. Technology related to CBAs can be defined as any electronic and/or web-based feature that is designed to support the assessment process (Bagnato et al., 2010). Technology features can range from low-tech options such as online tutorials or interactive web sites from which additional materials may be downloaded to high-tech options such as software programs that allow data to be stored, managed, and interpreted for use in program planning. Several programs (e.g., AEPSinteractive, CreativeCurriculum.net) can interface with state databases for reporting accountability. Some technology supports the link between assessment and instruction (i.e., the intent of assessment to assist with summarizing, interpreting, planning, and revising instruction). For example, the AEPSinteractive, a data management system for the AEPS, a common CBA, includes features such as scoring the AEPS Test; tracking, displaying, and recording a child's progress over time; providing eligibility reports for special education services; and creating customized individual and group reports to aid in planning and revising instruction.

Administering CBAs

Although CBAs are the most logical way to conduct assessment for program planning purposes, they involve two administration issues that must be addressed. First, CBAs are intended to be administered using authentic assessment strategies (i.e., observation, interview) in a child's natural environment, with materials that are familiar to the child. Given that there are clear parameters for administering CBAs, consideration should be given to the fidelity with which teachers conduct the assessment. Second, experience has shown that teachers sometime need support in gathering data on all CBA items. As a result, assessment activities are suggested as a method for gathering data on individuals or groups of children. We will discuss determining fidelity of administration and using assessment activities next.

Assessment Fidelity

The term *fidelity* often refers to instructional efforts and is commonly defined "as the determination of how well an intervention is implemented in comparison with the original program design during an efficacy and/or effectiveness study" (O'Donnell, 2008, p. 33). Issues surrounding fidelity, however, be they related to adherence, duration, quality, or program differentiation, are important when it comes to assessment practices (Grisham-Brown, Hallam, & Pretti-Frontczak, 2008). In other words, evidence is needed that an assessment such as a CBA is administered, summarized, interpreted, and used in the way that it was designed, intended, and validated:

> Fidelity of implementation of assessment helps to avoid having learners be provided a tier or level of instruction only to discover that it was a misguided decision due to lack of proper selection and/or use of assessment devises [sic] and practices . . . . A high level of assessment fidelity relates directly to more accurate decisions concerning the best method of choice for level, duration, and intensity of instruction for all learners." (Hoover, 2009, p. 52)

As stated by Montana's Office of Public Instruction (n.d.),

> Data that are generated by assessments can only be as reliable as the extent to which the assessments are implemented in a consistent and standardized way. Again, without measuring the fidelity of assessment implementation, it is not possible to evaluate student responses to any degree of reliability. Student test results depend on assessments being implemented and scored correctly. Ways to check integrity of assessment implementation include assessor checklists, outside observation, and random checks of scoring accuracy. Of course, initial training for an assessment tool should include practice sessions to achieve competency in administering the assessment. Periodic "booster sessions" in which assessors are retrained on assessments are an important way to prevent "drift" in the way that assessments are implemented and scored.

Variable	Indicators of Authentic Assessment Procedures	Indicators of Non authentic Assessment Procedures	Score
Set up and Preparation	❑ Assessment activity is set up within typical class-room environment/ routine (e.g., at the snack table, on the playground, at the reading corner). ❑ Teacher is familiar with the activity as evidenced by the flow (e.g., children are engaged; there are not long pauses in the activity; teacher refers to the activity protocol mostly for data recording purposes). ❑ Activity follows a plan or seems organized and items targeted seem appropriate to the activity.	❑ Assessment activity is set up outside the typical classroom environment/ routine (e.g., in hallway or empty room). ❑ Teacher is unfamiliar with the activity as evidenced by the flow (e.g., children are disengaged; there are long pauses in the activity, teacher constantly refers to the activity protocol). ❑ Activity does not seem to follow any set plan or organization and items targeted seem inappropriate to the activity.	0 1 2 3

Figure 7.1. Sample portion from an authentic assessment activity fidelity measure. (From Pretti-Frontczak, K. [2009]. *Authentic Assessment Fidelity Meausre*. Reprinted by permission from Center for Excellence in Early Childhood Research and Training web site, http://www.ehhs.kent.edu/ ceecrt/ index.php/research/current)

There may be any number of reasons that CBAs are not completed with fidelity. Teachers may find the actual implementation of a CBA to be overwhelming, particularly in classrooms where large amounts of data have to be collected on many children. Sometimes teachers lack the training or support to administer the CBA. In such a situation, the teacher may become frustrated and implement the assessment with low fidelity. Finally, if teachers do not understand the usefulness of the CBA, they may reluctantly use it but not as it was intended.

The likelihood that teachers complete CBAs with fidelity will increase if they are given 1) adequate support; 2) sufficient training; and 3) information regarding the usefulness of the CBA for identifying children's goals, curriculum planning, and progress monitoring. Grisham-Brown and colleagues (2008) used a fidelity measure to determine the assessment fidelity of Head Start teachers who used the AEPS. Figure 7.1 contains a sample of the measure, which rated the fidelity with which teachers *set up and prepared* assessment activities (i.e., the extent to which observations occurred in natural activities), selected *materials* that were part of natural activities, used *procedures* that elicited assessment items in a natural way, made *decisions* that allowed children to demonstrate behavior in numerous ways, *embedded* opportunities for child responses related to the activities in which they were engaged, and allowed for *child choice* about activities. A complete copy of the authentic assessment fidelity measure is available at http://www.ehhs.kent.edu/ceecrt/wp-content/uploads/2008/12/procedural-reliability-final.pdf. Again, decisions made from CBAs are only as credible and trustworthy as the data that guide them. Therefore, teachers must

---

BOX 7.2

Common pitfalls and remedies for increasing assessment fidelity

Pitfall 1: Most ECI assessments, even those with standardized procedures, do not include administration checklists that can be used for integrity/fidelity checks.

Remedies:
- Use the authentic assessment fidelity measure by Grisham-Brown and colleagues (2008).
- Use the checklist designed by Hoover (2009) to determine the degree to which the assessment itself, the assessment practices, and assessment accommodations (if applicable) were followed.
- Develop a fidelity measure that relates to procedures of the assessment being used by your program.
- Review procedures (often stated in the manual) ahead of time and avoid deviating from the directions, particularly for standardized tests.

Pitfall 2: Teams administer assessments without sufficient training or ongoing support.

Remedies:
- Build opportunities for frequent checks by "experts" for scoring accuracy and correct administration and use.
- Utilize a coaching system in which teachers check one another and provide support for those who are new to using the assessment.
- Engage in ongoing professional development to ensure accuracy in scoring and use and avoid drift over time.
- Keep up to date with changes in the assessment being used, including securing revised editions and/or new features as they become available.

---

make a concerted effort to avoid factors that lead to a lack of assessment fidelity. (See Box 7.2 for common pitfalls and remedies for increasing assessment fidelity.)

Assessment Activities

One way to make collecting information for a CBA more efficient is to collect data during pre-established assessment activities (Grisham-Brown, Hallam, & Brookshire, 2006; Grisham-Brown, Hemmeter, & Pretti-Frontczak, 2005). Assessment activities are semistructured events that allow teams to use observation as the primary method of gathering information. The intent is to structure observations by embedding assessment instrument items into commonly occurring home and classroom activities. Teachers can create assessment activities for individuals or groups of children. First, teachers identify activities that are motivating and interesting to young children and that offer opportunities for the teacher to observe skills related to several areas of development/content (i.e., many items from the CBA). Next, teachers embed skills that they would like to assess into the identified activities. Skills selected should be ones that can logically be observed during the selected activities. For example, teachers would likely observe certain adaptive skills (e.g., pouring liquids, eating

Examiner:	
AEPS Level: II	
Group Name:	Sample Level II
Status:	
Test Date:	02/17/2010 (mm/dd/yyyy)

Short Description:
story time provides opportunity to assess skills such as establishing joint attention, functional use of reading materials, locating objects, and sounding out words.

SYMBOL KEYS

Child's Name:	Damien Roberts	Bob Wire
Date of Birth:	07/09/03	09/22/05
Area: Cognitive	IFSP IEP S N	IFSP IEP S N
C. Sequencing		
⊞ 3. Retells event in sequence	☐ ☐ ☐ 🔘	☐ ☐ ☐ 🔘
⊞ 3.1 Completes sequence of familiar story or event	☐ ☐ ☐ 🔘	☐ ☐ ☐ 🔘
F. Play		
⊞ 1. Engages in cooperative, imaginary play [N]	☐ ☐ ☐ 🔘	☐ ☐ ☐ 🔘
⊞ 1. Enacts roles or identities	☐ ☐ ☐ 🔘	☐ ☐ ☐ 🔘
⊞ 1.2 Plans and acts out recognizable events	☐ ☐ ☐ 🔘	☐ ☐ ☐ 🔘
⊞ 1.3 Uses imaginary props	☐ ☐ ☐ 🔘	☐ ☐ ☐ 🔘
H. Phonological Awareness and Emergent Reading		
⊞ 1. Demonstrates phonological awareness skills [N]	☐ ☐ ☐ 🔘	☐ ☐ ☐ 🔘
⊞ 1.1 Uses rhyming skills	☐ ☐ ☐ 🔘	☐ ☐ ☐ 🔘
⊞ 1.2 Segments sentences and words	☐ ☐ ☐ 🔘	☐ ☐ ☐ 🔘
⊞ 1.3 Blends single sounds and syllables	☐ ☐ ☐ 🔘	☐ ☐ ☐ 🔘
⊞ 1.4 Identifies same and different sounds at the beginning and end of words	☐ ☐ ☐ 🔘	☐ ☐ ☐ 🔘
⊞ 2. Uses letter-sound association to sound out and write words [N]	☐ ☐ ☐ 🔘	☐ ☐ ☐ 🔘
⊞ 2.1 Writes words using letter sounds	☐ ☐ ☐ 🔘	☐ ☐ ☐ 🔘
⊞ 2.2 Sounds out words	☐ ☐ ☐ 🔘	☐ ☐ ☐ 🔘
⊞ 2.3 Produces correct sounds for letters	☐ ☐ ☐ 🔘	☐ ☐ ☐ 🔘

Save Test In Progress   Finalize Area

Figure 7.2. An example of an assessment activity administered during storytime. (From AEPSinteractive™ Storybook Samples, http://www.aepsinteractive.com; reprinted by permission.)

with utensils), social skills (e.g., initiating interactions, sharing materials), and social-communication skills (e.g., requesting assistance, answering questions) during snack time. After they have identified skills that may be embedded into selected activities, teachers choose materials that might be needed in order to observe the identified skills. For example, if teachers want to observe whether children pour liquids at snack time, they will need to have pitchers of preferred drinks and cups for pouring. Figure 7.2 shows an example of an assessment protocol for observing developmental skills during a storytime routine.

Teachers can plan assessment activities across the classroom routine to elicit information from groups of children. The assessment activities should be part of the classroom schedule. Teachers may elect to make two or three activities per week available as a way to elicit specific items from their CBA. Children should not be forced to participate in the activities, but when they decide to participate in an assessment activity, an adult can collect data on CBA items that are embedded in that particular activity. For example, if a group of children are playing with playdough, the observer could gather information regarding children's fine motor skills (e.g., removing lid from playdough), social/communication skills (e.g., asking for assistance), and concept knowledge (e.g., naming colors of playdough, identifying numbers on cookie cutters). The teacher also may want to assign specific team members to these centers to collect data (Grisham-Brown et al., 2006). He or she may place a teaching assistant in the writing center, a teacher in the art center, and an occupational therapist in the manipulative center.

Sometimes teachers may need to conduct an assessment activity during which various team members observe a child during a common activity. For example, if a team is trying to determine whether a child who is learning multiple languages has a language delay or whether a child who is having difficulty participating during a small-group activity needs a different type of instruction, a team approach may lead to greater insight. The teacher may use a transdisciplinary approach to collect data (Grisham-Brown, 2000) and may also use an assessment activity to guide the teams' observations and subsequent conclusions. The teacher would facilitate an assessment activity and invite all of the needed service providers (e.g., speech and language pathologist [SLP], occupational therapist, physical therapist [PT]) to observe the child. During the assessment activity, such as playing with playdough, the SLP could collect data on social/communication skills, the occupational therapist could collect data on fine motor skills, and the PT could collect data on gross motor skills, while the teacher collects data on concept knowledge.

Although the SLP may focus on social-communication skills and the PT may focus on gross motor skills, the transdisciplinary model encourages cross-role observations. For example, if the SLP notices that the child is using an abnormal movement pattern during the playdough activity, he or she would note it. Or if the PT notices that the child is making articulation errors in communications to peers while playing with playdough, he or she would note that. Using this model, team members provide input not only from their own domain, but other domains as well. With a transdisciplinary assessment approach, the teacher and therapists work and collaborate as a team, which is the best practice for collecting assessment data for programming purposes. Once the team has conducted the assessment through cross-role observations and has reached decisions about what skills to target, members can engage in role release for teaching the target skills. As a team, members can engage in role-release after target skills have been developed for the child. For example, the SLP may demonstrate specific skills to the teacher, such as how to produce the initial /l/ sound, and then the teacher can embed that skill within activities and routines across the child's day (Hawkins & Schuster, 2007). Similarly, the PT may demonstrate or model a specific positioning technique for a student and the teacher then can embed that technique within classroom activities and routines.

Parents also should be involved in role-release. If the therapist can model to the parents specific skills, then those skills will be addressed not only during the school day but in the home as well (Jung & Grisham-Brown, 2006).

USING INFORMATION FROM CBAs TO PROGRAM PLAN

As we noted earlier in this chapter, when teachers complete a CBA for program planning purposes, they should obtain and document information regarding children's overall development, their interests and preferences, and family priorities and concerns. To avoid the temptation of completing a CBA, putting it in the child's folder, and then planning instruction that is based on a holiday, favorite book, season, or idea discussed during an in-service rather than on elements suggested by the CBA, teachers must recognize that program planning involves much more than the completion of a CBA. The teacher must now finish the process by summarizing the information, analyzing patterns and trends, interpreting (i.e., explaining findings), and making a series of critical decisions. Specifically, teachers need to make decisions regarding the needs and priorities of individuals and groups of children and the level of instruction that is required to address these needs and priorities. Thus, the sections that follow provide suggestions and strategies for the other steps of a data-driven decision-making (DDDM) process for planning instruction (i.e., summarizing, analyzing, and interpreting the data). Appendix B contains a case study that demonstrates how one teacher engaged in a five-step DDDM process using a CBA. (See Chapter 2 for descriptions of, and strategies for, the first two steps, *gathering* (e.g., observing, interviewing, reviewing artifacts) and *documenting* data; see Chapter 8 for descriptions of, and strategies for, DDDM regarding performance monitoring.

DDDM Step 3: Summarizing

The information that is gathered and documented with a CBA must be summarized using a variety of methods and for both individual children and groups of children. Often, teachers will find that using a combination of summary strategies helps them make more accurate and less biased decisions. For example, they may assume from the many notes they've written that several children are presenting challenging behaviors, yet when they summarize the number of times that these behaviors occurred and the number of children who presented such behaviors, they may find that just two of the children exhibited challenging behaviors at such a high rate that it gave the appearance that more children were "misbehaving." Furthermore, mixing and matching summaries can lead to greater clarity that helps the teachers share the information with families and other team members. There are three main ways teachers can summarize information to guide program planning for individual and groups of children: numerical summaries, narrative summaries, and visual summaries. Again, using a combination of summaries helps teachers obtain a complete picture of children's performance and abilities.

Numerical Summaries

It may be necessary for teachers to reduce and consolidate the vast amounts of data documented on a CBA by creating numerical summaries. In other words, many CBAs are composed of hundreds of discrete skills, and making sense of who can do what or who needs to learn what can be overwhelming. Often, numerical summaries such as total numbers, averages, and/or percentages can aid in making sense of the data that are collected. For example, numerical summaries may include the total number of times a child performed a behavior across a set period of time (e.g., day, week, month), the number of activities during which the child performed the skill, the percentage of times the behavior was demonstrated correctly, or the percentage of words spoken by the child that were understood by others. Numbers in general, however, can be misleading. For example, summarizing a child's performance as an age equivalency (Chapter 6) or a percentile rank (Chapter 5) may lead to misunderstandings and short-change the rich behavioral repertoire of a child or group of children by reducing their performance to a number. Numerical summaries should be used in conjunction with narrative and/or visual summaries to provide the most meaning and guide program planning.

Narrative Summaries

As described in Chapter 2, there are a number of ways to document children's performance using written narratives (e.g., anecdotal notes). Written narratives can be combined into a single report to describe a child's performance across activities and events. In other words, as a teacher reviews CBAs for a child or a group of children, he or she may write several sentences that summarize strengths (e.g., "Data for all of the children suggest independence and consistency with following the daily routine."), emerging skills (e.g., "The 3-year-olds all need frequent reminders and models for how to prepare food at snack time."), and areas of concern (e.g., "A number of the children use objects functionally but were not observed using them to represent other objects or during cooperative play."). Teachers can also use narrative summaries to describe numbers (e.g., raw scores, percentages, total numbers, frequency counts, length of time recorded) or products such as drawings, pictures of structures the children have built, or clay figures made by children. For example, a teacher might take information from how a CBA was completed (including the numbers, notes, and artifacts) and create a narrative summary that describes how children selected which materials they wanted to use during art, how they negotiated where to stand or sit, which words and sentences they used during the activity, and any concerns that were observed.

Narrative summaries can be informative but are time consuming to create. They are, however, useful for sharing information about children with other team members and are necessary for analyzing patterns and trends. When teachers create a narrative summary, it is important for them to write specific, objective statements and avoid jargon, labels, or judgments. For example, a narrative summary that includes statements such as "the child can request food by pointing to desired items," "the child imitates a few two- and three-word phrases," or "the child is starting to draw and paint simple shapes such as crosses and circles" are preferable to statements such as "the child is overly active," "the child loves to play in the water," or "the child has a severe speech delay."

Visual Summaries

It is often said that a picture is worth a thousand words; thus, a powerful way to summarize CBAs is visually. Visual summaries include graphs, diagrams, and permanent products such as writing samples and photographs. For example, to describe a child's performance, a teacher can show the number of acquired skills, emerging skills, and skills that are not yet mastered in a bar graph. The teacher also can use permanent products to document mastered skills or skills that still need to be targeted. For example, the teacher may notice that the child wrote his or her name at the top of a piece of artwork in the wrong direction; therefore, writing letters from left to right may be a target area for the child, and the artwork may serve as a physical documentation of this need. Skill levels may also be recorded in photographs. The teacher may photograph the child in the writing center holding the writing implement incorrectly; therefore, holding a writing implement appropriately may be a skill to target. "Engaging in regular data-based decision making by collecting, graphing, and interpreting data is a significant and meaningful way to fully engage in the process of intentional, systematic, and effective intervention" (Gischlar, Hojnoski, & Missall, 2009, p. 3). "Organizing child performance data into graphic displays can promote the systematic use of data in educational decision-making, which enhances outcomes for all students" (Gischlar et al., p. 16). Graphs can easily be generated using a computer program or by hand. (See Gischlar et al. for specific directions for creating and interpreting graphs.) After information has been summarized visually in a graph, teachers can see whether a child's performance is consistent or not, occurs at a high level or low level, and is increasing or decreasing.

DDDM Step 4: Analyzing

After data have been documented and summarized, teachers are ready to analyze. Analysis is a process of inspecting data with the goal of highlighting useful information, suggesting conclusions, and subsequently supporting decisions. In other words, analysis is a process of looking at summarized data for patterns and trends. *Patterns* are events that reoccur, typically in a

predictable manner. For example, if every time a teacher asks a child to follow a simple direction like "put the toys away" the child falls to the ground
and cries, that is a pattern. Patterns can indicate strengths as well as areas
of concern. For example, a child's eager participation in any activity that
involves movement or music is a pattern of successful behavior. If a child
always needs teacher assistance to open doors or jars, take off the caps of
markers, or prepare food at snack time, that might be a pattern regarding
a need for assistance. There may also be patterns in terms of whether a
child is performing skills in the order and at a rate that is expected for the
child's age and family context or whether a child exhibits an atypical pattern of development. In general, teachers should look for patterns regarding when children are successful; which toys, materials, and/or situations
they prefer or choose to engage in; when they need predictable levels of
assistance or direction; when they are able to do something functionally
but the quality of their performance is poor; and, lastly, when challenging
behaviors such as acting out, ignoring, or refusing are likely to occur.

Analysis of summaries from CBAs also involves looking for *trends*.
Trends have to do with the general direction in which a value tends to
move (up, down, first up and then down, no movement, etc.). For example, if the number of times that a child cries when asked to put toys
away decreases, a trend is observed. Analysis is most commonly done
through visual inspection, but can also be done by comparing a child's
score with the mean of a normative group or criterion set forth in a measure (e.g., with a cutoff score), and/or through discussion with team members during which predictable actions by the children are recognized and
discussed. Gischlar and colleagues (2009) provide useful strategies for analyzing graphed data. Box 7.3 provides even simpler ways of looking at
graphed data to make decisions. Additional illustrations are given in the
case example found in Appendix B of this chapter and Appendix A of
Chapter 8.

DDDM Step 5: Interpreting

The final step related to program planning is to make meaning of all the
hard work that was involved in gathering, documenting, summarizing,
and analyzing data and information using a CBA. The final step, interpreting, is defined as explaining results or making sense of the information
(i.e., making sense of the patterns and trends). The types of decisions that
are made on the basis of the interpretations will vary according to purpose.
For example, interpretations of patterns and trends from CBA summaries
that are designed to guide instruction should lead to decisions regarding
who needs to learn what, whether certain outcomes are of a higher priority than others, and what type and level of instruction are needed, again
for both individual children and groups of children. The types of decisions
that are made when monitoring children's performance (i.e., when monitoring initial decisions regarding instruction) are described in Chapter 8.

BOX 7.3

**Suggestions for analyzing graphed data to plan
and subsequently revise instruction**

Before instruction:

- Examine the trend in the child's performance. Determine whether the behavior is increasing, decreasing, or not changing much. In other words, determine whether the line representing the child's performance is going up, going down, or staying the same.

- Calculate the child's mean performance. Add the number of times that a child demonstrated a particular behavior, divide the total by the number of days or sessions observed, and multiply by 100.

- Determine whether the child's performance is different or is staying consistent from observation to observation (i.e., day to day). If the line representing the child's performance has large peaks and deep valleys (e.g., the child doesn't perform the behavior one day, then performs the behavior 29 times the second day, 2 times the third day, and 15 times the fourth day), the behavior is considered variable. If the line representing the child's performance is fairly flat, the child's performance is considered stable (i.e., peaks and valleys aren't big). For example, if the child performed the behavior 1 time, then 2 times, then 1 time, then 2 times, the behavior would be considered stable.

After instruction:

- Again, examine the trend and determine whether there has been a change in direction and steepness. In other words, determine whether the line representing the child's performance has changed direction quickly or sharply after instruction was initiated.

- Again, examine the child's mean performance. Determine whether the mean is larger, smaller, or the same as before instruction was initiated.

- Again, determine whether the child's performance is variable (sharp peaks and valleys) or stable.

- Examine changes in level by comparing the line representing the child's behavior before and after instruction. As indicated by Gischlar et al. (2009), there are specific procedures for calculating the level; however, a less technical and more straightforward way to think about the level is to consider the space under the line before and after instruction. The greater the space, the greater the change in the child's performance.

- Examine how quickly the child's behavior did or did not change before and after instruction (i.e., determine the amount of time elapsed before instruction was provided and the point at which there began to be a change in the child's performance). The sooner there is a change in the child's performance, the greater is the indication that the instruction is having the desired effect.

Before teachers can act on what they have concluded from patterns and trends that were generated from summaries, they need to make sure that their interpretations are based on sufficient and accurate data. See Box 7.4 for examples of related and mediating factors that should be considered regarding steps taken to summarize, analyze, and interpret. After the teacher is confident that sufficient and accurate data were gathered, documented, summarized, and interpreted, he or she can make program planning decisions with confidence. The next section describes the decisions that teachers make in terms of planning instruction.

BOX 7.4

Questions to ask regarding related and mediating factors

- Was the CBA completed with fidelity?
- Were sufficient amounts of information collected to create rich summaries?
- Were summaries objective and free from bias?
- Did summaries provide a complete picture of the child or groups of children within the context of their family and community?
- During the analysis of patterns and trends, were factors such as attendance, change in medications, exposure to other therapies, fidelity of implementation, and health status considered?
- Was the influence of family and culture considered?
- Was the interrelatedness and interdependence of development considered?

Making Data-Driven Decisions for Program Planning

After teachers have made meaning (i.e., interpreted findings) from the CBAs, they are ready to begin planning instruction for individuals and groups of children. Regardless of how information is gathered, what information is gathered, or even how the information is summarized, if it isn't used to plan and guide instruction, then the process is a waste of the teacher's time and provides no advantage for young children. Thus, assessment information must be used to determine 1) who needs to learn what; 2) which skills, concepts, and dispositions are a priority; and 3) how to match instruction to identified need. Each decision is described in the discussion that follows.

Identifying Needs

Deciding who needs to learn what (that is, identifying needs for individuals and groups of children) is a necessary step for planning instruction. The more experienced the teacher, the more automatic the process will become; however, teachers who are new to the field may need to use a key part of their planning time (or to secure planning time) in order to "sort" children's needs. Creating an image of a tiered model or similar type of figure may help teachers identify and sort children's needs. At the bottom tier are common or universal outcomes that all children need to learn. Tier 1 needs are derived from federal outcomes, state standards, and developmental milestones that are considered to be appropriate for a given age group. When a child's needs are identified as Tier 1, it means that their development and growth is considered on track. Tier 2 needs are demonstrated when a preschooler has difficulty with a means of expression, is challenged by a component of a larger or more sophisticated concept or skill, or appears to have stalled growth or growth that is affected by a related set of concepts or skills (e.g., child counts repeatedly only to 5 and may need instruction on sequencing or recall in order to make further gains in counting). Tier 3 needs indicate that a child may be missing a foundational or prerequisite skill or concept that is keeping the child from accessing, participating, and making progress toward common outcomes. For example, a child may throw a tantrum every

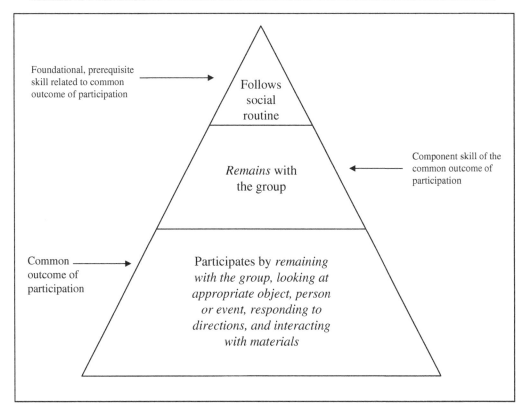

Foundational, prerequisite
skill related to common
outcome of participation

Follows
social
routine

Remains with
the group

Component skill of the
common outcome of
participation

Common
outcome of
participation

Participates by *remaining
with the group, looking at
appropriate object, person
or event, responding to
directions, and interacting
with materials*

Figure 7.3.   An example of sorting children's needs within a tiered model.

time that he or she is asked to follow a social routine, may lack joint attention or conversational turn taking, or still may be working on reaching and
grasping objects even though the child is of preschool age. When a child is
missing a foundational, prerequisite, or prosocial/age-appropriate skill, he
or she is demonstrating a Tier 3 need. Figure 7.3 provides one example of a
tiered model of sorting children's needs.

Prioritizing Needs

After the needs of individual children or groups are sorted, teachers may find
that several children have many Tier 2 and Tier 3 needs or even that a single
child has many such needs. Given the complexities of blended classrooms, it
is impossible for teachers to provide the instruction that is required to address
higher tiered needs when they have numerous Tier 2 and 3 needs for multiple children; thus, teachers should prioritize where to begin instruction.

When a teacher sets priorities for individuals and groups of children, he
or she has to determine outcomes that are a priority for all team members
and that will benefit the child in the home and community, as well as deciding what the child needs in order to access, participate, and make progress
in the classroom. Teachers may rely on developmental sequences to help
them prioritize pedagogical or logical sequences. *Sequence* refers to the order
in which skills and concepts across developmental and content areas are

taught or learned. When they are using developmental sequences to help prioritize, teachers should consider milestones and expected patterns of growth and learning in order to determine what a child may be ready to learn next. In other words, a team may prioritize engaging in cooperative play with objects as a Tier 3 need for a particular child, but may realize that the child is still learning to use toys for their intended purposes and is not yet ready for cooperative play with objects. Thus, the team must refocus its priorities and reconsider its decision about where to begin instruction. Pedagogical sequences are based on research and experience and describe how best to teach a particular skill or concept (e.g., rhyming). Again, teachers should consider the child's current abilities and then, using pedagogical sequences, prioritize which skills to target first (e.g., first alliteration, then segmenting and blending, then letter–sound correspondence). Lastly, teachers should consider logical sequences, which may not necessarily follow developmental expectations or pedagogical suggestions. Instead, they occur through a natural process as the teacher recognizes a necessary place to begin instruction for a given child's culture, experience, and need.

Matching Instruction to Children's Needs

After deciding on priorities for instruction, teachers are ready to consider the type and frequency of instructional efforts that they will implement. The level of intensity and frequency of instruction should match the level of the child's need. For example, more individualized, intensive, and intentional instruction should be provided for a Tier 3 need. Teachers should use a variety of evidence-based instructional strategies (from nondirected to directed again, matching frequency and intensity with level of need).

The bottom tier (Tier 1) is the set of skills that a child is likely to learn through incidental instruction at home and in any center-based program. These skills are part of the general curriculum in center-based programs and are the focus of instruction for all young children. For example, parents and teachers constantly talk about numbers, colors, and shapes as they interact with children, play on the playground, and engage in routine activities throughout the day. Within this tier, children do not receive any individualized instruction; the instruction is universally given to all children.

The second tier (Tier 2) includes skill needs of children for whom mere "exposure" is not enough. In that situation, the teacher may need to provide targeted instruction. This type of instruction includes additional learning opportunities and scaffolding to enhance the child's capacity to learn the skill. For example, the teacher may note that a child is not acquiring numbers through everyday instruction during circle time; therefore, the teacher provides additional opportunities to embed number instruction across activities and routines.

Sometimes, even with extra exposure and more frequent teaching opportunities, children do not learn a skill that they need. Under these circumstances, the teacher may move to Tier 3 and identify the skill as one that requires *intensive, intentional, individualized* instruction. The teacher must determine under what circumstances a child will be taught the skill (i.e., what the teacher will do to set the occasion for the child to learn the skill), consequences that will be provided during instruction, and how often the skill will be targeted across activities and routines. The determination of the skills that require this level of instruction will depend on the severity of the child's disability, the extent to which the child needs to learn the skill in order to participate in activities and routines, and the age of the child. After the team decides that the child has a Tier 3 need, it can then use that need to develop objectives for the child's Individual Education Plan (IEP) or Individualized Family Service Plan (IFSP). Because instruction has been intentionally planned and is intensive and individualized to the child, various components of the IEP or IFSP describe how often the child will receive instruction, where instruction will take place, what the specially designed instruction will look like, and what the actual objectives are. All of this information is useful to the team that is working to develop an IEP/IFSP for a child with a Tier 3 need.

SUMMARY

The purpose of Chapter 7 was to describe recommended practices for program planning for individuals and groups of children. First, the chapter defined and discussed assessment for program planning purposes. Next, we provided information on how to select and administer a CBA for program planning purposes and how to administer it with fidelity. We covered a review of CBAs and how to use a CBA Rating Rubric to choose and administer the assessment. Information was provided on using information from CBAs to program plan for individuals and groups of children, including how to summarize, analyze patterns and trends, interpret findings, and make decisions that are based on the results. When the CBA is holistically summarized, it provides the team with information on all areas of a child's development, interests, preferences, and family priorities and concerns. Lastly, the chapter included suggestions and strategies for making decisions around the needs and priorities of individuals and groups of children and matching needs to instruction. We concluded with a description of how to interpret, prioritize, and sort needs using a tiered system to match the instruction to the individual needs of the child or group of children.

REFERENCES

Bagnato, S.J., Neisworth, J.T., & Pretti-Frontczak, K. (2010). *LINKing authentic assessment and early childhood intervention: Best measures for best practices* (2nd ed.). Baltimore: Paul H. Brookes Publishing Co.

Bricker, D.D., Capt, B., Pretti-Frontczak, K., Johnson, J., Slentz, K., Straka, E., et al. (2002). *The Assessment, Evaluation and Programming System (AEPS) for infants and young children: AEPS test for birth to three years and three to six years* (2nd ed.). Baltimore: Paul H. Brookes Publishing Co.

Brigance, A.H. (2004). *BRIGANCE Inventory of Early Development-Second Edition (IED-II)*. North Billerica, MA: Curriculum Associates.

Brown, T., & Hubbell, S.P. (2010, January). *Evidence-base of commonly-used assessments in early childhood special education.* Center for Excellence in Early Childhood Research and Training, Kent State University, Kent, OH. Retrieved May 23, 2010, from http://www.ehhs.kent.edu/ceecrt/wp-content/uploads/2008/12/procedural-reliability-final.pdf

Giangreco, M.F., Cloninger, C.J., & Iverson, V.S. (1998). *Choosing Outcomes and Accommodations for Children (COACH): A guide to educational planning for students with disabilities* (2nd ed.). Baltimore: Paul H. Brookes Publishing Co.

Gischlar, K.L., Hojnoski, R.L., & Missall, K.N. (2009). Improving child outcomes with data-based decision making: Interpreting and using data. *Young Exceptional Children, 13*(2), 2–18.

Grisham-Brown, J., Hallam, R., & Brookeshire, R. (2006). Using authentic assessment to evidence children's progress toward early learning standards. *Early Childhood Education Journal, 34*(1), 45–51.

Grisham-Brown, J., Hemmeter, M.L., & Pretti-Frontczak, K. (2005). *Blended practices for teaching young children in inclusive settings.* Baltimore: Paul H. Brookes Publishing Co.

Grisham-Brown, J.L. (2000). Transdisciplinary activity-based assessment for young children with multiple disabilities: A program planning approach. *Young Exceptional Children, 3,* 3–10.

Hawkins, S., & Schuster, J. (2007). Using a mand-model procedure to teach preschool children initial speech sounds. *Journal of Developmental and Physical Disabilities, 19*(1), 65–80.

Haynes, D.G., & Grisham-Brown, J. (in press). *Reach for the stars: A transition process for families of young children.* Louisville, KY: American Printing House for the Blind.

Hoover, J.J. (2009). *RTI assessment essentials for struggling learners.* Thousand Oaks, CA: Sage.

Jung, L.A., & Grisham-Brown, J.L. (2006). Moving from assessment information to IFSPs: Guidelines for a family-centered process. *Young Exceptional Children, 9*(2), 2–11.

Montana's Office of Public Instruction retrieved February 6, 2010, from http://opi.mt.gov/Pub/RTI/EssentialComponents/Fidelity/Reading/Resources/Fidelity.pdf

NECTAC. (2005). *Norm-referenced versus curriculum-based assessment tools.* Retrieved December 23, 2010, from http://www.nectac.org/topics/quality/childfam.asp

O'Donnell, C.L. (2008). Defining, conceptualizing, and measuring fidelity of implementation and its relationship to outcomes in K–12 curriculum intervention research. *Review of Educational Research, 78*(1), 33–84.

Rous, B., & Townley, K. (Eds.). (2006). *Building a strong foundation for school success: Kentucky's early childhood continuous assessment guide.* Frankfort: Kentucky Department of Education.

APPENDIX A

Revised Curriculum-Based Assessment Rating Rubric and Glossary

Element	Unsatisfactory (0)	Basic (1)	Satisfactory (2)	Excellent (3)
Alignments with federal/state/ agency standards and/or outcomes	No alignments between standards/outcomes and assessment items **AND** little to no conceptual alignment possible (i.e., even on the face of it, the items on the assessment would not align with most state early learning content standards or federal outcomes).	No alignment between standards/outcomes and assessment items has been conducted; however, a conceptual alignment is possible (i.e., on the face of it, the items on the assessment would align with most state early learning content standards or federal outcomes).	Alignment between standards/outcomes and assessment items has been conducted; however, information or evidence regarding the alignment process/product is not provided.	Alignment between standards/outcomes and assessment items has been conducted **AND** information or evidence regarding most of the following is available: • Description of the steps taken to align components • Consistency of content in the outcomes and assessment • Comparable span of knowledge encompassed by both • Even distribution of assessment items across outcomes • Consistency between the cognitive demands of the outcome and the assessment items • Expert validation or other steps taken to validate alignment

(continued)

Element	Unsatisfactory (0)	Basic (1)	Satisfactory (2)	Excellent (3)
Collaboration	Assessment is completed and summarized by one team member.	Several team members work independently to complete the assessment (i.e., separate protocols or sections are completed by different professionals). Family members are not involved. Assessment reports are often created by individual team members.	Several team members (often from different disciplines) work together to complete the assessment. Family members are involved in the assessment process; however their role is prescribed, dictated, or limited. Assessment reports may be created by individual team members.	Assessment process encourages different recommended models of teamwork (e.g., transdisciplinary) and role sharing among parents and professionals. All team members work together to complete the assessment. Families have choices and can play a variety of roles. Assessment reports are summarized as a whole by the team.
Comprehensive coverage	Assessment items cover a single developmental area (e.g., communication) OR a single content area (e.g., literacy) AND many critical concepts and skills are missing.	Assessment covers either several developmental areas OR several content areas but not both, AND some of the areas may be missing critical concepts and skills.	Assessment covers many traditional developmental areas and some content areas, which may be missing critical concepts and skills. The assessment is fairly comprehensive but mostly covers traditional developmental areas with some inclusion of content areas.	Assessment covers the major areas of development (i.e., motor, adaptive, cognitive, communication, social) AND major content areas (e.g., early math, readings). Assessment may combine content and developmental areas (e.g., literacy may be covered under the cognitive domain); however, most critical concepts and skills are included.

Element	Unsatisfactory (0)	Basic (1)	Satisfactory (2)	Excellent (3)
Equitable design	Children are expected to demonstrate competence according to biased and narrowly defined criterion. Modifications are not allowed, thus a child is penalized due to sensory, physical, behavioral, social/emotional, linguistic, and/or cultural differences or functional limitations. Emphasis is on topographical content or form rather than the function of the child's performance.	Children are expected to demonstrate competence according to a predefined criterion. Extensive modifications would be needed to ensure that all children are able to show their competencies due to sensory, physical, behavioral, social/emotional, linguistic, and/or cultural differences or functional limitations. Emphasis is on topographical content or form rather than the function of the child's performance.	Children can demonstrate competence using a variety of expressions (verbal and nonverbal); however, some modifications may be needed to ensure that all children are able to show their competencies due to sensory, physical, behavioral, social/emotional, linguistic, and/or cultural differences or functional limitations. Emphasis is on the child's performance rather than topographical content or form.	Children can demonstrate competence using a variety of expressions (verbal and nonverbal). Children aren't penalized due to culture, language, or individual differences, making modifications or adaptations unnecessary. In other words, children are allowed multiple and alternate ways to show their competencies despite sensory, physical, behavioral, social/emotional, linguistic, and/or cultural differences. Emphasis is on the function of the child's performance rather than topographical content or form.
Family involvement	No opportunities for family involvement.	Minimal opportunities for involvement, mostly passive roles (e.g., answering questions, observing but not participating).	Several opportunities for passive and active involvement (e.g., families are encouraged to answer questions and to observe and participate by gathering information or scoring protocols).	Assessment practices enable the integral engagement of parents, family members, and friends via "friendly" jargon-free materials and procedures, and practices that respect cultural values, among which the family and partners can voice a preference. Specific supports, strategies, and/or content to help improve communication and partnerships with families are provided. Families are

(continued)

Element	Unsatisfactory (0)	Basic (1)	Satisfactory (2)	Excellent (3)
Multifactors	Uses a single method of gathering information at a single point in time, in an unfamiliar single setting, by a single and unfamiliar team member.	Uses a single method of gathering information in multiple settings, but with unfamiliar people.	Uses multiple methods of gathering information during a single setting or time period, with familiar people.	viewed as equal team members and have a variety of options or ways of participating in assessment and instructional efforts. Gathers information through multiple methods across time points in familiar settings/ situations with familiar people.
Professional development	Nothing in the assessment materials (manual, web site, etc.) addresses the need for training and/or approaches to training.	Very little in the materials (manual, web site, etc.) addresses the need for training and/or approaches to training.	Some of the materials (manual, web site, etc.) address either the need for training to ensure accuracy and fidelity of assessment OR suggestions and/or procedures for training (e.g., additional downloads, tutorials, list of trainers, menu of training options, training videos, self-study materials, FAQ blogs) are provided.	Considerable attention is given in the materials (manual, web site, etc.) to the need for training to ensure accuracy and fidelity of use without bias AND suggestions and/or procedures for training (e.g., additional downloads, tutorials, list of trainers, menu of training options, training videos, self-study materials, FAQ blogs) are systematically provided.
Reliability	Multiple assessors do not agree on the scoring AND child scores differently when reassessed within a short amount of time.	Multiple assessors do not agree on the scoring OR the child scores differently when reassessed within a short amount of time.	Multiple assessors agree on the scoring OR child scores similarly on items when reassessed within a short amount of time.	Multiple assessors agree on the scoring AND child scores similarly on items when reassessed within a short amount of time.

Element	Unsatisfactory (0)	Basic (1)	Satisfactory (2)	Excellent (3)
Sensitivity	Assessment does not contain a sufficient number of items to record low or high levels of functioning, items are not organized in sequences that guide instruction, AND ratings are dichotomous (e.g., yes/no, ready/not ready, mastered/not mastered, +/−).	Assessment contains a sufficient number of items to record low OR high levels of functioning, items are not consistently organized in sequences that guide instruction, AND ratings are dichotomous (e.g., yes/no, ready/not ready, mastered/not mastered, +/−).	Assessment contains a sufficient number of items to record low AND high levels of functioning, most items are organized in sequences that guide instruction, AND uses quantitative ratings (e.g., multipoint ratings) OR qualitative methods (rich anecdotal notes and permanent records).	Assessment contains a sufficient number of items to record low and high functional levels AND to detect the smallest increments of changes. Items are consistently organized in sequences that guide instruction. Child's performance is measured using a range of quantitative and qualitative methods (e.g., multipoint ratings or classifications are used as well as procedures to document the extent and conditions under which children demonstrate competence).
Technology	Assessment does not incorporate any electronic and/or web-based features.	Assessment incorporates only static technology options (e.g., CD-ROM of forms).	Assessment incorporates a single interactive/dynamic technology-based support, OR a combination of static options.	Assessment incorporates multiple interactive (e.g., blog, discussion board, online data management system, hand-held devises, etc.) AND static technology-based supports (e.g., downloads, FAQs, tutorials) exist, including materials that promote the link between assessment and instruction.

(continued)

Element	Unsatisfactory (0)	Basic (1)	Satisfactory (2)	Excellent (3)
Usefulness for intervention	Assessment information serves no purpose related to intervention (i.e., for planning or revising).	Assessment information has limited use and is not linked to daily plans, individual intervention plans, or performance monitoring efforts.	Assessment information can be used for multiple purposes (e.g., developing present levels of performance, identifying children's needs, planning instruction, monitoring progress) and is somewhat linked to daily plans, individual intervention plans, and performance monitoring efforts.	Assessment information can be used for multiple or inter-related purposes **AND** is linked to daily plans or individual intervention plans **AND** administration of the assessment leads to improved outcomes and measures important skills that accurately portray the child's abilities.
Validity	Little to no evidence exists to validate the tool for the purposes for which it was developed, designed, or intended **AND** there is little to no evidence that the assessment links well to instruction.	Little to no evidence exists to validate the tool for the purposes for which it was developed, designed, or intended but there is some evidence that the assessment links well to instruction.	At least some evidence exists to validate the tool for the purposes for which it was developed, designed, or intended **OR** there is evidence that the assessment links well to instruction.	Considerable evidence exists to validate the tool for the purposes for which it was developed, designed, or intended (e.g., eligibility, programming, outcomes evaluation, accountability) **AND** there is evidence that the assessment links well to instruction.

Alignment with federal/state/agency standards and/or outcomes—Alignment is the process of matching two or more educational components. For example, a teacher might align an assessment instrument's items with state standards. Alignment considers the degree to which children's performance toward federal, state, or agency standards or outcomes can be documented using a given CBA.

Collaboration—The assessment instrument can be used by a group of people (e.g., educators, service providers, professionals, assistants, family members, therapists) who engage in a process of planning, conducting, summarizing, interpreting, and using the assessment for a variety of purposes.

Comprehensive coverage—The assessment instrument encompasses all areas/competencies of children's early development and learning. In other words, the assessment instrument covers all content areas (e.g., literacy, mathematics, science) and developmental areas (e.g., motor, communication, social-emotional) and shows the interrelationships of early development.

Equitable design—All children are able to demonstrate their underlying and often unrealized functional capabilities. The assessment allows alternate and often multisensory means for children to show their competencies despite sensory, physical, behavioral, social-emotional, linguistic, and cultural differences or functional limitations. The CBA emphasizes functional rather than topographical content (form) and adheres to universal design concepts (i.e., it is designed for all children, including those with disabilities, without relying heavily on adaptations or special design; it promotes full integration; and it acknowledges differences as a part of everyday life). For example, an assessment would determine whether a child can *get or move across the room* vs. *walk across the room.*

Family involvement—Families are viewed as equal team members and given a variety of options or ways of participating in assessment and instructional efforts. Families (and other important caregivers) are included throughout the assessment process (e.g., asked to share information, be present during the assessment process, help administer assessment items, help with summarizing and interpreting).

Multifactors—Assessment information is gathered and recorded about children's competencies across diverse places (e.g., classroom, home, community), routines (e.g., group circle, playground, lunch), and situations (e.g., morning, evening). Information is pooled from several familiar caregivers (e.g., parents, family, friends, professionals) who have attachments to the child and interact with the child during daily events, life activities, and across different settings. Information is gathered through multiple methods (i.e., interview, direct probes, permanent products, observations).

Professional development—An assessment contains supports, strategies, and/or content related to its initial and ongoing use to ensure that it is conducted accurately, without bias, and with fidelity. For example, the publisher or authors provide access to ongoing professional development activities through live expert trainings, webinars, online tutorials, or instructional videos.

Reliability—CBA results are stable and consistent. The more reliable scores and procedures are, the more confidence users can have in their accuracy. Reliability correlation coefficients range from −1 (i.e., an inverse relationship) to +1.00 (i.e., a perfect relationship). Generally speaking, the higher the correlation coefficient, the better is the assessment. Furthermore, the higher the stakes in terms of the decisions made from the assessment, the higher the correlations should be.

Sensitivity—An assessment can differentiate between small variances in skills—there are a sufficient number of items to record low and high functional levels. Sensitivity can be measured by using quantitative methods that analyze the density of items in a skill hierarchy and using graduated scoring of children's performance on those items, as well as by using qualitative methods that document the extent and conditions under which children demonstrate competence.

Technology—The CBA has electronic and/or web-based features that are designed to support any aspect of the assessment process (e.g., online tutorials, interactive web site or even a place to download additional materials, scoring assist, handheld data-entry devices, online data management system and/or interface with state databases).

Usefulness for intervention—This measure refers to "the degree to which an assessment or assessment process is shown to contribute to beneficial treatment or intervention outcomes" (Meisels & Atkins-Burnett, 2000, p. 252). For example, teachers might be interested in the usefulness of the assessment process, often called its treatment validity, to accomplish specific early childhood intervention purposes, especially planning and evaluating interventions.

Validity—Evidence that an assessment instrument correctly and accurately measures what it was intended to measure (i.e., the overall degree of justification for test interpretation and use).

APPENDIX B

Case Study of Five-Step Data-Driven Decision-Making Process Using a CBA for Program Planning

Mrs. Donovan is a teacher in a blended preschool program. Her class consists of 12 children, some with and some without Individualized Education Plans (IEPs). On a daily basis, she works with a Speech and Language Therapist and a teaching assistant. In order to plan instruction for all the children, Mrs. Donovan and her team administered a Curriculum Based Assessment (CBA) in October. Mrs. Donovan and her team used the Assessment, Evaluation, and Programming System for Infants and Young Children (AEPS), Second Edition, as their program's CBA. To complete the AEPS, she *gathered* information about all children during daily activities, interviewed familiar caregivers, and conducted authentic assessment activities as needed. All children's performance was *documented* using numerical scores placed on the AEPS data recording form.

A score of 2 on the AEPS indicates that the child independently and consistently met item criteria. A score of 1 indicates that 1) the specific criteria were partially met, 2) the child needed assistance, 3) the child inconsistently performed the criteria, and/or 4) the child's performance toward the criteria was emerging. A score of 0 indicates that the child was not yet able to perform or meet the stated item criteria. AEPS scoring notes were used to indicate additional information regarding children's abilities. For example, a note of "Q" indicates that quality was of concern for the specific item; "B" indicates that the child's behavior interfered with his or her performance, and "D" indicates that a direct prompt was needed in order for the child to achieve the goal. Mrs. Donovan further elaborated on the scores by recording written comments that were related to the specific assessment items. In order to demonstrate how to use a CBA for program planning and performance monitoring for a specific skill set, the authors have chosen specific items of the AEPS that are related to a broad outcome (engaging in cooperative activities). Table 7.1 illustrates 3 of the 12 children's performance as documented on AEPS items related to the outcome during October.

Mrs. Donovan then *summarized* each child's performance using a combination of narrative, visual, and numerical summaries. The narrative summaries captured Mrs. Donovan's reflections regarding the performance

Table 7.1. AEPS results from October for three children

AEPS Items	Rob Time 1			Lisa Time 1			Chuck Time 1		
	Score	Note	Comments	Score	Note	Comments	Score	Note	Comments
Participation in small group (watches, listens, participates)	1		Inconsistent	1	Q	Participates nonverbally	1		Emerging
Interacts appropriately with materials during small-group activities	2			2			1		
Responds appropriately to directions during small-group activities	1		Inconsistent	1	Q	Difficult to understand when she responds verbally	1		
Looks at appropriate object, person, or event during small-group activities	2			2			2		
Participation in large group (watches, listens, participates)	1			1	Q	Participates nonverbally	1		
Interacts appropriately with materials during large-group activities	2			2			1		
Responds appropriately to directions during large-group activities	2			1	Q	Difficult to understand when she responds verbally	2		

Behavior	Score	Comment	Score	Q	Comment	Score	Comment
Looks at appropriate object, person, or event during large group activities	2		2			2	
Interacts with others as play partners	1		1	Q	Words are not recognizable by peers which interferes with ability to interact	1	
Responds to others in distress or need	1		1			1	
Establishes and maintains proximity to others	2		1			2	
Takes turns with others	2		1	Q	Difficult to understand when she requests items	1	
Initiates greeting to others who are familiar	2		1	Q	Difficult to understand	1	
Responds to affective initiations from others	2		1			2	
Initiates cooperative activity	1	Will initiate with favorite peer	0	Q	Does not initiate	1	Beginning to initiate
Joins others in cooperative activity	2		1	Q	Difficult to understand	1	Will join in favorite activities
Maintains cooperative participation with others	2		1	Q	Difficult to understand	2	
Shares or exchanges objects	2		1	Q	Difficult to understand	2	

Key: Q, quality was a concern

185

10/15—I've noticed that many of the children are having difficulty with cooperative inter-actions, specifically, with *initiating* social interactions. Jamel enters the classroom without acknowledging peers or teachers (unless directly prompted). Starr will respond to peers, but does not initiate. She will often sit and watch others play, but needs to be invited to join in. Jamie does not talk to peers during play unless prompted. Lisa will imitate greet-ings, but not initiate. Both Lisa and Jamie have trouble being understood by their peers, due to articulation difficulties. Trever plays alone, neither initiating nor consistently re-sponding to peer interactions.

Figure 7.4.   Narrative summary of performance of a group of children.

of a group of children. See Figure 7.4 for a sample of the narrations made by Mrs. Donovan. In her narration, Mrs. Donovan notes that several of the children were having difficulty with initiation, which is a specific aspect of the broad outcome. Expanding on her concern that was noted in the nar-rative summary, Mrs. Donovan chose to visually summarize the entire class's performance on initiation. (See Figure 7.5.) She also created a visual summary of all children's performance across the items that were docu-mented on the AEPS. The numerical summaries that she generated in-cluded information about the percentages of items that were achieved, emerging, and not yet demonstrated for each child. Table 7.2 shows the numerical summary for the entire class.

Mrs. Donovan and her team then *analyzed* the summaries to find pat-terns and determine trends regarding children's growth and develop-ment. She was particularly surprised to see the wide range of perform-ance on how the children engaged in cooperative activities. Cooperative activities are defined as activities that require one or more peers;

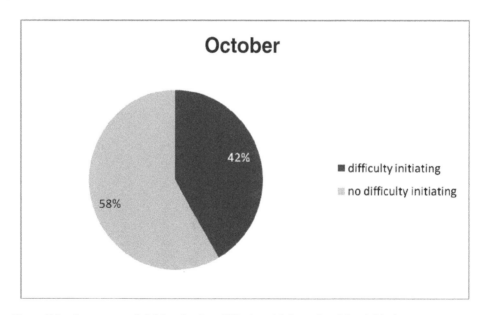

Figure 7.5.   Percentage of children having difficulty with items involving initiating.

Table 7.2. Numerical summary of children's performance on the AEPS.

	% of AEPS items achieved	% of AEPS items emerging	% of AEPS items not yet demonstrated
Gabriel	39	61	0
Jamie	11	83	6
Trever	0	61	39
Rosa	78	22	0
Starr	28	55	17
Chuck	39	61	0
Jamel	17	44	39
Rob	67	33	0
Jacob	78	22	0
Lisa	22	72	6
Jared	39	61	0
Heather	67	33	0

encourage children to share and exchange or assist one another with materials; contain jobs, roles, or identities for children to assume; and often lead to mutual benefit for those participating. In particular, she analyzed how the children interacted with one another as *play partners*, their ability to *initiate cooperative activities*, and their level and type of *participation during small-group and large-group activities*.

The results of her comprehensive assessment efforts indicated that all the children, regardless of gender, age, experience, or eligibility for special services, had a range of needs. In other words, her interpretation led to her recognition that some children had Tier 1 needs, some had Tier 2 needs, and some had Tier 3 needs. As she planned instruction she was able to determine that seven children (Chuck, Rob, Gabriel, Heather, Rosa, Jacob, and Jared) were demonstrating skills and abilities that were related to engaging in cooperative activities, as expected given their age and level of exposure to other children. Four of the children (Starr, Jamel, Lisa, and Jamie) either appeared to be missing a component of engaging in cooperative activities (i.e., initiating) or were having difficulty being understood by adults and peers, which was affecting their ability to engage in cooperative activities. One child, Trever, had behaviors that interfered with his ability to successfully engage in cooperative activities.

Tier 1 Program Planning

Because Chuck, Rob, Gabriel, Heather, Rosa, Jacob, and Jared were developing as expected given their age and experience, Mrs. Donovan determined that their needs were at the Tier 1 level. Mrs. Donovan planned activities and learning opportunities that allowed the children to continue to engage in cooperative activities.

Tier 2 Program Planning

Mrs. Donovan found that Starr and Jamel were missing a *component* of the common outcome of "engages in cooperative activities": initiating greetings or cooperative activities. While Lisa and Jamie also had difficulty initiating, Mrs. Donovan suspected that their difficulty was due to lack of intelligibility. In other words, Lisa and Jamie were having trouble with a means of expression; that is, they were *difficult to understand*. Therefore, all four children had a Tier 2 need. Mrs. Donovan realized that Starr, Jamel, Lisa, and Jamie would need more targeted instruction around initiating and intelligibility in order for them to become competent and consistent at engaging in cooperative activities.

Starr and Jamel

Mrs. Donovan utilized the five-step DDDM process in an effort to establish the baseline (i.e., determine what children's behaviors look like before instruction and during typical conditions) on the target behaviors for Starr and Jamel, which included initiating greetings and cooperative play with peers. She *gathered* information about Starr and Jamel during small-group centers, large-group circle time, and outdoor play to see when they initiated greetings and/or cooperative play with peers. Whereas her preferred way of documenting children's performance was through the use of learning stories in which she used written description and pictures to describe children's actions, she recognized that the amount of data she needed in order to know whether Tier 2 instructional efforts were having the intended impact was greater than she could manage by writing learning stories multiple times a day for several children. She also recognized that Starr and Jamel demonstrated some components of engaging in cooperative activities; therefore, she was interested only in increasing their initiations. Thus, she deemed a simple count and tally system sufficient. She documented the children's performance across 4 consecutive days during three different activities by recording the number of times each child initiated a greeting or initiated a cooperative activity. (See Table 7.3 and Figure 7.6.)

Table 7.3. Documentation sheet before Tier 2 instruction.

Date		Small-group centers	Large-group circle time	Outdoor play	Total
10/26	Starr	−	−	−	0
	Jamel	+	−	−	1
10/27	Starr	−	−	−	0
	Jamel	−	−	−	0
10/28	Starr	−	−	−	0
	Jamel	−	−	+	1
10/29	Starr	−	−	−	0
	Jamel	−	−	−	0

Key: + each time child initiated activity or greeting   − did not initiate during activity

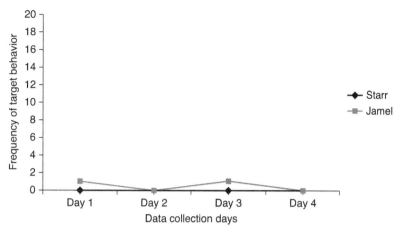

Figure 7.6. Frequency of target behavior for two children.

Mrs. Donovan numerically summarized the information she had documented on the tally sheet by adding the total number of initiations at the end of each day. Her *analysis* indicated a consistent pattern of no response across all three activities for Starr and minimal response across all three activities for Jamel. She *interpreted* that Starr and Jamel would need temporary, targeted instruction in order to address the missing component. She chose an instructional strategy, peer-mediated intervention, to address the children's needs, and decided to collect performance monitoring data 1 day per week and to analyze and interpret the data monthly.

Lisa and Jamie

Mrs. Donovan also engaged in the 5-step DDDM process to plan instruction for Lisa and Jamie. As a part of the assessment process, Mrs. Donovan and her team collected language summaries for all of the children. Specifically, they gathered information regarding each child during several brief periods (10 to 15 minutes) during familiar and routine activities. They *documented* at least 50 communicative utterances by scribing what the child said, using a particular notation if the communication attempt was unintelligible. They also recorded the context and function of each utterance. Mrs. Donovan summarized the information numerically by dividing the number of intelligible utterances by the total number of utterances and multiplied by 100, thereby determining the percentage of utterances that were intelligible. (See Table 7.4.)

Table 7.4 Percentage of intelligible utterances.

Child	Percent of Intelligible Utterances during October
Lisa	43%
Jamie	56%

Mrs. Donovan's *analysis* of the information indicated that both Lisa and Jamie were responding verbally and imitating during activities such as circle time, snack time, and small-group time, which are highly structured activities. Mrs. Donovan noted that both girls had difficulty being understood by peers, specifically during play activities, which are less structured. Her *interpretation* was that both children would need targeted instruction in order to increase their intelligibility. She decided to monitor each child's response to the instruction monthly.

Tier 3 Program Planning

When Mrs. Donovan examined the initial assessment for Trever, she discovered that several items related to the common outcome of engaging in cooperative activities were marked with a "B" on the AEPS data recording form, which indicated that his behavior interfered with his performance. Further examination revealed that Trever specifically had difficulty transitioning between activities, which adversely affected his ability to participate in cooperative activities. Specifically, he engaged in behaviors such as screaming, hitting, falling to the ground, and refusing to move when asked to transition between activities. Mrs. Donovan determined that Trever had difficulty following familiar one-step directions during transitions. Because following one-step directions is a foundational skill for engaging in cooperative activities, and because his current performance proved to be a barrier to engaging in cooperative activities, Mrs. Donovan determined that Trever had a Tier 3 need in this area.

Mrs. Donovan recognized the need to *gather* more specific information in order to establish a baseline of Trever's performance. She began the five-step process by *observing* Trever during common transitions in order to determine how often he demonstrated interfering behaviors as well as how often he followed one-step directions. She developed a data collection sheet to track Trever's behaviors during transitions. She *documented* his performance on the data sheet that is displayed in Table 7.5.

She *summarized* the data by comparing the number of times that Trever was able to transition without demonstrating an interfering behavior with the number of times that he engaged in an interfering behavior. Figure 7.7 is a visual summary of Trever's behavior during 1 week prior to receiving intensive instruction.

Mrs. Donovan *analyzed* the data by looking for patterns and trends. The visual summary revealed that Trever engaged in interfering behaviors consistently across 5 days and rarely followed one-step directions. There was little variability in his performance, meaning that the lines representing the frequency of behaviors did not have large "peaks and valleys." In order to further analyze the data, Mrs. Donovan examined the documentation sheet. She discovered that Trever did not demonstrate the interfering behaviors during transitions to activities that involved lots of movement (outdoor play and movement circle). He did not demonstrate the

Table 7.5. Documentation sheet before Tier 3 instruction was provided.

Daily Transitions	Date: 10/26	Date: 10/27	Date: 10/28	Date: 10/29	Date: 10/30
From bus to classroom					
From cubby to opening circle	–	–	–	–	+
From circle to centers/choice	+	–	–	–	–
Between activities during centers/choice	(demonstrated 4 interfering behaviors)	(demonstrated 3 interfering behaviors)	(demonstrated 5 interfering behaviors)	(demonstrated 4 interfering behaviors)	(demonstrated 5 interfering behaviors)
From choice to snack		–	–	–	–
From snack to outdoors					
From outdoors into class	–		–	–	–
From cubby to small group	–		–	–	–
From small group to movement circle					
From circle to cubby	–	–			
From cubby to bus			+		
Totals:	+ 1 – 8	0 7	1 9	0 8	1 8

Key: + followed one-step direction
– demonstrated interfering behaviors: screaming, hitting, falling, refusing
Blank cell indicates data not collected that day

191

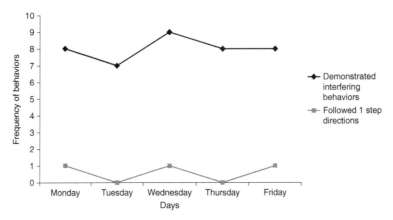

Figure 7.7. Frequency of behaviors prior to instruction.

interfering behaviors when he entered the classroom in the morning; however, he did demonstrate the behaviors when he entered the classroom after outdoor recess. He also demonstrated the interfering behaviors when he was transitioning to activities that required cooperative interactions (opening circle, centers/choice, time between activities during centers/ choice, and small-group time).

Mrs. Donovan's *interpretation* of the information was that Trever needed intentional, intensive, individualized instruction where specific antecedents, expected prosocial behaviors, and adult responses to Trever's behaviors were clearly articulated among team members. Mrs. Donovan recognized that she would need to teach Trever to follow single-step directions in order for him to be able to make progress toward the common outcome of engaging in cooperative activities. Due to the frequency of the behaviors and the intensity of the need, she decided to gather, document, and summarize information daily and to analyze and interpret it weekly.

Using the information that she had gathered through her comprehensive authentic assessment efforts, Mrs. Donovan was able to develop a holistic picture of all the children's needs in terms of engaging in cooperative activities. She was able to use the information she obtained from the assessment to sort and prioritize needs and plan instruction for each child. Chapter 8 explores how Mrs. Donovan monitored the children's performance over time.

CHAPTER 8

Performance Monitoring within a Tiered Instructional Model

Carrie Pfeiffer-Fiala, Kristie Pretti-Frontczak,
Lydia Moore, and Ashley N. Lyons

Mrs. Donovan is a teacher in a blended preschool classroom that serves children with and without disabilities. The classroom consists of children ages 3 through 6. Four of the children have individualized education plans (IEPs) with specific goals and outcomes; six of the children are developing typically, and two children do not currently have an IEP, but data are being collected on their performance due to concerns related to their development. As was described in Chapter 7, Mrs. Donovan assessed all of her children with the use of a curriculum-based assessment (CBA) and engaged in the data-driven decision making (DDDM) process to determine the children's needs and to match instruction to those needs.

At this point, Mrs. Donovan realizes that a systematic approach to plan instruction is vital. However, Mrs. Donovan isn't sure how to complete the task. The prospect of tracking so many children and different abilities makes Mrs. Donovan feel a little overwhelmed. Mrs. Donovan wonders: How will her instruction change the children's behavior. How will she monitor multiple children's progress towards different outcomes? What kinds of information assist in making good decisions about the impact of instruction and intervention? When should her instruction change, and how long should the current instruction and intervention continue?

Teachers make data-driven decisions on a regular basis. In fact, early research on teacher decision making and efficacy estimated that teachers made as many as 1,300 decisions daily (Jackson, 1968; Sandall & Schwartz 2002). Subsequent research has confirmed that both novice and experienced teachers make continuous decisions before, during, and after they provide instruction to their students (Ysseldyke, Thurlow, & Christenson, 1987). The types of decisions that teachers make are often quick and are done under ever-changing situations. Thus, teachers frequently rely on their past experience in order to make decisions.

The complexities of blended classrooms, however, have changed the types of decisions that teachers need to make. For example, when teachers serve children who are multi language learners, who may have a delay or disability, or who may exhibit challenging behaviors, the teachers need to rely on the systematic use of data, rather than their past experiences or intuition, to inform their decisions. Furthermore, the decisions that are made regarding instruction have implications for children's growth, development, and learning and thus should be based on valid, reliable, and sufficient evidence (Ysseldyke & Tardrew, 2007). To address the challenges of ongoing data collection and use, teachers need both informal and formal methods of gathering and using data to support instructional decisions, particularly until they become more experienced and the decisions become more common and automatic.

The processes and procedures for conducting assessment to plan instruction were addressed in Chapter 7. The purpose of Chapter 8 is to assist teachers in conducting assessment for the purpose of revising instruction (referred to as performance monitoring) in an effort to continuously support children. Chapter 8 is divided into four sections. First, we define assessment for the purpose of revising instruction. Second, we describe two broad recommended practices for performance monitoring. Third, we share a tiered model of performance monitoring as a means of addressing the challenges of systematically collecting data for children in blended classrooms. Last, we discuss suggestions and strategies for sharing performance monitoring reports.

PERFORMANCE MONITORING

Performance monitoring is an assessment process in which teachers revisit initial instructional decisions in terms of their accuracy and efficacy (i.e., they determine whether instructional efforts are promoting growth and development, leading to family satisfaction, and resulting in quality programming). Throughout the book, we will use the term *performance monitoring*, even though the term *progress monitoring* may be more familiar.

The term *performance monitoring* is used for three main reasons. First, performance views children's growth and development in terms of the acquisition of skills and also the use of functional abilities. In this context, the term *progress* may lead to thoughts about vertical gains in the development and acquisition of skills to a mastery criterion (i.e., as a child learns one skill, teams automatically move to the acquisition of the next and the next, without considering the child's developmental readiness or function) (Kearney, 2008). In other words, performance monitoring stresses the need to describe and examine changes in children's behaviors more broadly, in terms of acquisition and mastery as well as other critical and often qualitative attributes.

Second, many people associate the term progress with IEP data collection efforts. We prefer to use more blended or universal language, and performance seemed more applicable to all children. Performance emphasizes the continuous process of collecting and analyzing data on multiple and often interrelated domains of development. In addition, performance indicators can compare the impact of instruction on goals and objectives and compare actual results against expected results (achievement of outputs and progress towards outcomes).

Third, other terms, such as *formative assessment* and *summative assessment* (see Box 8.1), could be used for performance monitoring, but they may be unfamiliar to many teachers, may be used more often to refer to older students, and might not clearly convey or emphasize the type of practices that are necessary for use with young children, particularly those with diverse abilities (Fuchs & Fuchs, 1986: 1999).

Regardless of the term that is used, the notion of *monitoring* is key to understanding this assessment purpose. In general, monitoring refers to the systematic collection of information that provides ongoing feedback regarding children's performance over time. Monitoring allows teachers to track children's performance on individually targeted behaviors as well as on broad outcomes. Monitoring also allows for the systematic collection of comparative data to determine the significance or effect of instruction for individual children and groups of children (Raver, 2003).

Performance monitoring is applicable to all types of early childhood programs and philosophies. The implementation of assessment for performance

---

BOX 8.1

"What Is the difference?"
definitions of formative vs. summative assessment

Formative	*Summative*
Part of instructional practice	Given periodically to determine at a particular point in time what children know and do not know
Allows timely adjustments to instruction	Is an accountability measure that is generally used as part of the grading process
Helps teachers determine next steps during the learning process	Allows teachers to gauge child learning relative to content standards at a particular point in time
Provides information at the classroom level to assist in making instructional revisions	Provides a snapshot of the child's performance at a specific interval of time
Engages children in the assessment of their own learning through descriptive feedback	Illustrates cumulative representation of children's current competency through comprehensive monitoring

Source: Garrison & Ehringhaus (2007).

---

monitoring purposes, however, may vary in terms of who collects data; how they do so; and what information is gathered, documented, and summarized for use (McAfee & Leong, 2002; McConnell, 2000; McLean, Wolery, & Bailey, 2004). In other words, the recommended practices and tiered model of performance monitoring described here in Chapter 8 hold true regardless of the type of program or educational philosophy; however, the "look" or "feel" of performance monitoring may vary.

It is beyond the scope of the chapter to describe in detail how teachers working in different programs conceptualize and define performance monitoring. However, Table 8.1 highlights key characteristics of performance monitoring with regard to widely accepted early childhood programs and philosophies (e.g., High/Scope, Montessori). In general, although programs following particular philosophies may conceptualize and define performance monitoring differently, it is recommended that all teachers serving young children engage in a set of monitoring practices that are holistic and data driven (Branscombe, Castle, Dorsey, Surbeck, & Taylor, 2003; Copple & Bredekamp, 2009; Gestwicki, 1999; Grisham-Brown, Hallam, & Pretti-Frontczak, 2008; Grisham-Brown, Hemmeter, & Pretti-Frontczak, 2005; Pretti-Frontczak & Bricker, 2004; Sandall, Hemmeter, Smith, & McLean, 2005).

Recommended Performance Monitoring Practices

As in the case of any assessment process, there are recommended practices to guide teachers. In regard to performance monitoring, two recommendations are prevalent across the literature. First, performance monitoring should be conceptualized holistically and should use both qualitative and quantitative methods, consider mediating factors, and consider the interdependence or

Table 8.1. Illustration of how various program types conceptualize and define performance monitoring

Program Type	Who tends to gather information and how?	What information is documented and what methods are used to document?	How is information summarized for use in monitoring performance?
Activity-based Intervention (ABI) (Macy, 2007; Pretti-Frontczak, & Bricker, 2004)	WHO: Transdisciplinary teams that include family members HOW: Through observation of children during routine, planned and child directed activities; through interviews and conversations with familiar caregivers	WHAT: Children's strengths, interests, emerging skills, as well as their interests and preferences METHODS: Written descriptions, permanent products, and counts/tallies	Narratively, numerically, and/or visually most often by compiling information on a curriculum-based assessment (CBA)
Discrete Trial Training Programs (Eikeseth, Svein, Smith, Tristram, & Eldevik, Erik Jahr, Sigmund. 2002; Lovaas, 1987)	WHO: Therapist/consultant HOW: Through direct testing and prompting during intervention sessions	WHAT: Children's performance on individualized and discrete skills METHODS: Counts and tallies; time sampling procedures	Visually most often through graphs
Creative Curriculum (Trister Dodge, D., Colker, L., & Heroman, C. (2002). Curriculum Developmental Continuum for Ages 3–5. Washington, DC: Teaching Strategies, Inc. 2006; Heroman, C., Burts, D. C., B., K., Bickart, T. (2010). Teaching Strategies GOLD. Washington, DC: Teaching Strategies, Inc.)	WHO: Teachers and teaching assistants HOW: Through observation during classroom activities	WHAT: Children's actions and abilities METHODS: Written descriptions and numerical ratings	Narratively and visually most often through portfolios
HighScope (HighScope Educational Research Foundation, 2010; 2003; 2002)	WHO: Teachers and teaching assistants HOW: Through observation during the plan, do, review sequence of daily activities	WHAT: Children's actions and abilities METHODS: Written descriptions (i.e. anecdotal notes and interviews), and counts and tallies	Narratively and numerically most often through discussions of work time

(continued)

Table 8.1. (continued)

Program Type	Who tends to gather information and how?	What information is documented and what methods are used to document?	How is information summarized for use in monitoring performance?
Montessori (Montessori, 1976)	WHO: Directress HOW: Observe children engaged during individual work that follows their own natural interests	WHAT: Children's inner directives from nature METHODS: Written descriptions (i.e. interviews , portfolios, audio/visual recordings of children's work, individual conferences, anecdotal notes, and counts and tallies	Narratively, numerically, and/or visually most often through word task analysis journals, and panel boards
Project-based (Katz, & Chard, 2000)	WHO: Teacher and teaching assistants HOW: Observe children in classroom activities following children's interests	WHAT: Children's interest and involvement in their own learning METHODS: Anecdotal/observational notes and records, graphic organizers (e.g., curriculum web), interviews, permanent products, counts and tallies (i.e., interviews)	Narratively, numerically, and/or visually most often through a display of objects
Reggio Emilia (Fraser, & Gestwicki, 2000)	WHO: Teacher and parents HOW: Observation of children during daily activities, guided by specific questions and hypotheses	WHAT: Children's principles of respect, responsibility, and community METHODS: Family interviews, panel boards, photos, text, sculptures, drawings, and paintings	Narratively and visually most often through various media and symbols and display of objects

the relationship among development, culture, and experiences (Brinton & Fujiki, 2003; Hojnoski, Gischlar, & Missall, 2009(a),(b),(c); Klingner, Sorrells, & Barrera, 2007; Ross, Roberts, & Scott, 1998). Second, performance monitoring should be data driven and serve as a recursive process that involves gathering information, documenting, summarizing, conducting analysis, and interpreting data to inform and revise instruction (National Association for the Education of Young Children & National Association of Early Childhood Specialists in State Departments of Education, 2003; Rous & Hyson, 2007). Each of the recommended practices is described next.

Holistic Approach to Performance Monitoring

Recommended practices indicate that children's performance should be monitored holistically, meaning that teachers should understand the importance of viewing the whole child and the interdependence of all variables (e.g., all the factors that may affect performance (Copple & Bredekamp, 2009; Hojnoski & Missall, 2007). National Association for the Education of Young Children & National Association of Early Childhood Specialists in State Departments of Education, 2003; Rous & Hyson, 2007; Sandall et al., 2005). The first way to examine a child's performance holistically is to measure a child's performance *qualitatively* and *quantitatively*. The use of qualitative and quantitative measurement strategies provides a more complete picture of the child and the relative effectiveness of the instruction. Integration of both types of data informs and influences the development of an effective intervention. Qualitative data are rich descriptions of characteristics, cases, and settings (Blankenship, 1985). Quantitative data ascertain the magnitude, amount, or size of attributes, behaviors, or opinions. See Box 8.2 for an analogy of qualitative and quantitative measurement approaches to describe a farm.

In an effort to gather qualitative and quantitative information regarding children's performance, teachers should aim to examine more than the frequency of a child's performance, which tends to be quantitative in nature (e.g., the number of times that the behavior occurs), or the accuracy of a child's performance, which tends to be qualitative in nature (e.g., descriptions of how well a child performs an action). Teachers should consider qualitative attributes of frequency and quantitative attributes of accuracy, as well as the dimensions of latency (the time between a trigger and the occurrence of the target behavior), duration (how long the target or nontarget behavior lasts), and endurance (how long the target or nontarget behavior is repeated). Children's performance and abilities are quite complex; thus, it is necessary to look at multiple dimensions of a performance, using qualitative and quantitative measurement to understand those dimensions and make sound decisions. Teachers often use qualitative methods to assess all the children in their classroom. The qualitative method is based on observations, anecdotal notes, and family interviews, and it explores children's interests and preferences. Data collected through qualitative methods are often viewed as "richness of information" (Creswell, Plano, & Clark, 2007).

BOX 8.2
Qualitative and quantitative data example: The farm

Qualitative	*Quantitative*
Red and brown barn, red silo	2 buildings
Smells of mud and hay	3 pastures and 2 grassy areas
Picturesque scene of fields and animals	Costs $10,000 per acre to run
Peeling paint on barn	24 × 48 foot barn

Consider the example of a teacher who has decided that a child in his class needs instruction towards the common outcome of participation. The teacher will need to measure how many times the child participates; whether the child's participation was appropriate, maintained, and pleasurable; and whether it resulted in positive interactions among children (Ingersoll & Schreibman, 2006). By collecting both qualitative and quantitative information, the teacher is able to gain a complete picture of the child's performance. Both methods have utility within the early childhood setting. Table 8.2 provides several examples of the quantitative and qualitative information that is needed to understand changes in children's performance across dimensions.

When teachers monitor children's performance holistically, they also understand the importance of viewing the *interdependence* of all variables that may affect performance, sometimes called mediating factors (Ross, Roberts, & Scott, 1998). Mediating factors are the social and psychological conditions that moderate the effects of instructional efforts. In other words, mediating factors are integral elements that may influence or contribute to the child's overall performance. Mediating factors can include attendance, home or community situations, medications, past exposure to instruction, and even the novelty of the situation. The mediating factors directly affect the child's rate of performance. For example, if the child is absent numerous days and does not receive instruction, then monitoring the child's performance of the skills that were taught when the child missed instruction is somewhat futile. Likewise, if a child's medication has recently changed, the data collected on the child's current level of performance may not accurately depict the child's overall capability.

Another aspect of understanding performance monitoring holistically is to recognize the interdependence between development, culture, and experience (i.e., the variables form a mutual and reciprocal relationship) (Darling-Hammond & Snyder, 2000; Creswell & Plano Clark, 2007). The

Table 8.2. Examples of quantitative and qualitative information needed to understand changes in child's performance

Dimensions of behavior	Associated quantitative statements	Associated qualitative statements
Frequency (Number of times/how often)	• Number of times a child initiates • Number of times a child manipulates • Number of times a child participates • Number of times a child is successful	• Each morning • Each afternoon • During most structured activities • On each occasion • Daily • Weekly
Accuracy (How well/how intended)	• Number/percent correct • Number of steps completed correctly • Number/percent of trials completed correctly	• Independently • Recognizably • Correctly • Quickly • Intelligibly • Functionally • Purposively • Precisely
Latency (Length of time to respond)	• Time between direction and child response • Time between cue and child response • Time between direction and child response • Time between request and child response	• Within the allotted time • Within the given time • Within a reasonable time
Duration (How long behavior lasts)	• How long a child cries • How long a child participates • How long a child plays near peers • How long a child stays on task	• Across the majority of the school day • As long as expected • As long as expected of others • Throughout supper • During the field trip • While shopping at Target
Endurance (How many times behavior is repeated)	• Takes 10 steps • Communicates for 2 or more exchanges • Counts 10 objects • Remains seated for 3 minutes	• With persistence or perseverance • By overcoming challenges and increased difficulty • During most of the activity or event • With concentration or attentiveness • With sensitivity to physical stimuli

interaction of skills from developmental domains or areas means that multiple skills may need to be addressed before a child demonstrates improvement in a single skill. For example, Travis is missing both the skill of bringing hands to midline and the skill of joint attention (Godfrey, Grisham-Brown, Schuster, & Hemmeter, 2003; Ingersoll & Schreibman, 2006). Joint attention is defined as looking at appropriate object, person, or event during small-group activities (Bricker, 2002). Travis will need to make progress on both skills in order to attain either.

In addition to being affected by skill interrelatedness, children's development and growth are affected by culture. In the example of Travis, performance monitoring on the two skills—bringing hands to midline and joint attention—reveals that Travis is making significant progress on joint attention but minimal progress on the skill of bringing hands to midline. The teacher reviews the qualitative data from the family and discovers that the family feeds and dresses Travis, as is customary in their culture, so he has fewer opportunities to practice each skill than do other children his age, possibly contributing to a difference in Travis's performance.

Lastly, developmentally appropriate experiences promote children's active exploration of their world, manipulation of real objects, learning through hands-on activities, direct experiences, and exposure to contextual clues, all of which provide children with multiple opportunities to engage skills across developmental domains. Not all children may have had these experiences or any experience on a specific skill or outcome. Performance monitoring should occur across the child's experiences and consider the child's repertoire of learning in order to provide the teacher with accurate data. The recommended practice of being holistic is illustrated in a project approach for a group of children in Box 8.3.

BOX 8.3

Case example: holistic performance monitoring within a project-based approach

Ms. Wolf is a teacher in a blended preschool classroom that incorporates the project approach to plan, employ, and evaluate instruction. At the beginning of the year, Ms. Wolf assessed all the children in her classroom through quantitative methods regarding performance on specific skills. To do this, she completed the Get It Got It Go! and the Early Language and Literacy Classroom Observation. She qualitatively assessed all the children in her classroom through observations, anecdotal notes, family interviews, and an exploration of children's interests and preferences. Ms. Wolf determined the needs of each child in her classroom relative to specific skills and outcomes.

She then set up a bird feeder in an isolated spot on the playground. The children observed the bird feeder and the birds that visited it. Capitalizing on the children's interests in the birds and the bird feeder, Ms. Wolf prepared a project involving birds and bird feeders. She determined that the project integrated multiple content area outcomes, such as reading and math. She narrowed her focus within the content areas to address the outcomes of comprehension and counting. In her classroom, Ms. Wolf serves as a researcher and as a resource to children, providing guidance, information, and materials while stimulating independent thinking.

In order to assess the children's performance, Ms. Wolf sent home a questionnaire to the family to help inform her of the current children's knowledge and to continually inform her of mediating factors that might moderate the effects of instructional efforts. Concurrently, Ms. Wolf assessed the children to determine which topics were locally relevant and valued by them, by developing a web with the children. Ms. Wolf also considered the culture of the community and the children (e.g., do the children live in homes with windows through which they can see birds, do they have bird feeders at home, or do they live mainly on farms and view birds from a different perspective as a source of food?). Ms. Wolf's next step was to implement multiple activities throughout the classroom focused around the topics from the web and the chosen outcomes.

During the project, Ms. Wolf continued to use the recommended practices to track how and why the children were performing or not performing toward the outcomes of comprehension and counting (e.g., if a child is not performing toward an outcome, is it because he has been absent, because his medication has changed, or because the instruction has no relevance to him?) by discussing, expanding and/or narrowing the web with the children. Ms. Wolf also continually analyzes and interprets artifacts, experiences, discussions, and interviews with the children and the family to revise her instruction.

Ms. Wolf continued to consider the children's interest and involvement to revise instruction. The children continued to choose from a variety of activities provided by her. She capitalized on children's proficiencies as she considered their families' influence and the families' climate for learning. For example, she considered whether the family was providing additional instruction and whether there were any families that could share their knowledge of birds? When Ms. Wolf selected outcomes for the project, she was keenly aware that the children were the experts and that the mediating factors continued to influence the direction, activities, and outcomes of the bird project. The web she had created with her class demonstrated the way in which outcomes in different domains connect to one another. Ms. Wolf continued to monitor the performance of her students and revised instruction as necessary by observing the students, taking anecdotal notes, conducting family interviews, and taking into account children's preferences and interests; as well as summarizing, analyzing, and interpreting the children's pictures, narratives, bulletin boards, panel boards, and webs.

Data-Driven Decision Making

Chapter 1 stated that recommended practice includes making assessment for any data driven purposes; however, following the five-step DDDM process of gathering information, documenting, summarizing, analyzing, and interpreting is particularly critical with regard to performance monitoring. Unless teachers engage in DDDM to carry out performance monitoring, how will they make decisions regarding when and how to revise instruction? How will their instructional efforts be informed? How will a teacher know whether a child is responding to instructional efforts and when and how to change their approach? Chapter 7 described the five-step process to determine initial instruction that would meet individual and groups of children's needs. For performance monitoring, the process remains the same; however, the purpose is to revisit initial decisions and systematically modify teaching practices to ensure that all children are progressing toward identified outcomes. See Box 8.4 for an illustration of the decision-making model in action for monitoring a child's performance (i.e., monitoring the child's response to instruction by means of the five-step DDDM process).

BOX 8.4

Data-driven decision making in action: the case study of Mikey

Mikey is a 4-year, 3-month-old boy enrolled in a blended preschool program. Results from a CBA, family interviews, and team meetings suggested that there was concern regarding Mikey's ability to hold or steady an object with one hand while manipulating an object with the other hand. For example, he had trouble holding a bowl and feeding himself with a spoon and opening containers such as his milk carton, and he tended to avoid activities such as putting puzzles together and making jewelry. The ability to hold or steady an object with one hand while manipulating an object with the other hand is a **prerequisite** for Mikey to later create and represent ideas and concepts, play with toys cooperatively, and engage in more advanced fine motor activities such as writing, cutting, and zipping up a coat. Thus, Mikey's need was labeled a Tier 3 need and intentional, intensive, individualized instruction was planned. The following case example describes how Mikey's teacher went through the five-step DDDM process to 1) determine his starting performance, 2) track his subsequent response to instruction, and 3) revise instruction as needed.

Step 1: Gathering Information

The teacher and classroom assistant observed Mikey during a variety of daily activities to see when he was able to perform the target action or behavior (holding or steadying an object with one hand while manipulating an object with another). For example, they watched to see whether he would pour juice into a cup, hold a book and turn the pages, zip his coat, cut a piece of paper in half, hold a pot and stir, or hold a nail and hammer.

Step 2: Documentation

The teacher and classroom assistant created a simple data collection system of counts and tallies to document how often and where Mikey held or steadied an object with one hand while manipulating an object with the other hand. To minimize the time they spent writing, they created a checklist of possible ways that Mikey could demonstrate the target behavior. They walked around the room and made a comprehensive list of the different ways that Mikey could hold or steady an object with one hand while manipulating an object with the other hand by considering the opportunities at each classroom center and during the daily routine. (See Figure 8.1 for a copy of their data collection sheet.) The form also allowed them to indicate other examples when he demonstrated the target behavior and to indicate the setting or activity where the target behavior was observed. The teacher and classroom assistant merely marked whether they saw Mikey do any of the behaviors that were listed.

Step 3: Summarization

At the end of each day, the teacher and classroom assistant summarized Mikey's performance numerically by totaling the number of times he held an object with one hand and manipulated an object with the other hand. The total number for each day was then summarized visually by plotting the total number on a graph. Figure 8.2 illustrates Mikey's performance during baseline (i.e., his performance before more intensive and intentional instruction was provided). The period of time where data are collected and specific or targeted instruction is not provided, is referred to as baseline, and otherwise thought of as where a child started.

Step 4: Analysis

Mikey's teacher reviewed the daily visual summaries at the end of the week. She looked for patterns and trends that were related to Mikey's performance. At the end of a week of taking baseline data, she was able to determine that Mikey rarely

Examples of target behavior (holding or steadying an object with one hand while manipulating an object with the other)	Tally each time target behavior is observed	Setting/Activity
Hold backpack and unzip		
Hold paper and scribble		
Hold puzzle steady and place pieces		
Hold a book and turn the page		
Hold container (such as playdough) and remove lid		
Hold a cup and pour liquid		
Hold a bowl/container and use spoon		
Hold a container and stir		
Hold paper and tear		
Hold paper and peel a sticker		
Hold paper and crease		
Hold a lace and string beads onto it		
Hold workbench and use hammer		
Hold a block while stacking another one on top		
Hold pop-up toy and press button		
Hold bowl and scoop snack		
Hold bucket and scoop sand		
Other: _____		

Narrative Comments:

Mikey responds more often and with more success with increased prompts and continuous positive reinforcement.

_____

_____

Figure 8.1.   Documentation sheet for target behaviors.

demonstrated the target behavior across 5 consecutive days of data collection. She concluded that his predictable response (i.e., his patterned response) was either to avoid touching or manipulating objects and toys or to try once and give up. The teacher also concluded that the trend (the way the direction of his performance was going) was relatively flat (i.e., it was not going up or down). The data showed little variability in the number of times that Mikey exhibited the target behavior (holding or steadying an object with one hand while manipulating with another) over the 5 days. To better direct her instruction, she went back to her data collection sheets to review which activities Mikey was participating in when he did perform the skill, and she noted that all three times were during sand-play.

Step 5: Interpretation

On the basis of her analysis of the data, Mikey's teacher was able to make decisions concerning how to better address Mikey's needs. She chose to embed frequent learning opportunities across daily routines and activities, particularly

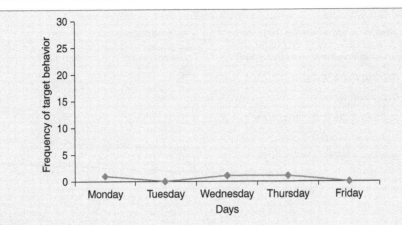

Figure 8.2. Mikey's baseline performance.

during sand-play. The embedded learning opportunities matched Mikey's interests and preferences and increased the chance that he would participate in the activities and demonstrate the target behavior.

First week: Instruction

As the individualized, intensive, and intentional instruction was provided, the teacher and classroom assistant continued to *gather* information about Mikey and *document* his performance using the checklist in Figure 8.1. At the end of each week they numerically *summarized* his performance by totaling the number of times Mikey held or steadied an object with one hand while manipulating an object with the other. Then they summarized the total number for each day visually by plotting that number on a graph as they had done during baseline. Figure 8.3 provides a visual summary of the data that were collected during the first week of instruction.

As she had done for the data collected during the baseline week, the teacher *analyzed* the data summaries, looking for patterns and trends related to Mikey's performance. She asked herself the following questions as a guide during the analysis: Is Mikey exhibiting the same behavior or lack of the same behavior across multiple settings? Is the intervention affecting the target behavior? When, why, and how is the intervention changing Mikey's performance? She expected, given the more intensive instructional efforts, that there would be a change in Mikey's performance. However, there were no changes during the first week of instruction (i.e., there wasn't a change in the pattern, trend, or variability

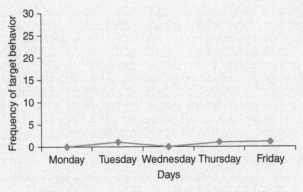

Figure 8.3. First week of intentional, intense, individualized instruction.

of his behavior compared with baseline). In other words, Mikey continued to rarely demonstrate the target behavior and to exhibit it in only one setting (sandbox). From the data, the teacher *interpreted* the situation as indicating that additional learning opportunities were needed and that she and the classroom assistant needed to consistently prompt and give feedback to Mikey. Therefore, she revised the intervention plan to include specific ways to prompt Mikey to engage in the target behavior. For example, the intervention plan included phrases that teachers could say or things that teachers could do during activities to prompt Mikey (e.g., help him hold an object while he acted on another, model how they held one object and acted on another, direct Mikey to demonstrate the target behavior). She also determined ways for classroom staff to consistently respond to Mikey depending on whether he demonstrated the target behavior. Staff responses would include providing Mikey with positive reinforcement (e.g., smiles, high fives, clapping) when he did demonstrate the target behavior and increasing the adult support when he did not.

Week 2: Instruction Revised

Because performance monitoring is a continuous process, the teacher and classroom assistant continued to provide Tier 3 instruction and to move through the five-step process. At the end of each week they summarized Mikey's performance on the target behavior. Figure 8.4 provides a visual summary of the data that were collected during the second week, following the implementation of the revised instruction plan.

Again, Mikey's teacher considered the guiding questions as she looked for patterns and trends. Furthermore, she considered whether there was a change in the level of his performance during the second week which might indicate that he was engaging in the target behavior more often and how quickly that change occurred. By the second week, Mikey began to predictably demonstrate the target behavior multiple times a day and during more than one activity (i.e., during housekeeping and sand-play). Week 2 data also showed an upward trend in terms of the frequency with which he demonstrated the target behavior. The visual summary also showed that the level increased rather quickly and consistently compared with the level in the first week.

On the basis of her *analysis* of the data, Mikey's teacher *interpreted* the situation as indicating that she should continue with the intervention as planned and implemented during the second week because Mikey appeared to be responding to the instruction. She made sure to focus on encouraging Mikey to engage in many activities that would require the target behavior, in order to increase his generalization and use of the target behavior.

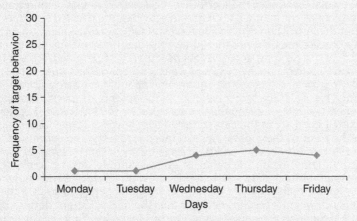

Figure 8.4. Second week of intentional, intense, individualized instruction.

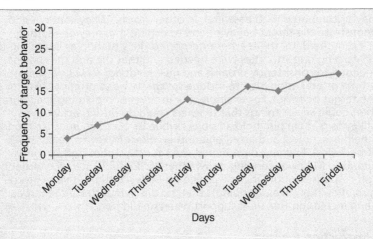

Figure 8.5. Third and fourth weeks of intentional, intense, individualized instruction.

The five-step process continued for 2 more weeks of instruction. Figure 8.5 shows a visual summary of the data collected during the third and fourth weeks. Because the teacher wanted Mikey to generalize the behavior (use it consistently across activities), she reviewed the checklists to see whether any new patterns emerged in terms of where the target behavior was being used. She discovered that Mikey was consistently demonstrating the target behavior across many settings and in a variety of activities. These settings and activities included snack time (pouring and using a spoon), art center (scribbling, tearing, opening the glue stick), and construction (building with blocks and using workbench). When she reviewed the data, Mikey's teacher was also able to see a continued upward trend, meaning that he engaged in the target behavior with increasing frequency. When she compared the summary from week 2 with those of weeks 3 and 4, Mikey's teacher saw that the level continued to increase and that there was little variability in performance from day to day.

Maintenance

On the basis of her analysis of 4 weeks of data, Mikey's teacher decided that the intervention plan continued to be effective. Because Mikey was demonstrating the target behavior across multiple settings and activities, she decided to reduce the intensity of the instruction. She decided to continue to provide many opportunities for him to practice the behavior throughout the day; however, she reduced the number of specific prompts and consequences that were provided. Mikey's teacher also decided to collect data by means of weekly probes of the target behavior. Thus, 1 day per week she gathered information about Mikey across activities and documented his use of the target behavior in the absence of specific prompts and consequences (i.e., she repeated the five-step process for 4 more weeks). Figure 8.6 shows a visual summary of the data collected over 4 weeks of maintenance.

On the basis of these data, Mikey's teacher saw that he continued to demonstrate the target behavior, and a review of the checklists revealed that he continued to demonstrate the behavior across multiple settings and activities. In all, the maintenance data continued to show an upward trend, meaning that he was continuing to increase his use of the target behavior. On the basis of her analysis, Mikey's teacher decided that she had sufficient data to conclude that Mikey had accomplished the target behavior. Thus, it was time for the teacher to reevaluate

Mikey's overall performance across common outcomes and determine what skill or concept he needed to learn next considering his developmental readiness and need to engage and participate during daily activities.

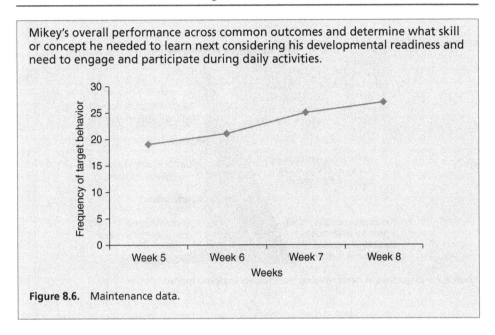

Figure 8.6.   Maintenance data.

Tiered Model of Performance Monitoring

A tiered model of performance monitoring provides a framework for making revisions to instruction and matches instructional efforts to children's needs. In other words, just as tiered levels of instruction were matched to identified needs, this model tiers performance-monitoring efforts and matches the frequency, intensity, and intent of efforts to the level of need and instruction. For example, if the needs of a child on a particular skill are determined to be at Tier 2 (targeted and temporary concentrated instruction), then performance monitoring efforts will also be at Tier 2 (targeted and temporary) so that the teacher can make timely decisions on whether the instruction is working and whether any changes in instruction need to occur. A tiered model of performance monitoring is illustrated in Figure 8.7, and each tier is described next.

Within Tier 1, all children's performance toward common outcomes is monitored. As defined earlier, common outcomes are the standards and milestones that all children are expected to achieve (regardless of ability) at a given age. Teachers monitor children's performance toward standards and developmentally appropriate milestones at least once a year, preferably (given the variability of development during the early years) three or four times a year. Tier 1 performance monitoring can include a readministration of an authentic and comprehensive assessment for all children (i.e., readministration of a CBA). Systematic monitoring of children's Tier 1 performance informs teachers whether children's needs have continued to develop as expected and whether they require a change in the frequency and intensity of instruction and/or the skills that are being targeted.

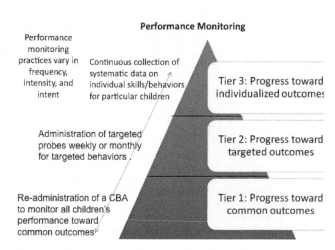

Figure 8.7.   Depiction of performance monitoring as tiered model.

For example, Ms. Grissom readministers a CBA to all children halfway through the year. Ms. Grissom summarizes and analyzes the information she collects. She then uses the information from the second administration of her CBA to determine whether any of the children who were previously determined to have a Tier 1 need now require a different level of instruction, given any of the mediating factors that were discussed earlier. For example, after interpreting Danny's information, she noticed that he fell below the cutoff score for the gross motor area of development that is provided in the CBA she uses. Back in October, Danny's gross motor skills were on track; however, after Danny had surgery to repair a tendon in his foot, he was unable to receive the Tier 1 instruction (i.e., missed several weeks of preschool). Now Danny's needs in gross motor development may require Tier 2 instruction for a temporary length of time while his foot is recovering.

Within Tier 2, performance monitoring consists of more frequent and targeted efforts and is not conducted on all skills for all children. In other words, at Tier 2, teachers gather information on select groups of children who may have similar needs related to a component of a common outcome, may be challenged to express themselves verbally or nonverbally as expected for their age, or may have a skill that has stalled and needs a boost of instruction to become more sophisticated and/or reach the expected level. At Tier 2, teachers may collect weekly or monthly data (i.e., administer targeted probes) to better track how children are responding to instructional efforts. In Danny's situation, for example, Ms. Grissom may determine a plan for targeted and temporary instruction to improve Danny's range of motion for his foot and ankle based on recommendations from his physical therapist. She may set a goal of having him kick a ball back and forth with a peer daily. Ms. Grissom then performs a weekly assessment of Danny's performance, measuring the frequency and duration that he can kick the ball back and forth with a peer. Each week after gathering information and documenting, Ms. Grissom summarizes, analyzes, and interprets the data. On the basis of the five-step process, Ms. Grissom may come to realize that Danny has increased the frequency (the number of times he kicks the ball back and forth) as well as the duration (how long he is able to continue kicking the ball back and forth). By the end of the third week, Ms. Grissom concludes that Danny no longer needs the temporary, targeted instruction, and Ms. Grissom and the physical therapist return Danny to Tier 1 instruction and monitoring.

Within Tier 3, performance monitoring consists of continuous collection of systematic data on individual skills and behaviors for particular children. (Refer to Figure 8.7.) In other words, at Tier 3 teachers gather data for individual children who are missing foundational or prerequisite skills that are deemed necessary for the children to make progress toward a common goal or outcome. The child may not have demonstrated performance within Tier 2 or may have a Tier 3 need that circumvented the implementation of Tier 2 efforts. At Tier 3, teachers may collect minute-by-minute, hour-by-hour, or daily counts and tallies, written narratives, and/or permanent products that are related to individualized skills. On the basis of the five-step DDDM process, Ms. Grissom will keep a tally sheet that records each time the correct or incorrect response occurred. She monitors performance on the skill every hour to inform instruction. At the end of the day, she summarizes, analyzes, and interprets the data sheet to determine whether Danny is performing the specific skill as expected (i.e., whether he is showing an immediacy of change and a positive trend line and/or pattern) or whether the instruction needs to be modified and, if so, how (i.e., through examination of antecedent, behavior, and consequence). Tier 3 performance monitoring is designed and employed to supplement, enhance, and support Tier 1 and Tier 2 instruction by remediation of the relevant area and development of compensatory strategies. Tier 3 performance monitoring (and instruction) on the same skill are intentionally revisited and modified on the basis of the present level of functioning. Closely monitoring performance allows teachers to revise instruction routinely to ensure that the child is reaching his or her maximum potential. Appendix A provides a case example of how to engage in a tiered model of performance monitoring for serving groups of children in a blended program.

Sharing Performance Monitoring Information

A logical step after decisions are made regarding children's performance may be to report the changes (good, bad, or otherwise). In actuality, family members and other team members should be involved throughout the performance monitoring process, thus making an additional step of reporting to others unnecessary. There are times, however, when teachers are expected to share performance monitoring information, such as during parent–teacher conferences, transition meetings, and IEP meetings. The next section provides suggestions and strategies for sharing performance monitoring information.

Communicating with families

As was noted in Chapter 3, teachers can employ a number of specific strategies to involve family members as partners in their children's education and to enhance communication with families (Woods & McCormick, 2002). Table 8.3 provides communication strategies that may be useful to

Table 8.3. Useful communication strategies for discussing a child's performance with families

Strategies	Teacher Actions
Active listening	• Allow for wait time (i.e., allow for time in between comments, questions, suggestions) • Be willing to listen to the family's concerns/questions/suggestions, and preferences • Demonstrate active listening through nonverbal communication (e.g., nodding head, eye contact) • Engage in reflective listening skills (i.e., repeat what was heard) to affirm understanding • Use verbal and nonverbal communication (i.e., lean forward and show interest, mirror the other's persons body language)
Acknowledgement	• Share relevant and pertinent data from the family • Recognize family's priorities and opinions through verbal and nonverbal means • Allow for differences in opinions • Mention child's strengths
Collaborate	• Seek alternative solutions aimed to meet the needs of families • Engage in a two-way process of information sharing and understanding (i.e., cultural reciprocity) • Adapt your professional recommendations to the value system of the family • Aim for consensus versus total agreement
Participation	• Actively participate in conversations, minimize distractions • Respond in a timely manner • Promote a positive atmosphere (welcome, reduce silence) • Allow access by families to data (qualitative and quantitative data)
Respect	• Allow for differences in opinions • Seek alternative solutions which meet the needs of families • Realize the family is the first teacher • Allow families to complete thoughts and sentences before responding • Minimize use of jargon
Sharing	• Maximize opportunities to use or enjoy something jointly with others • Communicate strengths of child and family • Keep information confidential • Share information in a variety of ways (i.e., in person, e-mails, notes, text, web sites)

teachers when they discuss performance monitoring information with families. The overarching suggestion is to ensure that communication is bidirectional, meaning that teachers should avoid a one-way reporting of information to families and should strive to have a conversation during which both parties share information, concerns, and ideas. Despite their best efforts to communicate effectively, teachers often express their concern about how to talk to families regarding a child who isn't making desired progress, how to deliver news about a child's lack of progress in development, and how to discuss challenging behaviors that are seen in the classroom. When families are involved throughout the processes of program planning, instruction, and performance monitoring, the conversations about difficult topics become less like meetings in which teachers are telling families something and more like a partnership in which each partner jointly recognizes when there may be reason for concern. Thus, sharing performance monitoring information should not be a point-in-time event, but rather a continuous effort (Wolery, 2004).

Teachers also express concern and frustration when they feel that their attempts to share information with families have been made to no avail. For example, a teacher may write notes home using a communication notebook, but family members "never write back," leading the teacher to assume that the notebook has never been opened. Before becoming frustrated, teachers need to consider several factors. First, has the teacher discussed with families the intent of the communication notebook? In other words, do families know what to expect from the teacher and what the teacher expects in return? Second, has the teacher considered literacy and language as possible barriers to a family member's access and participation in communicating through a written format? Third, has the teacher talked to the family about its preferences in terms of mode and frequency of sharing information? In other words, some families may enjoy communicating back and forth on a daily or weekly basis; others may appreciate a less interactive mode such as a monthly newsletter, an updated web site, or more personal, but less frequent, phone calls; while still others may want frequent informal modes of communication such as texting, twittering, and e-mailing.

Keeping the proper perspective on the interaction can make it easier for teachers to share difficult or sensitive information. For example, if a teacher has evidence that a child's development is delayed and that the child needs further testing or perhaps special services, the teacher may fear that the family will not agree or may become upset at hearing the news. Keep in mind that it is not the teacher's job to convince a family how it should feel or what it should think, or to keep family members from hearing objective concerns. It is the teacher's job, as a developmental specialist, to share all information as objectively and meaningfully as possible and then engage in a discussion with the family about what the information may mean, what the next steps might be, and how the family feels about the information. Sometimes families will need time to process the information or need to hear it again or in a different way, and they need to know that they can ask questions and express their own concerns. Thus, the key to any difficult situation is to ensure that there is a relationship of trust and open communication already in place.

How and When to Share Performance Monitoring Information

When teachers share performance monitoring information with families, as discussed in Chapter 7 with regard to summarizing, it is best for them to use a mixture of methods to convey children's strengths, emerging skills, and areas of continued need. For example, matching a picture with a few written notes or a graph with percentages may have more meaning than a picture, a note, a graph, or a percentage standing alone. Mixing and matching methods also ensures that the information is being conveyed through multiple means of representation. In other words, teachers should document performance data by varying portrayals of the child's current level of performance. Documenting data in a mixed manner helps teachers to prepare and articulate their findings to others.

Furthermore, as is the case with needs and instruction, performance monitoring, reporting efforts should be tiered (i.e., the frequency and intensity of sharing should be tiered). For example, Tier 1 performance toward common outcomes may be shared with all children's families two, three, or four times a year. Tier 2 performance monitoring information may be shared only with the families of select groups of children each month. Lastly, Tier 3 performance monitoring information may be shared with individual families on a weekly basis. Again, like other aspects of tiering, the frequency and intensity (meaning the amount of effort that is put forth) vary, given the tier of performance monitoring. Teachers should avoid a one-size-fits-all approach such as doing a comprehensive, detailed report on each individual child regarding all skills and abilities (Schwartz & Olswang, 1996). When common outcomes are being addressed through Tier 1 instruction, broad samples of a child's performance are sufficient.

Regardless of the format or frequency of sharing information, most teachers will be faced at one point or another with the task of creating a "report card" and sharing a child's "progress" with families. Unfortunately, report cards are a feature of push-down policies that may work in a K–12 environment but that are not very helpful in a blended early childhood classrooms (Cavallaro & Haney, 1999; Schwarttz & Olswang 1996). Given that young children who are served in blended classrooms have diverse abilities and that all children will have tiered needs, the idea of reporting

---

BOX 8.5

Suggestions for developing report cards within blended programs

1. Create report cards that contain information regarding children's performance on Tier 1 outcomes. For example, children's performance as measured by and summarized using a comprehensive curriculum-based assessment.

2. Organize Tier 1 outcomes into manageable parts of developmental domains and content areas (i.e., create classifications or strands that represent behaviors from a broad domain/content area, but not all the specific skills). For example, Tier 1 outcome reports should include what is expected of all children regarding participation, counting, classifying, one-to-one correspondence, and engaging in cooperative activities.

3. Include qualitative AND quantitative data regarding children's performance toward common outcomes. For example, information on how the child has increased the number of activities they participates in AND the types of activities (e.g., small group, large group, those with movement and music, those requiring manipulation of small objects) the child consistently participates in.

4. Include information as needed for subgroups or individual children regarding performances toward Tier 2 and Tier 3 outcomes. For example, include narrative, numerical, and/or visual summaries of a child's performance toward targeted or individualized outcomes such as degree to which they are understood by others, extent to which they have gained prerequisite or foundational skills that will increase their access, participation, and progress toward common outcomes, and/or how they have responded to instruction regarding a missing component of a common outcomes.

---

performance data for all children across levels can be an overwhelming task. Box 8.5 includes suggestions for developing report cards within blended programs.

SUMMARY

The purpose of Chapter 8 was to describe recommended practices for performance monitoring for individuals and groups of children. First, the chapter defined and discussed assessment for the purpose of revising instruction (i.e., for performance monitoring). Second, information was provided on two broad recommended practices for performance monitoring—a holistic approach and a data-driven process—and the recommendations were illustrated. Next, a tiered model of performance monitoring was shared as a means of addressing the challenges of systematically collecting data for children who are served in blended classrooms. Multiple case examples exemplified how to engage in the tiered model. Lastly, suggestions and strategies for sharing performance-monitoring reports were discussed.

REFERENCES

Alberto, P.A., & Troutman, A.C. (1999). *Applied behavior analysis for teachers* (5th ed.). Upper Saddle River, NJ: Prentice Hall.

Bagnato, S.J., Neisworth, J.T., & Pretti-Frontczak, K. (2010). *LINKing authentic assessment and early childhood intervention: Best measures for best practices* (2nd ed.). Baltimore: Paul H. Brookes Publishing CoBricker, D.D., Capt, B., Pretti-Frontczak, K., Johnson, J., Slentz, K., Straka, E., et al. (2002). *The Assessment, Evaluation and Programming System (AEPS) for infants and young children: AEPS test for birth to three years and three to six years* (2nd ed.). Baltimore: Paul H. Brookes Publishing Co.

Blankenship, C.S. (1985). Using curriculum-based assessment data to make instructional decisions. *Exceptional Children, 52*, 233–238.

Branscombe, N.A., Castle, K., Dorsey, A.G., Surbeck, E., & Taylor, J.B. (2003). *Early childhood curriculum: A constructivist perspective.* Boston: Houghton Mifflin.

Brinton, B., & Fujiki, M. (2003). Blending qualitative and quantitative methods in language research and intervention. *American Journal of Speech–Language Pathology, 12*, 165–171.

Cavallaro, C. C., & Haney, M. (1999). *Preschool inclusion.* Baltimore: Paul H. Brookes Publishing Co.

Creswell, J. W., & Plano Clark, V. L. (2007). *Designing and Conducting Mixed Methods Research.* Thousand Oaks, CA: Sage Publications.

Copple, C., & Bredekamp, S. (Eds.) (2009). *Developmentally appropriate practice in early childhood programs serving children from birth through age 8 (3rd ed.).* Washington, DC: National Association for the Education of Young Children.

Darling-Hammond, L., & Snyder, J. (2000). Authentic assessment of teaching in context. *Teaching and Teacher Education, 16*(5), 523–545.

Deno, S.Eikeseth, S., Smith, T., Jahr, E., & Eldevik, S. (2002). Intensive behavioral treatment at school for 4- to 7-year-old children with autism: A 1-year comparison controlled study. *Behavior Modification, 26*(1), 49–68.

Fuchs, L.S., & Fuchs, D. (1986). Effects of systematic formative evaluation: A meta-analysis. *Exceptional Children, 53*, 199–208.

Fuchs, L.S., & Fuchs, D. (1999). Monitoring student progress toward the development of reading competence: A review of three forms of classroom-based assessment. *School Psychology Review, 28*(4), 659–671.

Fuchs, L.S., Fuchs, D., Hamlett, C.L., & Stecker, P.M. (1991). Effects of curriculum-based measurement and consultation on teacher planning and student achievement in mathematics operations. *American Educational Research Journal, 28*(3), 617–641.

Garrison, C., & Ehringhaus, M. (2007). *Formative and Summative Assessments in The Classroom.* Retrieved from http://www.nmsa.org/Publications/WebExclusive/Assessment/ tabid/1120/Default.aspx

Gestwicki, C. (1999). *Developmentally appropriate practice: Curriculum development in early education* (2nd ed.). Albany, NY: Delmar.

Gickling, E.E., & Thompson, V.P. (1985). A personal view of curriculum-based assessment. *Exceptional Children, 52*(3), 205–218.

Godfrey, S.A., Grisham-Brown, J., Schuster, J.W., & Hemmeter, M.L. (2003). The effects of three techniques on student participation with preschool children with attending problems. *Education and Treatment of Children, 26*(3), 255–272.

Grisham-Brown, J., Hallam, R., & Pretti-Frontczak, K. (2008). Preparing Head Start personnel to use a curriculum-based assessment: An innovative practice in the "age of accountability." *Journal of Early Intervention, 30*(4), 271–281.

Grisham-Brown, J., Hemmeter, M.L., & Pretti-Frontczak, K. (2005). *Blended practices for teaching young children in inclusive settings.* Baltimore: Paul H. Brookes Publishing Co.

Hall, G.E., & Loucks, S.F. (1978). *Innovation configurations: Analyzing the adaptations of innovations.* Austin: University of Texas, Research and Development Center for Teacher Education.

Heroman, C., Burts, D. C., B., K., Bickart, T. (2010). *Teaching Strategies GOLD™ Objectives for development and learning: Birth through kindergarten.* Washington, DC: Teaching Strategies, Inc.

High/Scope Educational Research Foundation (2003). Preschool COR development and validation. In *User Guide: High/Scope Preschool Child Observation Record* (pp. 29–31). Ypsilanti, Michigan: High/Scope Press.

High/Scope Educational Research Foundation (2002). Development and validation. In *User Guide: High/Scope Child Observation Record for Infants and Toddlers* (pp. 31–36). Ypsilanti, Michigan: High/Scope Press.

Hojnoski, R.L., Gischlar, K.L., & Missall, K.N. (2009a). Improving child outcomes with data-based decision making: Collecting data. *Young Exceptional Children, 12,* 32–44.

Hojnoski, R.L., Gischlar, K.L., & Missall, K.N. (2009b). Improving child outcomes with data-based decision making: Graphing data. *Young Exceptional Children, 12,* 15–30.

Hojnoski, R.L., Gischlar, K.L., & Missall, K.N. (2009c). Improving child outcomes with data-based decision making: Interpreting and using data. *Young Exceptional Children, 13,* 2–18.

Hojnoski, R.L., & Missall, K.N. (2007). Monitoring preschoolers' language and early literacy growth and development. *Young Exceptional Children, 10,* 17–27.

Ingersoll, B., & Schreibman, L. (2006). Teaching reciprocal imitation skills to young children with autism using a naturalistic behavioral approach: Effects on language, pretend play, and joint attention. *Journal of Autism and Developmental Disorders, 36*(4), 487–505.

Jackson, P. (1968). *Life in classrooms.* New York: Holt, Rinehart, & Winston.

Katz, L. & Chard, S.C. (2000). *Engaging children's minds: The project approach* (2nd ed.). Stamford, CT: Ablex Publishing.

Kazdin, A.E. (1982). *Single-case research designs: Methods for clinical and applied settings.* New York: Oxford University Press.

Kearney, A.J. (2008). *Understanding applied behavior analysis: an introduction to ABA for parents, teachers, and other professionals.* Philadelphia: Jessica Kingsley Publishers.

Klingner, J.K., Sorrells, A.M., & Barrera, M. (2007). Three-tiered models with culturally and linguistically diverse students. In D. Haager, S. Vaughn, & J. Klingner (Eds.), *Validated practices for three tiers of reading intervention.* Baltimore: Paul H. Brookes Publishing Co.

Lovaas, O.I. (1987). Behavioral treatment and normal educational and intellectual functioning in young autistic children. *Journal of Consulting and Clinical Psychology, 55,* 3–9.

Macy, M. (2007). Theory and theory-driven practices of activity-based intervention. *Journal of Early & Intensive Behavior Intervention, 4*(3), 561–585.

McAfee, O., & Leong, D. (2002). *Assessing and guiding young children's development and learning.* Boston: Allyn and Bacon.

McConnell, S. (2000). Assessment in early intervention and early childhood education: Building on the past to project the future. *Topics in Early Childhood Education, 20*(1), 43–48.

McLean, M., Wolery, M., & Bailey, D.B. (2004). *Assessing infants and preschoolers with special needs* (3rd ed.). Upper Saddle River, NJ: Prentice Hall.

Montessori, M.M., Jr. (1976). *Education for human development: Understanding Montessori.* New York: Schocken Books.

National Association for the Education of Young Children & National Association of Early Childhood Specialists in State Departments of Education. (2003). *Early childhood curriculum, assessment, and program evaluation building an effective, accountable system in programs for children birth through age 8.* Retrieved November 5, 2008, from http://www.naeyc.org/files/naeyc/file/positions/CAPEexpand.pdf

Pretti-Frontczak, K., & Bricker, D. (2000). Enhancing the quality of individualized education plan (IEP) goals and objectives. *Journal of Early Intervention, 23,* 92–105.

Pretti-Frontczak, K., & Bricker, D. (2004). *An activity-based approach to early intervention* (3rd ed.). Baltimore: Paul H. Brookes Publishing Co.

Pretti-Frontczak, K.L. (2002). Using curriculum-based measures to promote a linked system approach. *Assessment for Effective Intervention, 27*(4), 15–21.

Raver, S. (2003). Keeping track: Using routine-based instruction and monitoring. *Young Exceptional Children, 6*(3), 12–20.

Teaching Strategies Inc. (2009). *Research foundation of the Teaching Strategies GOLD™ ssessment system* (field test ed.). Washington, DC: Teaching Strategies.

Ross, D., Roberts, P., & Scott, K. (1998). *Mediating factors in child development outcomes children in lone-parent families.* Ottawa: Human Resources Development Canada. Retrieved on January 17, 2009, from http://www.hrsdc.gc.ca/eng/cs/sp/sdc/pkrf/publications/research/1998-001259/page00.shtml

Rous, B., & Hyson, M. (Eds.) (2007). *Promoting positive outcomes for children with disabilities: Recommendations for curriculum, assessment and program evaluation.* Division of Early Childhood of the Council for Exceptional Children. Retrieved February 2, 2010, from http://www.decsped.org/uploads/docs/about_dec/position_concept_papers/Prmtg_Pos_Outcomes_Companion_Paper.pdf

Ross, D., Roberts, P., & Scott, K. (1998).*Mediating Factors in Child Development Outcomes Children in Lone-Parent Families.* Ottawa: Human Resources Development Canada.

Sandall, S., Hemmeter, M.L., Smith, B., & McLean, M. (2005). *DEC recommended practices: A comprehensive guide for practical application.* Longmont, CO: Sopris West.

Sandall, S., & Schwartz, I. (2002). Building blocks for teaching preschoolers with special needs. Baltimore: Paul H. Brookes Publishing Co.

Sandall, S.R., Schwartz, I.S., & LaCroix, B. (2004). Interventionists' perspectives about data collection in integrated early childhood classrooms. *Journal of Early Intervention, 26,* 161–174.

Schwartz, I.S., & Olswang, L.B. (1996). Evaluating child behavior change in natural settings: Exploring alternative strategies for data collection. *Topics in Early Childhood Special Education, 16*(1), 82–101

Trister Dodge, D., Colker, L., & Heroman, C. (2002). *The Creative Curriculum® Developmental Continuum for Ages 3–5.* Washington, DC: Teaching Strategies, Inc.

Wolf, M.M. (1978). Social validity: The case for subjective measurement or how applied behavior analysis is finding its heart. *General Applied Behavior Analysis, 11,* 203–214.

Wolrey, M. (2004). Monitoring child progress. In M. McLean, M. Wolrey, & D.B. Bailey (Eds.), *Assessing infants and preschoolers with special needs* (3rd ed., pp. 545–584). Upper Saddle River, NJ: Prentice Hall.

Woods, J.J., & McCormick, K.M. (2002). Toward an integration of child and family-centered practices in the assessment of preschool children: Welcoming the family. *Young Exceptional Children, 5*(3), 2–11.

Ysseldyke, J., & Tardrew, S. (2007). Use of a progress monitoring system to enable teachers to differentiate mathematics instruction. *Journal of Applied School Psychology, 24*(1), 1–28.

Ysseldyke, J.E., Thurlow, M.L, & Christenson, S.L. (1987). *Teacher effectiveness and teacher decision-making: Implications for effective instruction of handicapped students.* Monograph No. 5. Instructional Alternatives Project. Minneapolis: University of Minnesota.

Ziolkowski, R., & Goldstein, H. (2008). Effects of an embedded phonological awareness intervention during repeated book reading on preschool children with language delays. *Journal of Early Intervention, 31*(1), 67–90.

APPENDIX A

Case Example of Tiered Performance Monitoring

Chapter 7 described how Mrs. Donovan and her team used a CBA to follow all of her children's current abilities, interests, preferences, and family priorities and to design instructional opportunities to match each child's level of need (Gickling & Thompson, 1985; Pretti-Frontczak, 2002; Woods & McCormick, 2002). We now continue with the three case examples introduced in Chapter 7 to illustrate how Mrs. Donovan revised her initial instructional decisions with the use of a tiered model of performance monitoring. Specifically, case 1 illustrates performance monitoring related to Tier 1, case 2 relates to Tier 2 practices, and case 3 relates to Tier 3 practices.

TIER 1 PERFORMANCE MONITORING

Following several months of instruction, Mrs. Donovan and her team again *gathered* information on *all* children during daily activities, interviewed familiar caregivers, and conducted authentic assessment activities as needed. All children's performance was *documented* by means of numerical scores and written notes to complete the AEPS (i.e., the AEPS was administered for a second time to *all* children regardless of their abilities and level of need as determined earlier in the year). As noted in Chapter 7, a score of 2 indicates that the child independently and consistently met item criteria. A score of 1 indicates that 1) the specific criteria were partially met, 2) the child needed assistance, 3) the child inconsistently performed the criteria, and/or 4) the child's performance toward the criteria was emerging. A score of 0 indicates that the child was not yet able to perform or meet the stated item criteria. Specific notes were used to indicate additional information regarding children's performance. For example, a note of "Q" indicates that quality was of concern for the specific item, "B" indicates that the child's behavior interfered with his or her performance, and "D" indicates that a direct prompt was needed. Table 8.4 illustrates Starr's performance on a portion of AEPS items that are related to engaging in cooperative activities for both administration periods (i.e., October and March).

Mrs. Donovan then *summarized* each child's performance across major areas of the AEPS (e.g., engaging in cooperative activities), using a

Table 8.4. Starr's performance during October and March

	Starr					
	October			March		
AEPS Items	Score	Note	Comments	Score	Note	Comments
Participation in small group (watches, listens, participates)	1			1		
Interacts appropriately with materials during small-group activities	1		Will repeat actions she has seen others engage in	1		
Responds appropriately to directions during small-group activities	2			2		
Looks at appropriate object, person, or event during small-group activities	2			2		
Participation in large group (watches, listens, participates)	1		Will follow lead of other children	1		
Interacts appropriately with materials during large-group activities	1			2		
Responds appropriately to directions during large-group activities	2			2		
Looks at appropriate object, person, or event during large-group activities	2			2		
Interacts with others as play partners	1			1		With specific friends
Responds to others in distress or need	0			0		
Establishes and maintains proximity to others	1	D	Needs to be invited to be with others	1		With certain peers
Takes turns with others	1	D	Will give an item, but not request from others	1		Beginning to ask for turns
Initiates greeting to others who are familiar	0		Does not initiate	1		Beginning to demonstrate
Responds to affective initiations from others	2			2		
Initiates cooperative activity	0		Does not initiate	1		Beginning to demonstrate
Joins others in cooperative activity	1	D	When invited/ prompted	1		Specific peers/ activities

(continued)

Table 8.4. *(continued)*

| | Starr | | | | | |
| | October | | | March | | |
	Score	Note	Comments	Score	Note	Comments
Maintains cooperative participation with others	1	D		1		
Shares or exchanges objects	1	D	Will give an item if directly asked	1		With specific peers

Key: D, direct prompt needed

combination of narrative summaries, visual summaries, and numerical summaries. The narrative summaries captured Mrs. Donovan's self-reflections regarding the performance of the entire group of children. See Figure 8.8 for an example of a narrative summary regarding a group of children's performance related to engaging in cooperative activities. Since "initiation" was identified as a need for several children and is considered to be a key part of engaging in cooperative activities, Mrs. Donovan created a visual summary of the class' performance around items related to initiation. (See Figure 8.9.) Lastly, numerical summaries included each child's percentage of items mastered, emerging, and not yet demonstrated. Figure 8.10 shows the combined numerical summary for the entire class on the assessment items that are related to engaging in cooperative activities.

Mrs. Donovan then *analyzed* the summaries. She saw that Chuck, Rob, Gabriel, Heather, Rosa, Jacob, and Jared (i.e., the children who were originally identified as being at Tier 1 for engaging in cooperative activities) continued to demonstrate patterns of expected performance. The seven children showed an upward trend of development over time, as evidenced by an increase in the number of items that were marked "mastered." Starr, Jamel, Lisa, and Jamie also showed an increase in the number of items that were marked "mastered." Although Trever made only small gains numerically, the notes from the AEPS showed that he had fewer items affected by interfering behaviors.

> 3/12—Chuck, Rob, Gabriel, Heather, Rosa, Jacob, and Jared continue to engage in cooperative play, initiating activities and greeting one another regularly. Jamel now greets certain peers upon arrival. Starr responds to peers, and will initiate play with Heather and Rosa. Jamie's peers can now understand what she is saying therefore Jamie has begun to talk to peers during play. Lisa will initiate greetings, specifically to adults. Trever engages in elaborate play scenarios; however, he does not initiate or invite others into play.

Figure 8.8. Narrative summary of performance of a group of children.

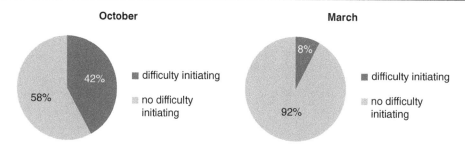

Figure 8.9. Percentage of children having difficulty with items involving initiation.

Using her analysis, Mrs. Donovan *interpreted* that in terms of Tier 1, all of the children made progress toward the common outcome of engaging in cooperative activities at different rates regarding different aspects of development. Specifically, Starr and Jamel made progress by beginning to demonstrate the ability to initiate greetings and cooperative activities. Furthermore, her analysis of the notes on the AEPS indicated that fewer Qs were noted for Lisa and Jamie, which she interpreted as showing growth since October, when they demonstrated a pattern of being difficult to understand. When she considered Trever's minimal numeric progress, she understood that Trever wouldn't show changes toward the common outcome until his Tier 3 needs were fully addressed. Trever's progress was

	% of items mastered		% of items emerging		% of items not yet demonstrated	
	Oct	March	Oct	March	Oct	March
Gabriel	39	61	61	39	0	0
Jamie	11	11	83	89	6	0
Trever	0	0	61	72	39	28
Rosa	78	83	22	17	0	0
Starr	28	33	55	61	17	6
Chuck	39	61	61	39	0	0
Jamel	17	22	44	78	39	0
Rob	67	72	33	28	0	0
Jacob	78	83	22	17	0	0
Lisa	22	22	72	78	6	0
Jared	39	61	61	39	0	0
Heather	67	72	33	28	0	0

Figure 8.10. Numerical summary of individual child's performance on the AEPS

evidenced by the fact that he was no longer demonstrating as many interfering behaviors and that he was beginning to follow one-step directions.

TIER 2 PERFORMANCE MONITORING

As Mrs. Donovan provided Tier 2 instruction, she continued to implement the five-step DDDM process. In addition to making efforts at Tier 1, she collected more frequent data on select children who had Tier 2 needs and received Tier 2 instruction.

Starr and Jamel

Mrs. Donovan monitored Starr and Jamel's performance on initiating greetings and/or cooperative activities with peers. First, she *gathered* information regarding Starr and Jamel's performance during three activities (small-group centers, large-group time in a circle, and outdoor play) on a designated day each week. She *documented* when each child either initiated a greeting or a cooperative activity. (See Table 8.5.)

At the end of each data collection day, Mrs. Donovan *summarized* the data by totaling the number of initiations made by each child. At the end of the first month of instruction, she summarized the numerical summaries visually by plotting the totals on a graph. Figure 8.11 shows the visual summary of the data collected during the first month of instruction for both children.

Mrs. Donovan used the information on the collection form, the numerical summaries, and the visual summaries to *analyze* the data. The visual summary revealed that Starr responded quickly to the instruction. The data and trend of the data points are evidence of Starr's positive performance on the target behavior. Mrs. Donovan also saw that Starr's performance was consistent and showed little variability. When she reviewed the data collection form, she noticed that Starr had begun to initiate greetings or cooperative activities during circle time and centers; however, she did not initiate interactions during outdoor play.

Table 8.5.   Documentation form of how often and when target children initiated greetings or initiated cooperative activities during first month of targeted instruction

Date	Name	Circle time	Center time	Outdoors	Total
11/3	Starr	−	+	−	1
	Jamel	+	−	+	2
11/10	Starr	++	++	−	4
	Jamel	−	−	−	0
11/17	Starr	++++	+++	−	7
	Jamel	++	++	++	6
11/24	Starr	+++	+++++	−	8
	Jamel	−	−	−	0

Key: + each time child initiated activity or greeting   − did not initiate during activity

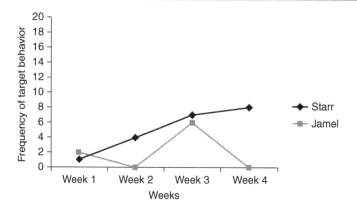

Figure 8.11. Visual summary for Starr and Jamel during first month of Tier 2 instruction.

The visual analysis revealed that Jamel responded to instruction initially; however, his performance was inconsistent across the first several weeks, as evidenced by the large "peaks and valleys" created by the data points and the lack of a desired trend line. The documentation form for Jamel revealed that although his initiations were inconsistent, he did greet and engage in cooperative activities in all three settings observed.

Because Starr began to demonstrate the target behavior and the data revealed an upward trend during circle time and center time, Mrs. Donovan interpreted the situation as indicating that the Tier 2 instruction was positively affecting Starr's performance, at least during two of the activities observed. Because Starr had not initiated during outdoor play, Mrs. Donovan decided to involve more peers in the peer-mediated intervention during outdoor time. Although Jamel had demonstrated the target behavior in all three settings, he did not do so with the frequency that would be expected or desired, given the level of targeted instruction he had received. Mrs. Donovan also noted that Jamel's attendance record was regular during the first month of instruction and that he experienced no changes in routine, medication, or other factors that could have affected or explained his inconsistent performance (Ross, Roberts, & Scott, 1998). She decided to revise Jamel's instructional plan to create more opportunities for peer-mediated intervention.

After revising her instructional efforts, Mrs. Donovan continued to *gather* information, *document* Starr and Jamel's performance (i.e., how often and where they initiated greetings or cooperative activities), and *summarize* the data both numerically (by adding the total number of initiations) and visually (by plotting the aggregated totals on a graph). The documentation form for the second month of targeted instruction is displayed in Table 8.6. Figure 8.12 is a visual summary of the data collected for both children over the second month of targeted instruction.

Table 8.6.   Summary of children's performance for second month of instruction

Date	Name	Circle time	Center time	Outdoors	Total
12/1	Starr	+++	+++++++		10
	Jamel	+		+	2
12/8	Starr	++	++++	+++	9
	Jamel	++	+++	+	6
12/15	Starr	++	++++++	+++++++++	16
	Jamel	+++	+++	+++	9
12/22	Starr	+++	++++++	+++++++++	17
	Jamel	+++	+++++	++++	12

Key: + each time child initiated activity or greeting   − did not initiate during activity

After the second month of Tier 2 instruction, Mrs. Donovan *ana-lyzed* the data and looked for patterns and trends to indicate whether the targeted instruction was affecting the children's performance. As during the first month of instruction, Starr continued to show an upward trend in performance with little variability. When Mrs. Donovan reviewed the data collection forms, she also saw that Starr was demonstrating the target behavior across all three settings. During the second month of instruction, Jamel began to show a consistent pattern of growth in his initiations across a variety of settings. The data revealed an upward and positive trend in the frequency of the target behavior, with little variability. Because both children were demonstrating the target behaviors across settings and doing so multiple times per setting, Mrs. Donovan *interpreted* the situation as indicating that the instruction was having a positive impact on both children's performance. She decided to reduce the data collection frequency to once a month in order to monitor the children's maintenance of the skill.

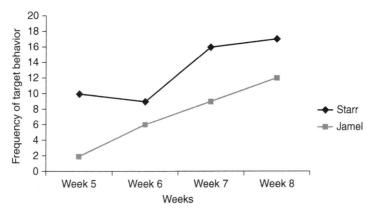

Figure 8.12.   Visual summary of children's performance during second month of targeted instruction following revision of intervention plan.

Lisa and Jamie

Mrs. Donovan *gathered* information about the performance of Lisa and Jamie by observing each child during play time for 15 minutes, 1 day per month. She *documented* what each child said by recording her utterances (i.e., each time she said a word, phrase, or sentence). She noted whether what was said was intelligible (i.e., understood by others). Mrs. Donovan summarized the information numerically by determining the percentage of utterances that were intelligible. Table 8.7 shows a numerical summary of the data that were collected during the first and second month of targeted instruction.

Mrs. Donovan *analyzed* the information by reviewing the written language records and the numerical summaries. When she reviewed the numerical summary in Table 8.7, Mrs. Donovan noticed that both children demonstrated an increase in the percentage of intelligible utterances. The written language records further showed that both children demonstrated decreased intelligibility as their phrase length increased. According to the speech and language pathologist, that pattern was to be expected, given each child's current level of performance.

Mrs. Donovan then *interpreted* the findings. Because both children were showing improved intelligibility but had not yet reached a level at which they could receive universal instruction along with typically developing peers, Mrs. Donovan decided to continue with Tier 2 instruction for both children and monitor monthly.

TIER 3 PERFORMANCE MONITORING

As was noted in Chapter 7, because Trever had difficulty following one-step directions (evidenced by his screaming, hitting, falling to the ground, and refusing to move during certain transitions) and because such an ability is a prerequisite to participation in cooperative activities, Mrs. Donovan determined that Trever had a Tier 3 need (Mrs. Donovan *gathered* information about Trever during transitions and *documented* his performance on the data collection form) shown in Table 8.8.

In order to address Trever's need, Mrs. Donovan decided to teach Trever to follow one-step directions during transitions. She continued to *summarize* the information by totaling the number of times that Trever demonstrated the interfering behaviors during transitions, as well as the number of times he followed the direction, and plotted the totals on a

Table 8.7. Percentage of intelligible utterances across 2 months of Tier 2 instruction

Name	November (First Month of Instruction)	December (Second Month of Instruction)
Lisa	50%	59%
Jamie	60%	68%

Table 8.8. Summary of children's performance for second month of instruction

Daily Transitions	Date: 11/2	Date: 11/3	Date: 11/4	Date: 11/5	Date: 11/6
From bus to classroom					
From cubby to opening circle	−	−	−	−	−
From circle to centers/choice		−	−	−	
Between activities during centers/choice	− − − (demonstrated 3 interfering behaviors)	− − − (demonstrated 3 interfering behaviors)	− − −− − (demonstrated 5 interfering behaviors)	− − − − (demonstrated 4 interfering behaviors)	− − − − − (demonstrated 5 interfering behaviors)
From choice to snack					
From snack to outdoors					
From outdoors into class	−	−	−	−	−
From cubby to small group	−		−	−	−
From small group to movement circle					
From circle to cubby	−	−		−	
From cubby to bus	+		+	+	
Totals: +	1	0	1	1	0
−	7	7	9	9	8

Key: + followed one-step direction   − demonstrated interfering behaviors: screaming, hitting, falling, refusing

graph. Figure 8.13 shows the visual summaries for the first week of Tier 3 instruction.

Mrs. Donovan *analyzed* the data by comparing the visual summary from the baseline with that of the first week. The summary showed her that there was little change in frequency of the measured behaviors (i.e., the lines representing the frequency of behaviors remained at the same level). Trever's performance did not change as a result of the instruction. The data collection form showed that Trever continued to engage in the interfering behaviors during specific transitions. When she *interpreted* the information, Mrs. Donovan determined that she needed to revise the instructional plan because Trever's performance remained relatively unchanged. The instructional change she made was to provide more visual structure for Trever before and during transitions. She also modified the consequences that were given to include stickers each time he followed a

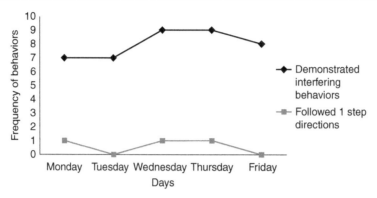

Figure 8.13. Frequency of behaviors during first week of Tier 3 instruction.

one-step direction during a transition. During the implementation of the revised plan, Mrs. Donovan continued to *gather, document,* and *summarize* Trever's performance. Figure 8.14 shows the visual summary for the second week of Tier 3 instruction.

Again, Mrs. Donovan looked for changes in the patterns and trends, which helped her to plan for Trever. During week 2, she noticed that Trever's performance began to change relatively quickly. The visual summary revealed an upward trend in following directions (meaning that he was engaging in that behavior more often) and a downward trend in the interfering behaviors (meaning that he was engaging in those behaviors less often). When she compared the visual summaries from the baseline, week one, and week two, Mrs. Donovan also saw changes in level of both behaviors. Specifically, she saw that the line representing the interfering behavior was much lower on the week 2 summary (indicating an overall lower frequency) and the line representing following directions was much higher (indicating an overall higher frequency). Furthermore, she saw that

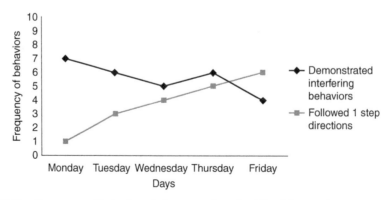

Figure 8.14. Frequency of behaviors during second week of Tier 3 instruction.

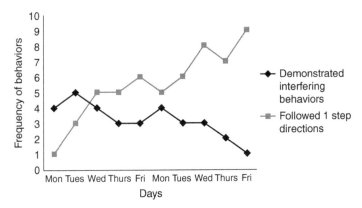

Figure 8.15. Frequency of behaviors: Third and fourth weeks of Tier 3 instruction.

the interfering behaviors continued to occur during predictable transitions. On the basis of her *analysis,* Mrs. Donovan *interpreted* the situation as indicating that the level and type of instruction she was providing were affecting Trever's performance in a positive way. She decided to continue with the intervention and performance monitoring as planned. Figure 8.15 depicts the frequency data over the next 2 weeks of Tier 3 instruction.

As Mrs. Donovan reviewed and *analyzed* the data, she discovered that the frequency of the interfering behaviors continued to decrease across all settings. Trever began to predictably transition between activities, given the supports and structure Mrs. Donovan had planned. He also was able to increase the frequency with which he followed one-step directions. Because Trever's behavior was no longer interfering with transitioning, Mrs. Donovan decided to reduce the amount of instruction that was provided to him during transitions and to monitor his performance monthly to ensure maintenance of the skill. She also decided that she would begin to teach Trever to follow directions given by a peer, as a next step to learning to engage in cooperative activities.

CHAPTER 9

Program Evaluation

Jennifer Grisham-Brown and
Kristie Pretti-Frontczak

The Building Blocks Preschool Program is a nonprofit community-based early child-hood center that contracts with the local public school to provide services to young children with disabilities. The program is accredited by the National Association for the Education of Young Children (NAEYC) and has been rated as a three-star (out of 4) center by the state's licensing agency. The program serves 70 children who are 2 to 5 years of age in mixed-age classrooms. Fifteen percent of the children have di-agnosed disabilities, and fifty percent of the children receive child care subsidy for low-income families. Twenty percent of the children are English-language learners. In addition to its contract with the local public school, and the child care subsidy, Building Blocks receives funding from the local United Way agency.

Ms. Lopez, Director of Building Blocks, is pleased with the progress the program has made since its inception 15 years ago. She believes that the mix of funding has af-forded the program the opportunity to provide high-quality early care and education to young children who are vulnerable to school failure. She is frustrated, however, about the amount of paperwork she must complete to maintain her contract with the school district, preserve NAEYC accreditation, and seek continued funding from United Way. Each entity requests multiple forms of data to support the effectiveness of the services provided by Building Blocks. Therefore, Ms. Lopez is seeking ways to provide the data that all these entities need in the most efficient way possible.

The scenario described in the vignette is not uncommon in blended pre-school programs. In an effort to provide high-quality inclusive services to young children, programs often collaborate with multiple entities and agencies. Local, state, and national agencies are increasingly requiring pro-grams to provide effectiveness data. Programs like Building Blocks need a comprehensive program-evaluation plan that will provide the data they need to make internal decisions about program enhancement and to sat-isfy funders and accreditation agencies.

Program evaluation has been defined as the process of "systematically collecting, synthesizing, and interpreting information about programs for the purpose of assisting with decision making" (Snyder & Sheehan, 1996, p. 359), as well as the process of "clearly articulating the services and de-sired outcomes of an intervention or program" (National Child Care Infor-mation Center [NCCIC], 2005, p. 1). The National Academy of Sciences (2008) details three primary purposes for collecting program evaluation data. First, data sometimes are collected to determine the *impact* of a pro-gram. This purpose is limited primarily to investigations in which re-searchers want to compare two (or more) programs and determine which program had the greatest impact. Second, program evaluations may be con-ducted for *social benchmarking* purposes. For example, if researchers want to find out whether today's 4-year-olds have better literacy skills than 4-year-olds did 10 years ago before the increased emphasis on literacy, they may compare data on children's literacy abilities now with data on a group of similar children from 10 years ago. Third, program evaluation data are collected for purposes of determining a program's *effectiveness.*

Chapter 9 focuses on program evaluation for the latter purpose. In addition, the program evaluation described here includes two approaches to monitoring trends and evaluating programs and services: "social indicators which are used to assess the adequacy of services to children or conditions in the environment and direct measures of children where children themselves are the sources of the data" (National Educational Goals Panel, 1998, p. 23). The chapter describes the types of program evaluations that early childhood intervention programs might undertake at the classroom, programwide, state, and national levels. Also described are methods for collecting program-evaluation data, including child assessment, program observations, stakeholder input, and record review. Finally, recommended practices used in conducting effective program evaluations will be discussed.

TYPES AND REASONS FOR CONDUCTING PROGRAM EVALUATION

As is evident from the vignette, blended programs often have multiple layers of program evaluation they must conduct. The Division of Early Childhood (DEC, 2007) represents the types of program evaluation as concentric circles indicating how information from each type can feed into the larger evaluation effort. Figure 9.1 is an adaptation from DEC showing the types or levels of evaluation that blended early childhood intervention programs might encounter and the reasons for collecting evaluation data at each level. In the sections that follow, we expand on each of these levels and their corresponding purposes.

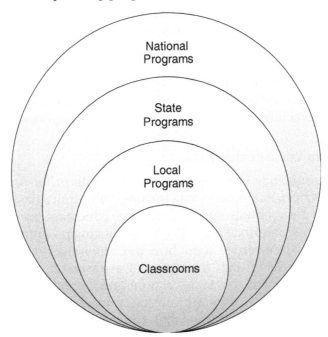

Figure 9.1. Relationship between levels of program evaluation. (Reprinted from Division of Early Childhood. [2007]. *Promoting positive outcomes for children with disabilities: Recommendation for curriculum, assessment, and program evaluation*. Missoula, MT; Author.)

Individual Classroom-Level Evaluations

For teachers, the most important form of program evaluation occurs at the classroom level. Teachers need information on the degree to which children are making progress, whether children are interested in curricular activities, whether instruction is being implemented properly, and whether the parents of their students are satisfied with the services provided. Data gathered from classroom program evaluations can be useful in making changes to the classroom curriculum. For example, if teachers determine that children are no longer engaging in activities and materials available to them, the activities and materials may need to be changed. If children have mastered the content associated with a particular topic of study, new goals need to be identified. If parents indicate that their children are really excited about coming to school and particularly enjoy an activity that has been introduced, then the activity might be maintained.

In addition to making changes to the curriculum, another important reason for collecting classroom-level program-evaluation data is to determine the degree of fidelity with which instruction is being delivered. Fidelity of implementation means "literature-based recommended practices" related to employing an intervention in the classroom (Campbell & Sawyer, 2007, p. 17). Some curricular approaches espouse specific instructional tenets that should be demonstrated. For example, research on the longitudinal benefits of the High Scope curriculum a child-centered curriculum that originated in Ypsilanti, Michigan showed that its benefits were dependent on teachers implementing the curriculum with fidelity (Schweinhart & Weikart, 1997). Similarly, when specialized instruction must be provided for individual children, the fidelity of implementation should be measured. This is often referred to as *procedural reliability,* which is the degree to which a person implements an intervention according to the plan (Billingsley, White, & Munson, 1980). Figure 9.2 shows an example of a procedural reliability checklist used to determine whether a teacher is implementing a procedure for teaching language to young children correctly.

Local Program-Level Evaluations

Local programs include those operated by nonprofit or for-profit agencies and school districts. Examples would include community-based child care, publicly funded preschools operated by local education agencies, home-visiting programs, and Head Start. When conducting program evaluations, local programs are concerned about how well children are doing, the quality of teaching or parenting, the utility of assessment, and staff morale (Bagnato and Neisworth, 1991). Local programs conduct evaluations for a variety of reasons. First, they are interested in determining the professional development needs of their staff. Child-assessment data that demonstrate consistent deficits in certain curricular areas (e.g., math) might indicate the need for staff development in that area of instruction. Observational data that demonstrate poor interactions between staff and child

Child's Name: Instructor: Date: Session #:

Are the materials ready? _____
Is the stop watch ready? _____
                    Key: + = Correct   − = Incorrect/No Response

Child's Name	Trial	Attentional cue provided?	3-second delay?	Response before CP	Response after CP	Controlling prompt provided, if needed?	Descriptive verbal praise given, if needed?	Continue activity?
	1.			+ − NR	+ − NR			
	2.							
	3.							
	4.							
	5.							
	6.							
Percent Agreement/Correct								

Figure 9.2. Intervention reliability data sheet: Small-group format 3 second delay.
Key: CP, controlling prompt; NR, no response.

would be indicative of a need for training in creating positive classroom environments for young children.

Local programs, particularly nonprofit programs, often receive funding from a variety of sources, including foundation grants. Under those circumstances, program-evaluation data are used to demonstrate that grant funds had an impact on the quality of the program or the children and families that receive services from the program. For example, if a local inclusive child care program receives funding from the United Way to purchase computers for each of its four preschool classrooms in order to support interactions between children with and without disabilities, it might need a variety of data to report to the funder. The program might show how interactions between children with and without disabilities increased as a result of having computers with interactive games. Similarly, the program might show gains in children's literacy scores on assessment measures as a result of having exposure to the technology. Finally, the program might show enhanced scores on environmental rating scales as a result of children having access to age-appropriate technology. Generally speaking, local program funders are interested in changes in scores that come about as a result of the funding they provided.

Evaluation data are needed in order for programs to obtain *accreditation* from some professional body. Most accrediting bodies provide specific guidelines about the type of data they need in order to document evidence of quality. The most common accreditation sought by early childhood intervention programs is from the NAEYC. The intent of the voluntary accreditation process is to improve program quality for young children, as program quality has been linked to children's outcomes (Groginsky,

Robison, & Smith, 1999). NAEYC accreditation establishes national standards of quality, as well as a process for improving program quality where
needed. NAEYC accreditation is being used in combination with state-
supported quality-rating systems. A program accredited by NAEYC is thought
to be of the highest quality; therefore, accreditation is generally a requirement of a high ranking in state quality-rating systems (e.g., North Carolina,
Kentucky). NAEYC accreditation involves self-evaluating classroom environments, gathering information from staff about their perceptions of the
program, and determining the satisfaction of families participating in the
program. Once programs have collected these data, NAEYC sends a representative to the program to validate the data collected by the program and
make a determination about accreditation.

Finally, local programs may collect program-evaluation data for the purpose of determining the degree with which they are meeting their program
goals. Often these data are reported to the program's stakeholders, such as a
board of directors or parent advisory board. For example, if one of the program's goals is to improve the literacy outcomes of all children who attend the
program, then child assessment pre- and posttest data would be needed to determine whether there has been growth in the area of literacy development.

State-Level Evaluations

In some states, agencies that oversee early childhood intervention programs (e.g., child care, Head Start, education) are working together to improve the quality of early education in order to ensure that young children
are ready to enter school (National Child Care Information Center, 2005).
Examples of initiatives that have been started include scholarship programs for teachers, quality-rating systems, and interagency councils. Most
of these initiatives are fiscally expensive programs; therefore, states engage
in program evaluation to determine the effect of such initiatives on the
quality of early childhood intervention programs, to measure stakeholders' satisfaction with the initiatives, and to determine the impact of the initiatives on children's school readiness.

One of the most widely investigated state initiatives was the Smart
Start Initiative in North Carolina, which began in 1993 with a vision that
"Every child reaches his or her potential and is prepared for success in a
global community" (Frank Porter Graham Child Development Institute,
2010). The Frank Porter Graham Child Development Institute conducted
approximately 35 studies of the Smart Start Initiative over a 10-year period, focusing on the effects of the initiative on the quality of child care,
family functioning, child health, and school readiness (Frank Porter Graham,
2010). The findings were as follows:

• Children have the skills and abilities deemed important for school success.

• Children have more options for receiving a high-quality child care
  experience under the initiative than if they did not participate.

- Children are accessing health care.

- Child care teachers have improved access to educational opportunities.

- Children with special needs are receiving a higher quality child care experience.

- Families benefit from Smart Start.

- Smart Start improves the collaboration and coordination of services.

There are two primary purposes for conducting state-level program evaluations. First, because of the amount of public resources that are used to implement these initiatives, state legislators are interested in understanding their impact on their constituencies. Some states have started cost–benefit analyses of early care initiatives (Groginsky et al., 1999). Second, evaluations of state initiatives can help set public policy. The KIDS (Kentucky Invests in Developing Success) NOW Early Care and Education Initiative has found improved program quality and superior social-emotional outcomes in programs and for children who attend the state's highest rated programs, those with three- and four-star ratings (Grisham-Brown, Gravil, Gao, & Townley, 2009). This type of data could be used to set policies regarding mandatory participation in quality rating systems that are now voluntary.

Local program administrators and teachers should willingly participate in state-level program evaluations because they provide an opportunity for stakeholders to voice their opinions about the usefulness of the initiative's programs, as well as discuss how they can be changed. In addition, participation in state-level program evaluations should be viewed as important to the sustainability of state-funded programs and services.

Federal Program Evaluations

During the Clinton administration, all federally funded programs became subject to the Government Performance Reporting Act (GPRA). As a result of that act and the No Child Left Behind (NCLB) Act, educational programs began reporting data to the federal government on students' performance on statewide tests. More recently, early childhood intervention programs have been held responsible for reporting data to the federal government about their success. Evaluations of federal programs are considered accountability assessments (DEC, 2007). Table 9.1 gives an overview of three federal early childhood programs that have created accountability assessment systems. The table describes each program, the evaluation system, and how local programs are affected by the evaluation.

From the federal government's point of view, the primary purpose for conducting accountability assessments is to determine whether the benefits outweigh the costs of the program. More specifically, federal program evaluations are conducted because "policymakers are asking two questions that are corollaries of their earlier readiness query: Are children learning?

Table 9.1. Federal early childhood programs, associated accountability system, and local requirements

Program	Accountability System	Requirements for Local Programs
Head Start—Program to provide services to low-income children to improve school readiness skills http://www.acf.hhs.gov/programs/ohs/legislation/HS_act.html#641A	Performance standards related to school readiness as defined by the Head Start Outcomes Framework	Local programs require assessment of child outcomes as they relate to school readiness
Office of Special Education Programs—Services provided through the U.S. Department of Education to children birth to 3 (Part C) and 3–5 (section 619) with disabilities http://www.fpg.unc.edu/~ECO/	Child outcome data on three outcomes Family outcome data	Local programs must provide child outcome data near entry and exit from early intervention (Part C) and 619 programs (Part C) and 619 programs (preschool)
Even Start—Services provided through the U.S. Department of Education and intended to break the cycle of poverty and illiteracy through early childhood education, adult literacy or adult basic education, parenting education, and parent–child interactive literacy activities http://www.ed.gov/programs/evenstartformula/index.html	Child outcome data on receptive and expressive language and early literacy outcomes	Local projects report data on recruitment and enrollment rates, hours of service offered, participant demographics, hours of participation for adults and children, retention rates, and indicators of developmental progress and achievement of goals for children

and, Are public funds being used wisely" (Meisels, 2006, p. 5). Sometimes accountability assessment is conducted in order to determine whether a program will continue to receive public funding. In other words, programs that are producing positive outcomes for children and families would continue to receive funding, and those which are not would lose funding. This type of high-stakes accountability assessment is part of NCLB. Schools showing progress or exceeding expected goals might receive rewards, and those schools not demonstrating progress might lose some portion of their federal funding.

Meisels (2006) warns against high-stakes accountability assessment for programs serving young children, for a variety of reasons. First, given that most accountability systems are based on child assessment data, there is a risk of *low-quality data* for decision making due to the fact that young children are not good test takers and there are no valid, reliable measures for assessing young children for accountability purposes. In addition, there could be unintended consequences of testing young children, the most disturbing of which is the possibility that teachers who administer the accountability tests might begin to view items on the test as curricular goals. This phenomenon was seen when the National Reporting System was implemented in Head Start. The test used included obscure vocabulary items (e.g., *swamp*) that were culturally insensitive to the experiences of many children. Head Start teachers, in an effort to ensure that their children did well on the test, began teaching irrelevant vocabulary as part of their curriculum. Another problem with high-stakes assessment in programs serving young children is the inconsistency in program accessibility and length, differences in teaching credentials, and availability of fiscal resources. The opportunities to learn, as well as the quality of instruction, vary so greatly that penalizing one program for not producing outcomes similar to those of another would be inappropriate. Finally, children from birth to 5 years of age vary, often unpredictably, in development. As a result, we expect some children in this age group to out-perform other children. Sometimes, the program has little to do with these developmental differences. For all these reasons, high-stakes accountability assessment is not recommended for programs serving young children.

A recent position paper by the National Early Childhood Accountability Task Force entitled *Assessing and Improving Early Childhood Learning and Program Quality* (Shultz, Kagan, & Shore, 2009) stated,

> Well-designed accountability efforts can enhance the credibility of early childhood programs, guide program improvements and generate data to support continued public investment. On the other hand, poorly conceived accountability initiative can produce misleading feedback, impose onerous burdens, and lead to misguided decisions. (2009, p. 17)

The task force made five recommendations regarding the establishment of accountability systems for young children that are appropriate in today's context of blended programming. First, there should be a unified system across sources of funding. Rather than having separate accountability systems for child care, publicly funded prekindergarten, and Head Start, one system should be in place. Second, standards, curriculum, and assessment should be aligned from prekindergarten to grade 3. Vertical curriculum alignment ensures that children are prepared for the next educational level. Third, like all assessments, accountability assessment should be valid and reliable. Given the potential high-stakes nature of accountability assessment, it is very important that data be accurate and provide the intended information. Fourth, as with K–12 accountability systems, all children should be included in accountability efforts, including those children with diagnosed disabilities. In fact, there is evidence that including children with disabilities in high-stakes assessment can have positive benefits for them (Cole, 2006) because doing so ensures that assessment results for children with disabilities are valued as much as those of their nondisabled peers. Similarly to recommendations for K–12 systems, appropriate accommodations should be made. Finally, accountability systems should provide for the necessary resources to ensure that programs can adequately implement the system. Resources are needed for data management, professional development, and oversight of accountability systems.

METHODS FOR COLLECTING PROGRAM EVALUATION DATA

In deciding which assessment method to use to collect program evaluation data, a number of issues must be taken into account. Program evaluation *questions* will drive assessment methods. Bagnato and Neisworth (1991, p. 178) provide examples that might be appropriate in blended programs:

- "Is the staff:child ratio adequate to deliver the program?"

- "Are staff inservice activities scheduled and/or completed?"

- "Does the program have an overall curriculum that meets the needs of enrolled children and staff capabilities?"

- "Are proper ancillary services available to the children who need them?"

- "Are program goals and procedures acceptable to parents and staff?"

- "Are follow-up procedures and information in place for children who have left the program?"

The *audience* also will affect the methods used. Programs providing program-evaluation data to groups such as funders that are unfamiliar with early childhood intervention assessment and practices would want to use methods that are understandable to those groups. In addition, those implementing program evaluations must consider available *resources* for collecting data. Some measures and methods require that someone outside of the program collect the data. Programs with limited funds may not have the fiscal resources to hire data collectors. Similarly, measurement systems may be cost prohibitive for some programs: Some measurement methods have expensive data management systems. Also, adequate staff training in program-evaluation measures can be costly to programs. Finally, it is important to consider the need for methods that produce both *quantitative* and *qualitative* information. Quantitative data produce information such as how often something happens, how much someone likes something, and whether children make progress. Qualitative data provide information on the impact of the program on the lives of the children and families that receive its services. In the sections that follow, we describe methods of collecting child outcome data and program-observation data, gathering information from stakeholders, and conducting record reviews.

Child Outcome Data

Given that child outcome data are used for program-level decision making, it is extremely important to ensure that data have been collected with fidelity and reliability. (See Chapter 5 for a discussion of the latter.) Ensuring that child assessment data are accurate is extremely important in conducting program evaluations because inaccurate data might lead to inappropriate decisions about services for children. For example, if child outcome data indicate that all children in a program are making substantial gains when in fact they are not, program funders might believe that certain services are unnecessary and cut funding as a result.

Programs need to adhere to recommended assessment practices when assessing young children for program-evaluation purposes. In addition to those practices described in detail in Chapter 1, other practices should be followed during program evaluation, particularly when the evaluation is part of an accountability system. First, child outcome data need to be aggregated, meaning that all individual scores are combined and reported (National Child Care Information Center, 2005, p. 1). Individual children's scores should be unrecognizable to program evaluators. In addition, when considering the impact of a program on child outcomes, program evaluators must take into account the length of time children have been in the program and the quality of services they have received. Children who have received high-quality early intervention services for 1 year will likely have better outcomes than those who have received low-quality early childhood interventions services for 3 months. Adequacy of services and quality of care must be considered when child outcome data are used for program evaluation purposes.

One of the most important considerations programs must make when collecting child outcome data for program-evaluation purposes has to do with the type of instrument that will be used. In a document entitled *Principles and Recommendations for Early Childhood Assessment*, the authors indicate that standardized, norm-referenced assessments should not be used with children younger than age 8 (National Education Goals Panel, 1998). Bagnato & Neisworth (1991) suggest that such tests are not tied to program goals and, therefore, lack content validity when they are used for program evaluation. In addition, many norm-referenced tests can be difficult to conduct, require special training for administrators, and are insensitive to small changes. The tests are especially problematic for children with disabilities: Items on many conventional assessments require children to speak, use their hands, and ambulate, so children who are nonverbal or nonambulatory may lack the capacity to demonstrate their true cognitive abilities. Accordingly, norm-referenced tests should be avoided at all cost (Cole, 2006).

The NCCIC (2005) provides some guidance for program evaluators who may be required to use standardized norm-referenced assessment measures with young children. First, evaluators should collect data on a sample of children, rather than trying to assess all of them. Graham, Taylor, Olchowski, and Cumsville (2006) describe a process called *matrix sampling* in which different groups of children are administered parts of a norm-referenced assessment so that none have to complete the entire test. The NCCIC (2005) also indicates that traits associated with the goals of the program should be assessed to the extent possible. For example, if the focus of a program is on improving the language and literacy outcomes of young children, then a child outcome measure that tests children's language and literacy abilities should be considered. Also, norm-referenced tests that are selected for program evaluation purposes should be normed on populations that include children like those in the program. Finally, there should be sufficient item density on selected tests so that detecting change is likely. Collecting pre- and posttest data at the beginning and end of a program's school year is another strategy for increasing the probability of detecting changes in children, through norm-referenced assessments (Donna Bryant, personal communication).

Still, instead of using norm-referenced assessment instruments, four different approaches are recommended. First, programs should consider using data collected from the curriculum-based assessment (CBA) they use for program planning purposes. Bagnato and Neisworth indicate that CBAs are the "most relevant, direct, and sensitive measure of the program's influence on the child's performance" (1991, p. 171). By demonstrating children's achievement of objectives on CBAs, programs can show a direct correlation between child outcomes and program quality. Second, judgment-based assessments, such as the Developmental System to Plan Early Intervention Services (Bagnato and Neisworth), are an alternative to norm-referenced assessments. Scores on judgment-based assessments are based on the perceptions of those who know the children on whom the data are being collected. Third, Sherow (2000) indicates that adopting goal attainment scaling is preferable to using standardized measures for program-evaluation purposes because it measures the impact of services provided and the actual goals that learners acquired. According to Bagnato and Neisworth, "goal attainment scaling techniques involve identification of individual child goals and the specification of five levels of possible attainment for each along a continuum of worst to best" (p. 171). Finally, general outcomes measures can be used to examine children's progress toward specific program goals (e.g., indicators of early literacy). General outcome measures are standardized measures that can be quickly administered to large groups of children over time to show the effectiveness of a curriculum or specific intervention (Hojnoski & Missall, 2007).

Program Observations

A common way program-evaluation data are collected is from program observations. Program-observation measures generally fall into two categories. The first set of measures assesses the *global,* or *macro,* aspects of the program. The most common global measures of program quality are the *Early Childhood Environmental Rating Scale–Revised* (Harms, Clifford, & Cryer 1998) and the *Infant Toddler Environmental Rating Scale–Revised* (Harms, Cryer, & Clifford, 2006); both scales measure space and furnishings, personal care routines, language reasoning, activities, interaction, program structure, and parents and staff. The second set of measures assesses *specific,* or *micro,* aspects of program quality. For example, the *Classroom Assessment Scoring System* (Pianta, La Paro, & Hamre, 2007) assesses interactions between teachers and children across academic areas, as well as classroom management strategies. Tables 9.2 and 9.3 summarize program observation

Table 9.2.   Global measures and description

Measure	Description
Assessment Profile for Early Childhood Programs (Abbot-Shinn M. & Sibley, 1992)	Observational checklist that gives measure of overall preschool quality. Subscales include the following: • Learning environment • Scheduling • Curriculum • Interactions • Individualizing
A Developmentally Appropriate Practices Template (ADAPT; Van Horn & Ramey, 2004)	Measures the degree to which practices in the preschool classroom are developmentally appropriate on the basis of the National Association of the Education of Young Children recommendations. Three scales: • Integrated curriculum • Social-emotional emphasis • Child-centered approaches
Early Childhood Environment Rating Scale (Harms, Clifford, & Cryer, 1998)	Evaluates the overall quality of the preschool environment primarily on the basis of interactions between teacher and children and activities that occur in the classroom. Seven subscales: • Space and furnishings • Personal care routines • Language–reasoning • Activities • Interaction • Program structure • Parents and staff
Infant Toddler Environmental Rating Scale (Harms, Cryer, & Clifford, 2006)	Evaluates the overall quality of the infant or toddler environment primarily on the basis of interactions between teacher and children and activities that occur in the classroom. Seven subscales: • Space and furnishings • Personal care routines • Language–reasoning • Activities • Interaction • Program structure • Parents and staff
Preschool Program Quality Assessment (High Scope, 2003)	Evaluates the overall quality of preschool classrooms on seven dimensions: • Learning environment • Daily routines • Adult–child interaction • Curriculum planning and assessment • Parent involvement and family services • Staff qualifications and development • Program management

(continued)

Table 9.2. *(continued)*

Measure	Description
DEC Recommended Practices Program Assessment: Improving Practices for Young Children with Special Needs and their Families (Hemmeter, Joseph, Smith, & Sandall, 2001)	Evaluates the quality of services provided to young children with disabilities and their families in any early childhood environment such as Head Start, child care, or public preschool on the basis of the Division of Early Childhood Recommended Practices. Divided into five strands: • Interdisciplinary models • Family-based practices • Assessment • Child-focused practices • Technology applications

instruments commonly used for evaluation purposes. Table 9.2 describes instruments used to measure global quality, and Table 9.3 lists measures used to assess specific program components, including parent–child interactions, teacher–child interactions, content-specific evaluations, behavior, and administration.

Stakeholder Input

Program-evaluation data also can be collected through stakeholder input. Stakeholders are those who benefit from the program's services and include family members who pay for the services, staff who deliver the services, and community constituents who advise and sometimes fund the program's services. In some situations, children who receive services from the program might provide input into the quality of the program.

There are three primary ways that information from stakeholders can be gathered. First, someone can conduct individual interviews with stakeholders. For program-evaluation purposes, interview questions are generally open ended and about the stakeholder's satisfaction or dissatisfaction with the program. The questions are often directed at focus groups, which generally involve 7–10 people who provide the evaluator information that will be useful in determining the effectiveness of the program. Focus groups are frequently utilized for local, state, or federal program evaluations. Table 9.4 provides sample questions for an evaluation of a state-level program evaluation.

Finally, information from large numbers of stakeholders can be gathered with a survey. Survey questions often require respondents to answer on the basis of some type of rubric or Likert scale. For example, when a program is going through the NAEYC accreditation process, both staff and families are asked to complete a comprehensive survey requesting their input into the degree with which the program is meeting certain standards. The staff survey asks questions about curriculum, family involvement, leadership, and management, among other aspects of the program. One item related to leadership and management is "Program staff are involved

Table 9.3.   Measures that target program components and description

Parent/Child Interactions	
Measure	Description
Home Observation for Measurement of the Environment (HOME; Caldwell & Bradley, 1984)	Examines infants and toddlers (birth to 3) by measuring the following: • Parent responsivity • Acceptance of child • Organization of the environment • Learning materials • Parental involvement • Variety of experience Uses the following early childhood (3–6) measures: • Learning materials • Language stimulation • Physical environment • Responsivity • Academic stimulation • Modeling • Variety • Acceptance

Teacher/Child Instruction	
Measure	Description
Caregiver Interaction Scale (Arnett, 1989)	Examines caregiver interactions with young children in home- and center-based settings, measuring the following: • Sensitivity • Harshness • Detachment • Permissiveness
Classroom Assessment Scoring System (Pianta, La Paro, & Hamre, 2007)	Examines teacher's interactions with child across all academic areas, as well as classroom management. Three subscales: • Emotional support • Classroom organization • Instructional support
The Early Childhood Classroom Observation Measure (ECCOM; Stipek & Byler, 2004)	Examines teacher sensitivity and management style in preschool classrooms. Measure includes three subscales: • Management • Social climate • Learning climate Also includes a classroom resources checklist that is used to determine the materials in the classroom for various activities (e.g., literacy, dramatic play, art)
Emerging Academics Snapshot (Richie, Howes, Kraft-Sayre, & Weiser, 2001)	Focuses on the extent to which individual preschool children are exposed to instruction and engagement in academic activities. Subcategories include the following: • Children's activity setting • Engagement with adults • Engagement with activities • Peer interaction

(Continued)

Table 9.3.   *(continued)*

Measure	Description
Observation Record of the Caregiving Environment (NICHD Early Child Care Research Network, 1996)	Focuses on the sensitivity and responsiveness of caregivers in their interactions with infants, toddlers, and preschoolers. Different subscales are scored depending on the age of the child. The following are among the variables examined: • Positive caregiving • Language development • Fostering child's exploration • Stimulation of cognitive development • Positive talk and physical contact

Content-Specific Instruction

Measure	Description
Early Childhood Environment Rating Scale—Extension (Sylva, Siraj-Blatchford, & Taggart, 2003)	Developed as an extension of the ECERS-R to examine the quality of instruction in preschool classrooms. The measure emphasizes instruction in four content areas: • Literacy • Mathematics • Science/environment • Diversity
Early Language and Literacy Classroom Observation—PreK (Smith, Brady, & Anastasopoulos, 2008)	Designed to measure the quality of the language and literacy environment and teacher practices in preschool classrooms. Measure examines five elements: • Classroom structure • Curriculum • Language environment • Books and book reading opportunities • Print and early writing supports
Observation Measure of Language and Literacy Instruction (OMLIT; Abt Associates Inc., 2006)	The OMLIT is an observational tool that measures the degree with which the early childhood environment is supporting language and literacy instruction for young children. There are five instruments: • Classroom literacy opportunities checklist • Snapshot of classroom activities • Read aloud profile • Classroom literacy instruction profile • Quality of instruction in language and literacy
Preschool Classroom Mathematics Inventory (National Institute for Early Education Research, (2007)	The Preschool Classroom Mathematics Inventory examines the quality of mathematics instruction and learning opportunities in preschool classrooms. Items are grouped into five categories: • Number • Mathematical concepts • Parent involvement
Supports for English Language Learners Classroom Assessment (National Institute for Early Education Research, 2005).	The Supports for English Language Learners Classrooms Assessment assesses the following: • Degree with which teacher incorporates culture of children in classroom • Degree with which teacher encourages parent participation

Behavior

Measure	Description
	• Degree with which teacher encourage children's use of native language and offers literacy materials in their native language
	• Degree with which the teacher supports English development
Teaching Pyramid Observation Tool for Preschool Classrooms (Hemmeter, Fox, & Snyder, 2008)	Assesses the degree with which preschool teachers are implementing the teaching pyramid for supporting young children's social emotional development. The tool measures four components:
	• Responsive interactions
	• Classroom preventive practices
	• Social-emotional teaching strategies
	• Individualized interventions

Administration

Measure	Description
Program Administration Scale: Measuring Early Childhood Leadership and Administration (Talan & Bloom, 2004)	Evaluates the overall quality of administrative practices in early care and education programs using 10 subcales:
	• Human resource development
	• Personnel costs and allocation
	• Center operations
	• Child assessment
	• Fiscal management
	• Program planning and evaluation
	• Family partnerships
	• Marketing and public relations
	• Technology
	• Staff qualifications

in a comprehensive program evaluation that measures progress toward program goals and objectives." Staff indicate a "yes," "no," or "don't know" response. Similarly, families complete a 26-question survey for NAEYC program accreditation. A sample item from that survey is "Teachers often share information about things happening in the program and want to know things my child is doing at home."

Information from stakeholders can provide both quantitative and qualitative information. Quantitative data may give program administrators information about the number or percentage of parents in a program who are satisfied with the services they received. Qualitative data can provide administrators with information about the impact that program services have had on their child or family. The following statement from a parent suggests the impact that the program has had on the child and family: "My child has gained so much since start[ing] Building Blocks. The staff are great about meeting her individual needs and listening to our concerns." One of the greatest benefits of surveying stakeholders is that it provides information not just about what the program is, but also about what

Table 9.4. Sample focus group questions

Components of Statewide Early Care and Education Initiative	Focus Group Questions
Quality Rating System	1. What supports are available that encourage participation in the STARS for KIDS NOW Quality Rating System?
	2. What makes participation in the STARS for KIDS NOW Quality Rating System challenging?
	3. What might the state do to encourage or support your continued participation in the STARS for KIDS NOW Quality Rating System?
Scholarship Program for Early Care and Education Providers	1. What supports are available to encourage participation in the scholarship program?
	2. What makes participation in the scholarship system challenging?
	3. What might the state do to encourage or support your (or your staff members') participation in the scholarship program?
Community Early Childhood Councils	1. What incentives or supports are available that encourage you to participate in your local Community Early Childhood Council?
	2. What makes participation in the local Community Early Childhood Council challenging?
	3. What might the state do to encourage or support your participation in the Community Early Childhood Council?
Healthy Start	1. What incentives or supports are available that encourage you to participate in your Healthy Start program?
	2. What makes participation in the Healthy Start program challenging?
	3. What might the state do to encourage or support your participation in the Healthy Start program?

difference the program makes. A high-quality program evaluation includes both quantitative and qualitative information. In a recent evaluation of an early reading program for English-language learners, Llosa and Slayton (2009) indicate that the only way to understand all of the variables that affect program implementation is to utilize a multimethodological approach to program evaluation.

Record Review

Finally, a review of program documents is a common component of many program evaluations. A review of a program's policies and procedures will provide information about the program's philosophy, goals, and intensity and duration of services. The handbook for parents has information about family-involvement options that the program offers. Information about employee professional development can be found in the program's employee records. Other administrative records will provide evidence of staff evaluations and associated professional-development plans. All of these documents can give program evaluators the information they need to understand the structural variables that affect program quality.

In an evaluation of an early childhood gifted education program, Hertzog & Fowler (1999) used semistructured interviews, focus groups, and surveys conducted during classroom observations to collect data from stakeholders (i.e., teachers and parents). However, prior to conducting the evaluation, they collected and reviewed program documents including previous evaluation reports, program pamphlets, and the program's policy and procedures manual. These documents provided the evaluation team members with information about the program's philosophy, curriculum design, and staffing patterns.

RECOMMENDED PRACTICES

Certain practices should be adhered to in conducting a program evaluation. More specifically, guidance is given on how to plan the evaluation, how to conduct it, and how to use the data collected. All three topics will be covered in the next section.

Planning for Program Evaluation

There are many things to consider in planning a program evaluation. A thorough evaluation should begin prior to the start of a new program and should be designed so that it will help to improve the program (Bagnato & Neisworth, 1991). The evaluation should focus on the program's goals, and its purpose should be clear to key stakeholders, who should be actively involved in the evaluation process (DEC, 2007). The National Forum on Early Childhood Program Evaluation (2007) indicates that improving the program should be the goal of all program evaluations. Often, there is a tendency to utilize comparative research design (i.e., comparing one program against another) as the model for evaluating federal programs. This approach is problematic because there may be variables that affect program quality but that are beyond the control of the program (e.g., the quality of the service delivered, whether the children or families in the program actually received the service).

Conducting a Program Evaluation

As previously stated, a high-quality program evaluation focuses on both outcomes (the product) as well as procedures (the process), using a variety of measures (Bagnato & Neisworth, 1991); therefore, collecting both qualitative and quantitative data is important. Regardless of what measures are used, all should be valid and reliable (DEC, 2007). A high-quality program evaluation should consider not only child outcomes (Bagnato & Neisworth), but also variables that mediate outcomes (e.g., length of time in the program) as well as the degree of fidelity with which interventions were provided (DEC).

Using Program Evaluation Data

The DEC (2007) indicates that a high-quality program evaluation should facilitate making decisions about the program. A common way to determine how to use program-evaluation data to improve programs is to develop a *logic model,* a clear and logical explanation of how the goals of the program link to the services provided and produce the expected results" (National Child Care Information Center, 2005, p. 2). DEC describes the components of a logic model. The *inputs* are the programs resources, which may include the people who work in the program or fiscal resources. The *activities* are what the program does with its inputs to carry out its goals. For example, the staff of the program implement developmentally appropriate curricula, and resources may be used to design outdoor learning environments. "Outputs are the direct products of program activities and typically are measured in terms of the amount of services or supports provided to participants" (p. 23). For example, the output of staff implementing a developmentally appropriate curriculum might be the number of children in a 1-year period who received access to a developmentally appropriate curriculum. Finally, the outcomes are the results generated during or after the program's implementation. The DEC describes two types of outcomes. *Proximal* outcomes are generated from consumers of the services and are intermediate. Parents' level of satisfaction with a program's curriculum would be an example of a proximal outcome. *Distal,* or end, outcomes are related to the expected impact of the activity. For example, a distal outcome of a developmentally appropriate curriculum might be that preschoolers possess the necessary skills to transition easily to kindergarten. Kingsbury (2002) suggests that when systems are being evaluated, *external influences* be included in the logic model. External influences are those variables which might be supporting or exacerbating the implementation of the activities. For example, if the goal of a statewide preschool program is to implement developmentally appropriate curricula in blended preschool programs, an influence which might affect that goal is the absence of state funding to appropriately train teachers to implement the curricula. Policy issues are often affected by external influences.

SUMMARY

This chapter has described program-evaluation systems at the classroom, programwide, state, and national levels. Among the methods examined for collecting program-evaluation data were child assessment, program observations, the use of stakeholder input, and a record review. Readers were cautioned to be selective in determining the type of assessment tool to use, and in interpreting child assessment data, for program evaluation purposes. Finally, recommended practices for conducting effective program evaluations were discussed, with an emphasis on using program-evaluation data to improve programs for young children and their families.

Program evaluation is a form of assessment that teachers sometimes believe does not affect them. However, teachers are an integral part of program-evaluation assessment at all levels. Teachers collect data for many levels of program evaluation, and they provide data to program administrators for some program-evaluation levels. Most importantly, teachers are consumers of program-evaluation data. Information gained from program evaluations can assist early childhood intervention teachers in improving services to children and their families. For that reason, an understanding of program evaluation is essential for teachers who work with young children.

REFERENCES

Abbot-Shinn M., and Sibley, A. (1992) *Assessment profile for early childhood programs.* Atlanta, GA: Quality Assist, Inc.

Abt Associates, Inc. (2006). *Observation training manual: OMLIT early childhood.* Cambridge MA: Author.

Arnett, J. (1989). Caregivers in day-care centers: Does training matter? *Journal of Applied Developmental Psychology, 10,* 541.

Bagnato, S.J., & Neisworth, J.T. (1991). *Assessment for early intervention: Best practices for professionals.* New York: The Guilford Press.

Billingsley, F.F., White, O.R., & Munson, R. (1980). Procedural reliability: A rational and an example. *Behavioral Assessment, 2,* 229–241.

Caldwell, R.H. and Bradley, B.M. (1984). *Home Observation for Measurement of the Environment (HOME).* Little Rock: University of Arkansas.

Campbell, P.H., & Sawyer, L.B., (2007). Supporting learning opportunities in natural settings through participation-based services. *Journal of Early Intervention, 29*(4), 287–305.

Cole, C. (2006). Closing the achievement gap series: Part III What is the impact of NCLB on the inclusion of students with disabilities? *Center for Evaluation and Education Policy, 4*(11), 1–12.

Division of Early Childhood. (2007). *Promoting positive outcomes for children with disabilities: Recommendations for curriculum, assessment, and program evaluation.* Missoula, MT: Author.

Frank Porter Graham Child Development Institute. (2010). *Early childhood outcomes center.* Chapel Hill, NC: Author. Retrieved January 24, 2010 from http://www.fpg.unc.edu/~ECO/

Graham, J.W., Taylor, B.J., Olchowski, A.E., & Cumsville, P.E. (2006). Planning missing data designs in psychological research. *Psychological Methods, 11*(4), 323–343.

Grisham-Brown, J., Gravil, M., Gao, X., & Townley, K. (2009). *The KIDS NOW Evaluation.* Lexington: University of Kentucky.

Groginsky, S., Robison, S., & Smith S. (1999). *Making child care better: State initiatives.* Denver, CO: National Conference of State Legislators.

Harms, T., Clifford, R., & Cryer, D. (1998). *Early childhood environment rating scale* (Revised ed.) New York: Teachers College Press.

Harms, T., Cryer, D., & Clifford, R. (2006). *Infant toddler environmental rating scale* (Revised ed.) New York: Teachers College Press.

Hemmeter, M.L., Fox, L., & Snyder, P. (2008). *The teaching pyramid observation tool.* Nashville, TN: Vanderbilt University.

Hemmeter, M.L., Joseph, G.E., Smith, B.J., & Sandall, S. (2001). *DEC recommended practices program assessment: Improving practices for young children with special needs and their families.* Longmont, CO: Sopris West.

Hertzog, N.B., & Fowler, S.A. (1999). *Roeper Review, 21*(3), 222–27.

High Scope. (2003). *Preschool program quality assessment.* (2nd ed.). Ypsilanti, MI: High/Scope Press.

Hojnoski, R.L., & Missall, K.N. (2007). Monitoring preschoolers' language and literacy growth and development. *Young Exceptional Children, 10*(17), 17–27.

Kingbury, N. (2002). Program evaluation Strategies for assessing how information dissemination contributes to agency goals. Washington DC: General Accounting Office.

Llosa, L., & Slayton, J (2009). Using program evaluation to improve the education of young English language learners in US schools. *Language Teaching Research, 13*(1), 35–54.

Meisels, S.J. (2006). Accountability in early childhood: No easy answers. Chicago, IL: Erikson Institute.

National Academy of Sciences. (2008). *Early childhood assessment: Why, what, and how.* Washington DC: Author.

National Child Care Information Center. (2005). *Assessment and evaluation: Becoming an educated consumer.* Fairfax, VA: Author.

National Education Goals Panel. (1998). Principles and recommendations for early childhood assessments. Washington DC: Author.

National Forum on Early Childhood Program Evaluation. (2007). *Early childhood program evaluation: A decision-making guide.* Center on the Developing Child at Harvard University, MA: Author.

National Institute for Early Education Research.(2005). *Support for English Language Learners Classroom Assessment.* Rutgers, NJ: National Institute of Early Education Research.

National Institute for Early Education Research. (2007). *Preschool mathematics inventory.* Rutgars, NJ: National Institute for Early Education Research.

NICHD Early Child Care Research Network. (1996). Observational record of the caregiving environment. *Early Childhood Research Quarterly, 11*(3), 169–306.

Pianta, R.C., La Paro, K.M., & Hamre, B.K. (2007). *Classroom assessments: Scoring system* Baltimore, MD: Paul H. Brookes Publishing Co.

Richie, S., Howes, C., Kraft-Sayre, M., & Weiser, B. (2001). *Emerging academic snapshot.* University of California at Los Angeles.

Schweinhart, L.J., & Weikart, D.P. (1997). The High/Scope preschool curriculum comparison through age 23. *Early Childhood Research Quarterly, 12*(2), 117–143.

Sherow, S.M. (2000). Adult and family literacy adaptations of goal statement scaling, *Adult Basic Education, 10*(1), 1–4.

Shultz, T., Kagan, S.L., & Shore, R. (2009). *Taking stock: Assessing and improving early childhood learning and program quality. Washington, DC:* National Early Childhood Accountability Task Force.

Smart Start: The North Carolina Partnership for Children, Inc. (2010). Families benefit from Smart Start. Raleigh, NC: Author. Retrieved January 24, 2010 from http://www.smartstart-nc.org/about/familyresults.htm

Smith, M.W., Brady, J.P., & Anastasopoulos, M.P.P. (2008). *Early language and literacy classroom observation—Pre K.* Baltimore: Paul H. Brookes Publishing Co.

Snyder, S., & Sheehan R. (1996). Program evaluation in early childhood special education. In S.L. Odom & M.E. McLean (Eds.), *Early intervention for infants and young children with disabilities and their families: Recommended practices* (pp. 359–378). Austin, TX: PRO-ED.

Stipek, D., & Byler, P. (2004). The early childhood classroom observation measure. *Early Childhood Research Quarterly, 19*, 375–397.

Sylva, K., Siraj-Blatchford, I., & Taggart, B. (2003). *Assessing quality in the early years: Early childhood environment rating scale—Extension (ECERS-E): Four curricular subscales.* Trentham Bookes, Stoke-on Trent.

Talan, T.N., & Bloom, P., J. (2004). *Program administration scale: Measuring early childhood leadership and administration.* New York: Teachers College Press.

Van Horn, M., & Ramey, S. (2004). A new measure for assessing developmentally appropriate practices in early elementary school, A developmentally appropriate practice template. *Early Childhood Research Quarterly, 19*, 569–587.

Index

alternative responses, 75–76
in children with diverse abilities
assessment, 63–65
cuing systems, 74–75
effective, 64
eligibility, 142–144
framework adoption, 64
influences and biases, 73–74
role release, 65t, 65
structure variations, 143
Treatment validity, 96t
Trends, 168
True negatives/correct rejection, 132
True positives, 132
True Score Theory, 101

Unidiscipinary teaming, 143
Universal newborn screening, 129
Universality, 77, 78
Universally designed assessments, 78
Unplanned moments, 20
Unstructured information gathering,
51–52t
Usefulness of intervention
defined, 182
revised CBA rating rubric, 180

VABS (Vineland Adaptive Behavior
Scales), 102
Validity
accountability assessments, 239
basic tenant of, 94

concurrent, 95t
construct, 96t
content, 95t
convergent, 96t
criterion, 95t
defined, 94, 182
discriminant, 96t
examination suggestions, 97
face, 96t
forms of, 94–95
predictive, 95t
revised CBA rating rubric, 180
social, 96t
in technical adequacy, 94–97
treatment, 96t
Vineland Adaptive Behavior Scales
(VABS), 102
Visual summaries, 167
Vulpe Assessment Battery-Revised, 102

Work Sampling System (WSS),
102, 156t
Written descriptions
ABC analysis, 28f, 28–29
anecdotal notes, 24–27, 25f, 26t, 27f
in authentic assessment practices,
24–29
defined, 24
examples, 24–25
running records, 27f, 27–28
types of, 24
WSS (Work Sampling System), 102, 156t